# FOLLOWING THE CULTURED PUBLIC'S CHOSEN ONE

# Following the Cultured Public's Chosen One
## Why Martensen Mattered to Kierkegaard

Curtis L. Thompson

Museum Tusculanum Press
Søren Kierkegaard Research Centre
University of Copenhagen
2008

Curtis L. Thompson
*Following the Cultured Public's Chosen One*
*Why Martensen Mattered to Kierkegaard*

© Museum Tusculanum Press and Curtis L. Thompson, 2008
Layout and cover design by Katalin Nun
Printed in Denmark by AKA-PRINT
ISBN 978 87 635 1097 4
ISSN 1903 3338

*Danish Golden Age Studies*
vol. 4

*Danish Golden Age Studies* is a publication of the
Søren Kierkegaard Research Centre

*General Editor*
Jon Stewart

*Editorial Board*
Finn Gredal Jensen
Katalin Nun

Cover illustration: Detail from
J.P. Lund's *Nørregade with the Church of Our Lady* (ca. 1830)
Reproduced courtesy of Copenhagen City Museum

This volume is published with financial support from
Carlsen-Langes Legatstiftelse
Lillian og Dan Finks Fond

Museum Tusculanum Press
126 Njalsgade
DK-2300 Copenhagen S
Denmark
order@mtp.dk
www.mtp.dk

# Table of Contents

*Abbreviations* — *ix*
*Preface* — *xiii*

*Chapter 1. A General Introduction of Martensen and His Literary Production* — *1*
   I. Philosophy of Religion within the Academy: 1833-1841 — *1*
   II. Dogmatic Theology in Relation to the Church: 1842-1850 — *29*
   III. Practical Theology Directed to Society: 1851-1884 — *74*

*Chapter 2. Martensen in Kierkegaard's Writings* — *91*
   I. The Early University Years: 1834-1841 — *92*
   II. Establishing the Authorship: 1842-1846 — *100*
   III. Criticizing the Established Order: 1847-1855 — *122*

*Chapter 3. A General Interpretation of Kierkegaard's Use of Martensen* — *145*
   I. The Tradition of Interpreting Kierkegaard's Use of Martensen — *145*
   II. Contributing to the Thought-World of Kierkegaard's Reflections — *155*
   III. Empowering Nihilism and the Possibilities of a Dipolar God — *162*

*Postlude* — *181*
*Bibliography* — *185*
*Index* — *207*

# Abbreviations

### *Kierkegaard's Writings*

*CA*     *The Concept of Anxiety*, trans. by Reidar Thomte in collaboration with Albert B. Anderson, Princeton: Princeton University Press 1980 (*KW*, vol. 8).

*CI*     *The Concept of Irony; Schelling Lecture Notes*, trans. by Howard V. Hong and Edna H. Hong, Princeton: Princeton University Press 1989 (*KW*, vol. 2).

*CUP1*  *Concluding Unscientific Postscript*, vols. 1-2, trans. by Howard V. Hong and Edna H. Hong, Princeton: Princeton University Press 1992, vol. 1 (*KW*, vol. 12.1).

*CUP2*  *Concluding Unscientific Postscript*, vols. 1-2, trans. by Howard V. Hong and Edna H. Hong, Princeton: Princeton University Press 1992, vol. 2 (*KW*, vol. 12.2).

*EO1*   *Either/Or 1*, trans. by Howard V. Hong and Edna H. Hong, Princeton: Princeton University Press 1987 (*KW*, vol. 3).

*EO2*   *Either/Or 2*, trans. by Howard V. Hong and Edna H. Hong, Princeton: Princeton University Press 1987 (*KW*, vol. 4).

*EPW*  *Early Polemical Writings: From the Papers of One Still Living; Articles from Student Days; The Battle between the Old and the New Soap-Cellars*, trans. by Julia Watkin, Princeton: Princeton University Press 1990 (*KW*, vol. 1).

*EUD*    *Eighteen Upbuilding Discourses*, trans. by Howard V. Hong and Edna H. Hong, Princeton: Princeton University Press 1990 (*KW*, vol. 5).

*FT*    *Fear and Trembling; Repetition*, trans. by Howard V. Hong and Edna H. Hong, Princeton: Princeton University Press 1983 (*KW*, vol. 6).

*JP*    *Søren Kierkegaard's Journals and Papers*, vols. 1-6, ed. and trans. by Howard V. Hong and Edna H. Hong, Bloomington and London: Indiana University Press 1967-78. Cited by volume number and entry number. *Index and Composite Collation*, vol. 7, by Howard V. Hong and Edna H. Hong, Bloomington and London: Indiana University Press 1978.

*KW*    *Kierkegaard's Writings*, vols. 1-26, trans. by Howard V. Hong and Edna H. Hong, Princeton: Princeton University Press 1978-2000.

*LD*    *Kierkegaard: Letters and Documents*, trans. by Henrik Rosenmeier, Princeton: Princeton University Press 1978 (*KW*, vol. 25).

*M*    *The Moment and Late Writings*, trans. by Howard V. Hong and Edna H. Hong, Princeton: Princeton University Press 1998 (*KW*, vol. 23).

*P*    *Prefaces*, trans. by Todd W. Nichol, Princeton: Princeton University Press 1998 (*KW*, vol. 9).

*Pap.*    *Søren Kierkegaards Papirer*, vols. 1-16, ed. by P.A. Heiberg, V. Kuhr and E. Torsting, Copenhagen: Gyldendal 1909-48; supplemented by Niels Thulstrup, Copenhagen: Gyldendal 1968-78.

| | |
|---|---|
| PC | *Practice in Christianity*, trans. by Howard V. Hong and Edna H. Hong, Princeton: Princeton University Press 1991 (*KW*, vol. 20). |
| PF | *Philosophical Fragments; Johannes Climacus, or De omnibus dubitandum est*, trans. by Howard V. Hong and Edna H. Hong, Princeton: Princeton University Press 1985 (*KW*, vol. 7). |
| PJ | *Papers and Journals: A Selection*, trans. by Alastair Hannay, Harmondsworth: Penguin Books 1996. |
| SKS | *Søren Kierkegaards Skrifter*, vols. 1-28, K1-28, ed. by Niels Jørgen Cappelørn, et al., Copenhagen: Gad Publishers 1997- . |
| SL | *Stages on Life's Way*, trans. by Howard V. Hong and Edna H. Hong, Princeton: Princeton University Press 1988 (*KW*, vol. 11). |
| SUD | *The Sickness unto Death*, trans. by Howard V. Hong and Edna H. Hong, Princeton: Princeton University Press 1980 (*KW*, vol. 19). |
| SV1 | *Samlede Værker*, first edition, vols. 1-14, ed. by A.B. Drachmann, J.L. Heiberg, and H.O. Lange, Copenhagen: Gyldendal 1901-1906. |

## Other Works

| | |
|---|---|
| ASKB | *The Auctioneer's Sales Record of the Library of Søren Kierkegaard*, ed. by H.P. Rohde, Copenhagen: The Royal Library 1967. |
| BHK | *Between Hegel and Kierkegaard: Hans L. Martensen's Philosophy of Religion*, trans. by Curtis L. Thompson and David J. Kangas, Atlanta: Scholars Press 1997. |

HSL  *Heiberg's Speculative Logic and Other Texts*, ed. and trans. by Jon Stewart, Copenhagen: C.A. Reitzel 2006 (*Texts from Golden Age Denmark*, vol. 2).

IL  *Heiberg's Introductory Lecture to the Logic Course and Other Texts*, ed. and trans. by Jon Stewart, Copenhagen: C.A. Reitzel 2007 (*Texts from Golden Age Denmark*, vol. 3).

OSP  *Heiberg's On the Significance of Philosophy for the Present Age and Other Texts*, ed. and trans. by Jon Stewart, Copenhagen: C.A. Reitzel 2005 (*Texts from Golden Age Denmark*, vol. 1).

# Preface

Søren Aabye Kierkegaard (1813-1855) had a fascinating relationship with Hans Lassen Martensen (1808-1884). Martensen—through his person, his tutoring, his teaching, his writing, his cultural contributions, and his church leadership—was an important source for Kierkegaard's development as a religious thinker. In fact, the case could be made that he was among a tiny group of people who most influenced the feisty Dane. This relationship, though volatile, was one in which Kierkegaard carefully attended to the activities of the other and in the process received information that helped determine the thought-world and pressing issues for his own agenda. The intent of this monograph in source-work research is to identify Kierkegaard's sources of information, including experiences in relation to Martensen the person and to his writings and writings about him, which might have influenced his own life and work as an intellectual. The monograph's three chapters will endeavor respectively to introduce Martensen as a thinker, to account for Kierkegaard's sources of information about Martensen, and to interpret Kierkegaard's use of Martensen as a source for his thinking and writing.

The title of this book comes from an undated journal entry Kierkegaard wrote between 1849 and 1851, in which he refers spitefully to Martensen in his function as Court Preacher: "In the splendid cathedral a handsome Royal Chaplain, the cultured public's chosen one, appears before a chosen circle of the chosen, and preaches movingly" on the apostle's words that "God has chosen the lowly and the despised in the world—and no one laughs."[1] Irritatingly handsome and handsomely rewarded priest of bourgeois culture, Martensen struck Kierkegaard as the epitome of selling out to the status quo establishment. And yet, this chosen one possessed charisma and was not to be ignored. Martensen mattered to Kierkegaard, and that is why he followed him.

---

[1] Kierkegaard, *Pap.* X-6 B 253; *JP* 6, 6787.

Kierkegaard's "following" of Martensen can be understood in at least four senses. First, Kierkegaard follows Martensen simply in the sense of coming after him. Martensen was in fact five years Kierkegaard's senior. Being a half decade younger than Martensen, Kiekegaard followed him chronologically.

Second, Kierkegaard would gradually arrive at an awareness of the utter depravity of Danish church life and culture in relation to the ideal set forth by New Testament Christianity. Christendom or a bland form of cultural Christianity prevailed in the land rather than genuine Christianity. Eventually he would understand that he was charged with the task to introduce Christianity into Christendom. Integral to this process of vocational or spiritual discernment was interpreting the spirit of the time. To know his context intimately, it was essential that Kierkegaard follow very carefully the leaders of the cultured public, and Martensen, along with J.L. Heiberg and Jakob Peter Mynster, constituted "the great clique" of the established order.[1] In this regard, then, he needed to follow Martensen in order to know the enemy. Kierkegaard followed Martensen intensely in order to arm himself for his attack.

We misconstrue Kierkegaard's relation to Martensen if we regard it strictly in negative terms. The next two senses in which Kierkegaard followed Martensen are more positive. Kierkegaard knew that Martensen was at the cutting edge of constructive theological developments going on in Copenhagen. Therefore, he followed him in the sense of tending to the issues and themes on which Martensen was writing in order to keep abreast of the times theologically. This third form of following Martensen, then, was Kierkegaard's implicit acknowledgement that Martensen as speculative theologian was determining the agenda of the day for the Danish world of theological thinkers including himself. While Kierkegaard developed a theological position at odds with that of Martensen, the issues which emerged as worthy of Kierkegaard's most serious consideration were ones that arose in relation to following deliberations Martensen was working out in his writings.

There is yet another way in which Kierkegaard followed Martensen. One could contend that the third sense of following just discussed—

---

[1] Kierkegaard, *SKS* 21, 39-41, NB6:55.

that is, following in the sense of Kierkegaard having his theological agenda of the day established by Martensen—did not result in any real appropriation, that even though Kierkegaard inherited issues from Martensen, he at every turn took a path which diverted from that of Martensen. In fact, this has been the position taken by a good many of the scholars who have considered the Kierkegaard-Martensen relation. I wish to maintain, though, that Kierkegaard appropriated ideas and insights from Martensen. In spite of his great dislike of and disdain for Martensen as a person and his criticisms of him as a theologian, Kierkegaard actually learned much from Martensen and affirmed many of the ideas and principles standing at the center of Martensen's theology. In the course of the account to be given here of Kierkegaard's relation to Martensen, it will be shown that Kierkegaard followed Martensen on many key substantive matters.

Besides these four ways in which Kierkegaard follows Martensen, I can point out one additional "following" of lesser significance but nevertheless meriting mention. I too believe that some of Martensen's ideas are worth following, especially after those ideas have been cleansed of their cultured public's taintedness via a Kierkegaardian critique and reformulated. A post-Kierkegaardian return to Martensen could be no less productive theologically than a post-Kierkegaardian return to Hegel could be philosophically. There are reasons why Martensen should matter to us and why we no less than Kierkegaard should engage in critically "following the cultured public's chosen one."

I am grateful to the Søren Kierkegaard Research Centre and Museum Tusculanum Press for publishing this monograph as a volume in the series, *Danish Golden Age Studies*. This piece of writing, which began as an essay but rather naturally grew into a monograph, has been the occasion for associating more closely with Jon Stewart and Katalin Nun. I wish to express my special thanks to the two of them for all that they have done to prepare the manuscript for press and for all the encouragement they have given along the way.

I also want to express my appreciation to the leadership of Thiel College where I have been privileged to work over the past quarter of a century. In ways large and small they have helped to facilitate my work as a scholar. Student assistants Brittany Chill and Meredith Nagle are to be thanked for the fine work they did on the Index of this book. I also want to thank my wife, Kathy, for the inexhaustible energy of embrace she lovingly shares with me daily, which carries over into unsullied support for larger projects such as this. While I have worked on this project a grandson, Soren Kristian Hedderick, has made his way into the world, and I would like to dedicate this monograph to him.

# Chapter 1

# A General Introduction of Martensen and His Literary Production

This overview of Hans Lassen Martensen is a general introduction to his life and work intended to familiarize the reader with a Danish contemporary of Kierkegaard who greatly influenced his thinking, even though the two never really saw things eye to eye.[1] Martensen's career is here divided into three periods: 1833-1841, 1842-1850, and 1851-1884, with the first period being devoted to the philosophy of religion and aimed at the public of the academy, the second period dedicated to dogmatic theology and addressed to the public of the church, and the third period committed to practical theology and directed to the public of society. Since Kierkegaard died in 1855, the third period of Martensen's career overlapped with Kierkegaard for only a few years, so the account of that period will be somewhat shorter.

### I. Philosophy of Religion within the Academy: 1833-1841

Hans Lassen Martensen has been called "the North's king of the Romantic world of ideas."[2] He was born in Flensburg, the gateway to Germany, to

---

[1] For a very good overview of Martensen's life and thought see Jon Stewart's "Kierkegaard and Hegelianism in Golden Age Denmark," *Kierkegaard and His Contemporaries: The Culture of Golden Age Denmark*, ed. by Jon Stewart, Berlin and New York: Walter de Gruyter 2003 (*Kierkegaard Studies. Monograph Series*, vol. 10), pp. 106-145, and especially pp. 116-129. See also my "Introduction," in *BHK*, pp. 1-71, and especially "An Intellectual Biography of Martensen," pp. 5-17.

[2] Bente Nilsen Lein, "Biskop Martensen og den etisk-kristelige sosialisme," *Norsk Teologisk Tidsskrift*, vol. 81, 1980, p. 233.

Anna Marie and Hans Andersen Martensen.[1] His mother spoke German and never fully mastered the Danish language, while his father preferred to speak Danish, the language in which he wrote on such subjects as seafaring and commerce.[2] Martensen's bilingual experience during these early, formative years endowed him with a natural power of assimilation for his later encounter with the intellectual world of Germany. At the age of nine he moved with his family to Copenhagen, where he attended the von Westen School (1817-1823), the Metropolitan School (1823-1827), and was matriculated into the University of Copenhagen on October 18, 1827 after passing the entrance exam with honors.[3]

During these early years Martensen's developing interest in poetry mirrored the general flourishing of humanistic and aesthetic studies in Copenhagen as the intellectual community opened itself to the romantic movement in reaction to the rationalism that had long dominated Danish culture. Along with his friend Frederik Christian Bornemann, Martensen became acquainted with "all the Danish poetic literature as well as a great deal of the foreign. Besides Shakespeare, according to Foesom's translation, we also became acquainted with most of Schiller and Goethe as well as the Romanticists Werner, Tieck, Novalis."[4] Bornemann, who later was to become a famous lawyer in Denmark, was also interested in theology and thus became a reading partner with Martensen:

---

[1] Flensburg was located in the duchy of Schleswig, which with Holstein, the other duchy of southern Jutland, was a point of political contention between Germany and Denmark during the nineteenth century. In reminiscing on his childhood years in Flensburg, Martensen recalls in his autobiography, *Af mit Levnet: Meddelelser*, vols. 1-3, Copenhagen: Gyldendal 1882-1883, vol. 1, p. 3, that "at school Danish was treated as a foreign language. Only a couple of times a week did we have a period in Danish where we used a Danish reader, which was published with German notes by the minister at the Danish church."

[2] Martensen, *Af mit Levnet*, op. cit., vol. 1, pp. 1-3. Hans Andersen Martensen was a seaman and shipowner until sometime between December 1808 and June 1812, when, after Denmark had sided with Napoleon in the war with the British, his ship was captured and he was imprisoned, thus losing wealth and health. He died in 1822.

[3] Martensen, *Af mit Levnet*, op. cit., vol. 1, pp. 8-23.

[4] Ibid., vol. 1, p. 19.

*The University of Copenhagen*
(The Royal Library, Copenhagen)

With Bornemann, my school fellow and friend, I shared everything spiritual. He also strove after the highest, and although absorbed in law studies, he went through the Introduction to Schleiermacher's Dogmatics in order to discuss with me the concept of religion, the feeling of absolute dependence. Fichte's popular writings on *The Vocation of Man*, on *The Blessed Life* and *The Speeches to the German Nation*, as well as Schelling's *Academic Studies* and his *Of Human Freedom* we read with shared enthusiasm. We sought with each other to enter into Hegel, for which we received a preliminary help in J.L. Heiberg's treatise *On Human Freedom*, which led into the Hegelian dialectic and taught us the meaning of the antinomies.[1]

The time was alive with new exciting thoughts coming from the rational elements of the Enlightenment and from the romantic figures who were rebelling against the universals of reason, and Martensen was ready to digest them all.

---

[1] Ibid., vol. 1, p. 80.

Martensen had shown great promise as a student from early on. In December of 1833 he wrote an essay, "An Attempt at a Response to the Theological Prize Subject," in response to the question "What is the basis of natural theology, its scope, and its relation to positive theology?"[1] Robert Leslie Horn sets out the conclusions the young theologian arrives at in this manuscript of eighty-nine quarto pages written in Danish. This creative writing contends that reason and revelation must be understood as working together and charts out a definite position in philosophical theology that sets the stage for constructive theological work to be engaged in over the next half-century. Martensen concludes in his essay, showing the clear influence of Hegel upon him, that all religion, including natural theology, is grounded in revelation; that a primitive religious consciousness within the human issues in "revealed" content as an awareness of the human's simultaneous separation from and unity with God; that this revealed awareness is rational in that it comes about through personal experience and thus is a religious *a priori*; that grasping the essential form of the religious consciousness in concept is the Idea; that the highest development in conceptual form of the religious consciousness is found in the Christian religion wherein revelation is God as infinite personality placing finite personality outside Godself, yet eternally overcoming this opposition in bringing the finite personality back into Godself, so that religion involves this sundering, overcoming, and return of God and world to the eternal; that natural theology is speculative theology or the science which unfolds the content of the religious consciousness into intelligible form according to the necessity of thought; that such natural or speculative theology possesses a certain autonomy but requires a unification with dogmatic theology in order for the great organism of Christian theology to find its true

---

[1] *Forsøg til en Besvarelse af den theologiske Priisopgave*, unpublished handwritten manuscript dated December 1833, in the Martensen archives of the Royal Library, Ny Kgl. Saml., 3434,4. Skat Arildsen, *H.L. Martensen. Hans Liv, Udvikling og Arbejde*, Copenhagen: G.E.C. Gads Forlag 1932, pp. 59-72, and Robert Leslie Horn, *Positivity and Dialectic: A Study of the Theological Method of Hans Lassen Martensen*, Copenhagen: C.A. Reitzel 2007 (*Danish Golden Age Studies*, vol. 2), pp. 44-55, have considered this essay very carefully.

*Søren Kierkegaard (1813-1855)*
(The Royal Library, Copenhagen)

fulfillment.[1] The last point—that natural or speculative theological reflection needs to tend to the positive content of human experience, including the perceptions or intuitions of God's presence in phenomenal experience, and thus needs to tend to dogmatic theology as the province of Christian thinking that has traditionally dealt with such positive content—should be underscored because it indicates that Martensen, already at this early stage of his thinking, affirmed the deliverances of the Christian faith as an objective reality that relativized the autonomous endeavors of the subjectively speculating thinker.

The early months of 1834 found the young Martensen taking on the task of tutoring a theological student, one Søren Kierkegaard, who was five years younger. Fifty years later in his autobiography he recalls the experience:

---

[1] Horn, *Positivity and Dialectic*, op. cit., pp. 45-47. My long sentence summarizes Horn's sixteen-point summary of Martensen's conclusions.

> He [Søren Kierkegaard] had his own way of arranging his tutoring. He did not follow any set syllabus, but asked only that I lecture to him and converse with him. I chose to lecture to him on the main points of Schleiermacher's dogmatics and then discuss them. I recognized immediately that his was not an ordinary intellect but that he also had an irresistible urge to sophistry, to hairsplitting games, which showed itself at every opportunity and was often tiresome.[1]

During these same months of tutoring Kierkegaard, Martensen was writing an article on biblical interpretation or biblical theology. In July of 1834 this critical review of an argument for the Johannine authorship of the Revelation was published, but as with most of Martensen's articles this is more an opportunity to express his own thoughts than a rigorous analysis of someone else's.[2] In the Prize Essay Martensen had claimed that "the positive element in all religion is to be found in the way in which that which is natural is discovered, its disclosure in time and space, in history."[3] These thoughts are developed further in this review of a text relating to the Bible's last book, which deals with God's relation to history. Martensen argues that Kolthoff's book had not made a convincing case for the apostle John as the author of the Christian Apocalypse.

A critical reading of the Revelation is called for in the review, because this biblical book has been taken literally for too long. He looks to J.G. Herder's work on Hebrew poetry as providing a responsible form of inquiry that counters the rationalist type of biblical criticism and considers the book of the Revelation in its genuine historical context:

> The historical interpretation must certainly be acknowledged as a necessary condition, but yet has only a subordinate worth. Namely, just as that which moves the historical poets is not the mere historical facts but the Idea, or the eternal history, which through the individual empirical event is revealed,

---

[1] Martensen, *Af mit Levnet*, op. cit., vol. 1, p. 78. For the English translation see *Encounters with Kierkegaard: A Life as Seen by His Contemporaries*, ed. by Bruce H. Kirmmse, trans. by Bruce H. Kirmmse and Virginia R. Laursen, Princeton: Princeton University Press 1996, p. 196.
[2] H. Martensen, "E.G. Kolthoff, *Apocalypsis Joanni Apostolo vindicate*," *Maanedsskrift for Litteratur*, 12, 1834, pp. 1-31.
[3] Horn, *Positivity and Dialectic*, op. cit., p. 47.

and just as the same thing applies to the deepest historical myths, where the mythical persons represent life's spiritual powers, which under manifold changing shapes produce anew the same spectacle, so was it also the great universal churchly ideas that the Seer vaguely sensed, but wrapped in the symbols, for which his age and its history had to give him the material.[1]

An appropriate theological interpretation of history in any epoch demands construing the particular empirical givens in light of the Idea. That is what the apocalyptic Seer did. "For empirically the prophet did not view farther than his earthly eye could reach; but as he comprehended it, thus in the mirror of the Christian Idea he saw it reflected as a view in which he grasped the fundamental spiritual powers which constitute the crisis of the eternal world, which each of the church's universal historical evolutions strives to realize."[2]

The essay continues with Martensen making the case for the Protestant principle as the principle of subjectivity, by which the conscience, the witness of the Spirit, in short, the life of faith is emphasized as demanding that the individual must have the conviction of the authority of the biblical canon at first hand.[3] The authority of the canon or of a canonical book such as the Revelation cannot ultimately be grounded in an external judgment of the Christian tradition to which the individual acquiesces; within Protestantism the investigation must always be freshly reproduced anew so that the truth might be experienced within the person through freedom, and this holds for the endeavors of theological science as much as for religious experience.[4] The point here lifts up the place of the church as being critical for the life of faith, for scriptural authority is not to be divorced from participation in the Christian community which engenders the experiential basis for acknowledging the Bible as the Word of God.[5]

---

[1] Martensen, "E.G. Kolthoff, *Apocalypsis Joanni Apostolo vindicate*," op. cit., p. 3.
[2] Ibid., p. 5.
[3] Ibid., p. 21.
[4] Ibid., p. 22.
[5] Ibid., pp. 28-29. Martensen, p. 30, criticizes the Grundtvigian emphasis on canonizing a churchly symbol, the Apostolic Creed, as not taking the subjective moment seriously enough.

At the end of this review essay the case is made for the diversity of biblical interpretations, since through such pluralism the church reaps the benefits of garnering the insights of all:

> With the idea of Protestantism is necessarily given pluralism [*Mangfoldighed*], not merely of formal but actual differences in the conception of revelation, and where these differences as such are found unjustifiable, Protestantism itself must be rejected, which clearly enough is what several of the Protestants who fled into Catholicism were themselves disposed to do, just as in time it also has been set forth by the Catholic polemicists against our church, except that they do not have an eye for the truth which underlies this and through this wants to be developed. Protestantism has before itself the Christian revelation's infinite content which is to be appropriated, but since it has its peculiar character in the fact that it shall be appropriated by the free *individuality*, this naturally must be released from the bound condition in which it is held under Catholicism, and be given room for developing itself in agreement with the delivered content. By this process the emancipated individuality's striving after an independent appropriation of the Christian revelation is itself allowed to account for its most important phenomena.[1]

Individual freedom is to be genuinely affirmed, and this stress on the individual need not be regarded as taking away from but rather as contributing to the community:

> Each person will here express his or her religious peculiarity, and this gives us both in life and literature the entire plurality of different views of Christianity, from the most profound and most sensitive to the most spiritless and most empty. Therefore, the universal Protestant church community also individualizes itself in a pluralism of lesser communities, which, namely, the church history of Germany and England sufficiently shows, a process of individuation that already commenced in the lifetime of the Reformation at one of Christianity's principal points of development. Therefore, if one wants to caricature Protestantism, one can with the Catholic polemicists present it as sectarianism. However, the essential thing is not contradiction

---

[1] Ibid., p. 30.

and difference, but the free appropriation of the gospel's truth. Tolerance and mutual recognition are closely bound up with this, since the opposed churchly systems move themselves around the Christian revelation's common center, and individuality must be conscious of its limit.[1]

Subjectivity and individuality are obviously very important to Martensen's understanding of Protestant Christianity, and this leads to multiple interpretations and views of truth, which he affirms as the situation of a pluralism of perspectives that will surely make for a conflict of interpretations but that will also finally enrich the Christian community.

Both Martensen and his friend Bornemann were awarded travel scholarships; as true friends they resolved to travel together and share their funds.[2] In the autumn of 1834 Martensen left his homeland for a two-year study trip that enabled him to further his education at the feet of many of Germany's leading scholars.[3] The encounter with Franz von Baader in Munich was especially influential on Martensen becoming more of an independent thinker and not functioning "merely as an enthusiast for Hegel's philosophy";[4] and yet, Martensen reports in his memoirs: "Baader himself demanded that one study Hegel and said that Hegel, with his dialectic, had lit a fire which everything that was to be proved as having validity in science must pass through."[5] In

---

[1] Ibid., pp. 30-31.
[2] Martensen, *Af mit Levnet*, op. cit., vol. 1, p. 84.
[3] Hermann Brandt, *Gotteserkenntnis und Weltentfremdung: Der Weg der spekulativen Theologie Hans Lassen Martensens*, Göttingen: Vandenhoeck & Ruprecht 1971, p. 34, summarizes the "envious series" of personal acquaintances made by Martensen during these years 1834-1836: "Claus Harms in Kiel, Marheinecke, Steffens, Gossner, Droysen, Göschel in Berlin, Tieck in Dresden, Daub, both of Hegel's sons, H.E.G. Paulus in Heidelberg, D. Fr. Strauss, F.Chr. Baur, L. Uhland in Tübingen, in Munich Baader, Schelling, G.H. v. Schubert, J. v. Görres, and no doubt, also Julius Hamberger. Then, in the winter of 1835-36, the friendship with Lenau, in connection with which Martensen's first booklet *Ueber Lenau's Faust* originated, and finally, in Paris, the meeting with Mr. and Mrs. J.L. Heiberg."
[4] Jon Stewart, *A History of Hegelianism in Golden Age Denmark,* Tome I: *The Heiberg Period: 1824-1836*, Copenhagen: C.A. Reitzel 2007, p. 540.
[5] Martensen, *Af mit Levnet*, op. cit., vol. 1, pp. 146-147; English translation cited in Stewart, *A History of Hegelianism in Golden Age Denmark*, op. cit., p. 541.

a letter to F.C. Sibbern dated January 26, 1836, Martensen refers to his having "gotten beyond Hegel."[1] Then, a few weeks later in another letter to Sibbern, Martensen explains his newly adopted critical stance over against Hegel:

> With what concerns my studies, what I no longer find satisfying in Hegel is the autonomic principle of his philosophy, and I have come more and more to the view that it cannot be made consistent with any positive religion.... In Hegel there is no creator and no creation, but only a cosmogonic and theogonic process, and through all of these systems conscience is only demonstrated as reason's *immediate* certainty of its own reality, but not as a proclamation of a higher will. Therefore, I think that it is no more a question of beginning philosophy by abstracting from God and religion or of philosophizing as if Christianity did not exist, than it is a question of acting in praxis as if there were no conscience. The act of philosophizing must also be a *religious* act.[2]

Martensen was on his way to developing a theonomous theology that stood in critical judgment of the autonomous systems of thinking that dominated the day.

The writing Martensen published while on his study trip abroad, written in German, analyzed *Faust*, a work by Lenau, the poetic name of the Austrian poet whose full name was Nikolaus Franz Niembsch Edler von Strehlenau (1802-1850).[3] Martensen had become acquainted with Lenau in the context of frequenting a café in Vienna, where leading intellectuals would gather for conversation.[4] Hermann Brandt

---

[1] "Letter from Martensen to Sibbern," January 26, 1836, in Skat Arildsen, *Biskop Hans Lassen Martensen. Hans Liv, Udvikling og Arbejde*, op. cit., p. 508; English translation in Stewart, *A History of Hegelianism in Golden Age Denmark*, op. cit., p. 542.

[2] "Letter from Martensen to Sibbern," Vienna, March 19, 1836 in C.L.N. Mynster (ed.), *Breve til og fra F.C. Sibbern*, vols. 1-2, Copenhagen: Gyldendal 1866, vol. 1, pp. 181-182; English translation in Stewart, *A History of Hegelianism in Golden Age Denmark*, op. cit., pp. 542-543.

[3] Johannes M.......n, *Ueber Lenaus Faust*, Stuttgart: Verlag der J.G. Cotta'schen Buchhandlung 1836.

[4] See Martensen, *Af mit Levnet*, op. cit., vol. 1, pp. 167-193, which tells about this relationship.

has indicated the high esteem Lenau had for Martensen as a fellow comrade in the search for truth.[1] During his stay in Berlin, Martensen had suffered from frequent skeptical moods that developed into a major existential crisis of belief, a crisis that took the form of a choice between the pantheistic and the theistic standpoint.[2] In the battle of worldviews or life-orientations the principle of personality was at stake, for Martensen understood pantheism as a highly impersonal perspective and theism as centered on a personal God. Will it be pantheism or personality that is to receive the last word or to provide one with what contemporary philosopher Richard Rorty calls one's "final vocabulary"?[3] This inner turmoil experienced by Martensen was evidently real for Lenau as well, and continued for him, for in 1850 the Austrian poet committed suicide. Since Lenau's *Faust* was an apocalyptic poem, Martensen's writing on this work occasioned further reflections on apocalyptic poetry, and once back in Denmark he revised the essay and published it in Heiberg's *Perseus*.[4]

Martensen's affinity for German thought and culture years later would prompt a disparaging assessment of him as "half German by study and intellectual persuasion,"[5] but on returning to Copenhagen

---

[1] Hermann Brandt, *Gotteserkenntnis und Weltentfremdung*, op. cit., pp. 66-75 discusses Martensen's writing on Lenau's *Faust*, and he quotes two interesting statements from *Lenau's sämtliche Werke und Briefe*, ed. by Eduard Castle, vols. 1-6, Leipzig: Insel Verlag 1910-1923, vol. 4, p. 227. The first quotation is cited on p. 66: " 'I have never found a human,' so wrote Lenau on April 29, 1836 to Em. Reinbeck, 'whose whole life so steadfastly redounded with the Ideal, with innocent piety and a fascinating purity of heart combined with such a persistent power of thought. A conversation with him is truly a bath of reason.'" The second quotation is cited on p. 74: " 'I have never found a more speculative thinker.' "

[2] See Martensen, *Af mit Levnet*, op. cit., vol. 1, pp. 98-106.

[3] See Richard Rorty, *Contingency, Irony and Solidarity*, Cambridge and New York: Cambridge University Press 1989

[4] The work by Nicolaus Niembsch's pseudonym Nicolaus Lenau is *Faust*, Stuttgart: Verlag der J.G. Cotta'schen Buchhandlung 1836, and it is considered by Martensen in his *Ueber Lenau's Faust* and in the Danish rewriting of that work, "Betragtninger over Ideen af Faust, med Hensyn paa Lenaus Faust," published in J.L. Heiberg's *Perseus*, no. 1, June 1837, pp. 91-165 and printed in Julius Martensen, *Mindre Skrifter og Taler af Biskop Martensen. Udgivne med en Oversigt over hans Forfattervirksomhed*, Copenhagen: Gyldendal 1885, pp. 29-88.

[5] W. Krogh, *Biskop Martensen og Kong Frederik den Syvende*, Copenhagen: A. Giese 1883, p. 24. This comment is made in comparing Martensen to King Frederik the Seventh who is depicted as being "genuinely Danish."

from his study trip in 1836 those close ties to Germany lent authenticity to his university lectures which introduced his listeners to the latest German thought. With Martensen's appointment at the University of Copenhagen, writes Leif Grane in a history of that University's Theology Faculty, a new period began in Danish theology.[1] Once home from his study trip Martensen set to work on his dissertation in the winter of 1836-1837, defending it successfully on July 12, 1837.[2] The dissertation was written in Latin and translated four years later into Danish.[3] This work on autonomy examines carefully the philosophy of Kant and the theology of Schleiermacher, finding both thinkers guilty of not operating out of a fully theonomous perspective. These two thinkers have shortchanged the concept of personality as concerns both the divine and the human. Human self-consciousness only finds its fulfillment in relation to its source in the divine self-consciousness. Human self-consciousness and human self-determination are to be granted their relative independence, but freedom is not absolute, and freedom's striving to be absolutely free is what sin is all about. He makes the case that in his understanding of method, theology and philosophy have methods that are not substantially different from one another. Martensen identifies Creation and Incarnation, revealing respectively the beginning as grounded in God's essence and the end as grounded in God's kingdom, as the two primary focal points of Christian theological understanding. Christian revelation is about the full disclosure of freedom as finding its true fulfillment in the reality of love. The Idea designates the absolute personality of God, which is manifest in the personality of Christ, and

---

[1] Leif Grane, "Det teologiske Fakultet 1830-1925," *Københavns Universitet 1479-1979*, ed. by Leif Grane, et al., vols. 1-14, Copenhagen: G.E.C. Gad 1980, vol. 5, p. 360.

[2] *Den Danske Kirkes Historie*, ed. by Hal Koch and Bjørn Kornerup, vols. 1-8, Copenhagen: Gyldendal 1950-66, vol. 6, p. 328, and Morten Borup, *Johan Ludvig Heiberg*, vols. 1-3, Copenhagen: Gyldendal 1946, vol. 2, p. 175.

[3] Johannes Martensen, *De autonomia conscientiæ sui humanæ in theologiam dogmaticam nostri temporis introducta*, Copenhagen: J.D. Quist 1837 (*ASKB* 648). Danish translation: *Den menneskelige Selvbevidstheds Autonomie i vor Tids dogmatiske Theologie*, trans. by L.V. Petersen, Copenhagen: C.A. Reitzel 1841 (*ASKB* 651). English translation: *The Autonomy of Human Self-Consciousness in Modern Dogmatic Theology*, in *BHK*, pp. 73-147.

this manifestation is the basis for the Idea becoming manifest in the world as the kingdom of God. Hegel's understanding of Absolute Spirit is briefly discussed at the end of the dissertation. But even here in dealing with the Hegelian perspective one encounters the need to go beyond the Hegelian viewpoint, because what is espoused is an understanding of autonomy that grants too much place to the creature and is not finally able to confess that true autonomy is only God's own autonomy.

Besides working on his dissertation, Martensen also wrote a review of a lecture on Hegel's logic that J.L. Heiberg had given, and this was published in 1836.[1] When the traveling scholar had met the Heibergs in Paris, the encounter had gone well.[2] Now he had an opportunity to do Heiberg the favor of writing a review article in relation to his introducing of Hegel to Danish students. In the review Martensen clarifies that he wants to support Heiberg's "efforts to evoke a deeper and more fundamental interest in" Hegelian philosophy, not because he thinks that Hegel's

> system is the messianic kingdom in science, but because it has an infinite meaning for our times since it contains the most complete and comprehensive development of rational knowledge. With this it thinks that an entire era in the history of philosophy, which sought to solve the riddle of existence

---

[1] Hans Lassen Martensen, "*Indledningsforedrag til det i November 1834 begyndte logiske Cursus paa den kongelige militaire Høiskole. Af J.L. Heiberg, Lærer i Logik og Æsthetik ved den kgl. Millitaire Høiskole,*" *Maanedsskrift for Litteratur*, vol. 16, 1836, pp. 515-528; English translation: "Review of the *Introductory Lecture to the Logic Course,*" in *IL*, pp. 73-86.

[2] Fru Heiberg, one of Denmark's most famous actresses, relates in her memoirs, *Et liv genoplevet i erindringen*, vols. 1-4, Copenhagen: Gyldendal 1973, vol. 1, pp. 281-282, how it was twelve o'clock noon, as she and her husband were sitting down for coffee in their hotel, when a strange young man entered their room; for the first time they saw the theological candidate Martensen whom they had heard about. The conversation began, and soon it was flowing and lively, moving from one topic to another; finally, it turned to Hegel's philosophy, and it was soon five o'clock and time for dinner. Martensen stayed for a good meal, at which Heiberg did not spare the champagne, after which the three went to a café. When Martensen at last looked at his watch, it was twelve midnight. This twelve-hour initial visit with the Heibergs was the beginning of a life-long friendship. See Martensen, *Af mit Levnet*, op. cit., vol. 1, pp. 219-226, for his account of this initial visit.

*Johan Ludvig Heiberg (1791-1860)*
(The Royal Library, Copenhagen)

independently of all tradition and any given positivity, comes to a close. But the new era which we await in science cannot come about before the old has ended. Hegelian philosophy is in this respect unavoidable for anyone who has participated in modern scientific reflection.

Who can deny that German philosophy has had great influence on our scholarly character and that in the greater part of what here in Denmark has passed for and counted as a system one can point out at least *disjecta membra* of older, now antiquated systems of German philosophy? It is important to take the newest philosophy into consideration not only for the so-called systematic sciences but also for the so-called positive sciences. That is to say, it is nothing but a prejudice to think that philosophy should be a single science alongside the others since, on the contrary, it is the intelligence in them all. One can, to be sure, disregard its principles, but one cannot escape the consequences. As experience teaches has always been the case, with every actual philosophy, these consequences would meanwhile expand their conquests in the realm of the real siences; if one does not want to yield to them blindly, as though to some inevitable power of fate, or seek salvation in a bad eclecticism, then one must strive to know their deeper ground, the soul in them whose essence can only be seen in philosophy.[1]

Hegelian philosophy, as the worldview that best comprehends the scientific nature of the day, is dismissed at one's own peril.

The reviewer maintains that rationalism is not able to capture the full range of life, that poetry and religion give expression to ways of thinking that simply cannot be exhaustively comprehended by any rational philosophical system, and this is because there are elements of life that elude the system:

> If only the logical is the soul of existence, then poetry remains only the reflection of the Concept and religion its symbol. Yet we cannot give up the demand that the soul of poetry be more than merely rational and that the consolation which religion gives us contain more than what logical consistency necessarily produces. There is in both something inexplicable which can only be understood by faith, a freedom which includes but is infinitely more than necessity.[2]

Again we see Martensen being critical of Hegel for reducing Christianity to the concept: "If religion is only a symbolic form for eternal concepts or reason, then it *is* not the truth itself but only the reflection of the truth. Similarly, it cannot be the absolute *power* in our consciousness but merely an object for speculative or aesthetic interest."[3]

A month after his dissertation was approved, Martensen was appointed to lecture as part of the Faculty of Theology. In his lecturing, especially important in Martensen's eyes was the history of modern philosophy from Kant to Hegel, for this intellectual tradition provided the

---

[1] Martensen, *Indledningsforedrag til det i November 1834 begyndte logiske Cursus paa den kongelige militaire Høiskole*, op. cit., pp. 515-516; *IL*, pp. 75-76.
[2] Martensen, ibid., p. 525; *IL*, p. 83.
[3] Martensen, ibid., p. 525; *IL*, p. 84.

*Hans Lassen Martensen (1808-1884)*
(The Royal Library, Copenhagen)

background for comprehending the new speculative approach to theology that he believed was demanded by the contemporary situation. Martensen's first set of lectures as a *Privatdocent* in theology was his "Introductory Lectures to Speculative Dogmatics" delivered in the winter semester of 1837-38 at the University of Copenhagen.[1] The second set of lectures, now given as a *Lektor* in theology, was his "Lectures on the History of Philosophy from Kant to Hegel," in winter semester 1838-39.[2] The third set was "Lectures on Speculative Dogmatics," presented in the summer semesters of 1838 and 1839.[3] In the late 1830s he also

---

[1] Kierkegaard, *SKS* 19, 125-143, Not 4.3-4.12; *JP* 5, 5277.
[2] *Pap.* II C 12-24 in *Pap.* XII, pp. 280-331; *JP* 5, 5353.
[3] *SKS* 18, 374-386, KK:11. *Pap.* II C 26-27 are included in *Pap.* XIII, pp. 3-43, and II C 28 is in *Pap.* XIII, pp. 44-116; *JP* 5, 5299.

held lectures on moral philosophy for incoming students in place of the recently deceased Poul Møller. These lectures were extremely popular: they were some of the best-attended and most admired lectures in the history of the University, ranking with those of Henrik Steffens and Georg Brandes at least as far as the sensation they caused.[1] Martensen introduced the theological students to the fundamental problems he was dealing with and the solution as he understood it, but this was only possible after bringing them through the history of modern philosophy. Martensen's teacher, colleague, and, later, a rival candidate for succeeding Mynster as Bishop, Henrik Nikolai Clausen, writes in his memoirs that the brilliant lecturer was supported by the freshness of the subject, and that, however significantly modified the Hegelian dress of these lectures were, the fact is that here the content of the Christian revelation made its appearance as something until then unknown and unheard of, and the new form of the gospel evoked the greatest of interest among the students.[2]

The revised essay on Lenau's *Faust* written in Danish and published in 1837 had included a long introduction on apocalyptic poetry.[3] Poetry, as we saw in the case of the apocalyptic poetry of the Revelation, strives to represent the speculative Idea. The ultimate goal of speculative poetry is to lift up the Idea by which the poem's or the play's characters are illuminated rather than to center on the characters themselves. *Faust* is a paradigmatic example of the third and highest type of poetry concentrating on the Idea as the principle of history, on the Idea of Absolute Spirit that is freedom. The Faust-poem gives artistic expression to a theological vision via speculative poetry, which discloses the nullity of the world but as anticipating the judgment of the end, thereby manifesting a religious nihilism.

---

[1] Harald Høffding, *Danske Filosofer*, Copenhagen: Gyldendal 1909, p. 141 and Henning Fenger, *The Heibergs*, trans. by Frederick J. Marker, New York: Twayne Publishers 1971, p. 139.
[2] Henrik Nikolai Clausen, *Optegnelser om mit Levned og min Tids Historie*, Copenhagen: G.E.C. Gad 1877, p. 211.
[3] See Julius Martensen, *Mindre Skrifter og Taler af Biskop Martensen*, op. cit., pp. 27-54. For a helpful discussion of this work, see George Pattison, *Kierkegaard, Religion and the Nineteenth-Century Crisis of Culture*, Cambridge: Cambridge University Press 2002, pp. 101-103.

*Henrik Nicolai Clausen (1793-1877)*
(The Royal Library, Copenhagen)

Closely related to the *Faust* work in aesthetics are two other articles, both reviews of Heiberg's creative productions. In 1838 Martensen published his review of two of Heiberg's plays, *Alferne*, and *Fata Morgana*, although the focus falls on the latter.[1] Brian Soderquist has helpfully dealt with Martensen's view of comedy,[2] and he sees it intended as a solution

---

[1] H.L. Martensen, *"Fata Morgana. Eventyr-Comedie af J.L. Heiberg," Maanedsskrift for Litteratur*, 19 (1838), pp. 361-397. George Pattison summarizes "Fata Morgana" in *Kierkegaard: The Aesthetic and the Religious*, New York: St. Martin's 1992, pp. 18-21.

[2] K. Brian Soderquist, *The Isolated Self: Irony as Truth and Untruth in Søren Kierkegaard's* On the Concept of Irony, Copenhagen: C.A. Reitzel 2007 (*Danish Golden Age Studies*, vol. 1), pp. 181-200. See also Soderquist's "Irony and Humor in Kierkegaard's Early Journals: Two Responses to an Emptied World," *Kierkegaard Studies. Yearbook*, 2003, pp. 143-167.

to the crisis of the age, a crisis centered on the nihilistic consciousness resulting from irony situated at the heart of romanticism. Martensen lauds Heiberg for his attempt to create a new art form, speculative poetry, which unites the romantic poets' striving for the infinite and Goethe's concern for form:

> Speculative poetry can be defined as central poetry—in contrast to peripheral poetry which holds us enclosed within particular circles in life where it is as if the light of the idea only shines through the cracks, while speculative poetry, light and ethereal by nature, breaks down every barrier which robs us of a view of the infinite.…Speculative poetry…takes the form of a harmonious illuminating light which transfigures life's darkness.[1]

Art, then, can be transformative; it can refigure reality as well as prefiguring and configuring it, as Paul Ricoeur suggests.[2] Art can impact on praxis, and comedy is more effective at doing this than tragedy. Tragedy is tied to a merely ethical view of the world, presupposes a conventional ethical view, and subscribes to norms but is not well-suited to prompting philosophical reflection on those norms; comedy on the other hand operates in a sphere beyond the ethical, in the "speculative consciousness," and relativizes the ethical consciousness, making it as nothing, and communicating a sense for what is of ultimate worth.[3] In artistic comedy "the free spirit hovers above the phenomena of worldly life, and inasmuch as it perceives the finite and illusory elements in human endeavors which perpetually seek reality where it cannot be found, it posits *its own* higher *perspective* as the authentic absolute.… It is infinite freedom which is elevated above all finite conditions, the purely *irresponsible* freedom."[4] It is the infinitude of subjective thought,

---

[1] Martensen, "Fata Morgana," p. 367, cited in Soderquist, *The Isolated Self*, op. cit., p. 181. See Pattison's treatment in *Kierkegaard, Religion and the Nineteenth-Century Crisis of Culture*, op. cit., pp. 103-107.
[2] Paul Ricoeur, *Time and Narrative*, vols. 1-3, Chicago: University of Chicago Press 1984-1988, especially vol. 1. pp. 52-87, where Ricoeur discusses prefiguration, configuration, and refiguration as three moments of *mimesis*.
[3] Martensen, "Fata Morgana," pp. 377-378 and Soderquist, *The Isolated Self*, op. cit., pp. 182-183.
[4] Ibid., p. 379 and ibid., p. 183.

the infinity of freedom, that can finally satisfy, and comedy certifies us in the consciousness of that infinitude. Comedy is an inclusive category that encompasses irony and humor. Irony, on the one hand, opens up subjective freedom by bringing a sense of superiority, but it can quickly slide into a self-absorbed, atheistic nihilism that ends up attached to the finite world it has rendered hollow; humor, on the other hand, involves a transforming of the ironic consciousness into a comprehensive grasping and affirming of the finite world, into, namely, a metaphysical perspective in which the finite is brought into a unity with the infinite.[1]

The discussion of irony and comedy is continued three years later in 1841 with Martensen's review of Heiberg's *New Poems*.[2] Again apocalyptic poetry is the artistic means of bringing emancipation. The focus in this review falls on Heiberg's classic "A Soul After Death: An Apocalyptic Comedy." Martensen portrays the way in which the comedy discloses a kingdom of triviality, supported by a metaphysics of triviality that is singular in its vision. "Genuine science and poetry, just like faith, sees all objects in a twofold way, sees them simultaneously under the gestalt of eternity and temporality. This double view appears on the whole in everything that is called witty. The bad, flat view of the world, on the other hand, sees everything in a single way."[3] The singular consciousness is flat, unable to avail itself of the richness of the comical, which includes both the ironic and the humoristic consciousness. If "the opposite of irony is common sense,"[4] then irony, like comedy and humor, opens one to the whole larger world that transcends the conventional. The entire world of double vision is the gift of the idealist worldview, which is set over against the monistic worldview resulting in triviality. The double-eyed viewpoint culminates in a perspective that is comical and sometimes humoristic, where the humoristic is understood as a

---

[1] Soderquist, *The Isolated Self*, op. cit., pp. 184-185.
[2] Martensen's review, "*Nye Digte* af J.L. Heiberg," appeared in *Fædrelandet*, vol. 2, no. 398 (January 10, 1841), columns 3205-3212; no. 399 (January 11, 1841), columns 3213-3220), and no. 400 (January 12, 1841), columns 3221-3224. See Pattison's elaboration of this review in *Kierkegaard, Religion and the Nineteenth-Century Crisis of Culture*, op. cit., pp. 111-113.
[3] Martensen's review, "*Nye Digte* af J.L. Heiberg," op. cit., column 3208.
[4] Rorty, *Contingency, Irony and Solidarity*, op. cit., p. 74.

positive, speculative form of the comical, just as irony is a negative form of the same, as we saw articulated in the earlier review. Humor is capable of possessing a salvific dimension:

> The dialectic between comedy and tragedy will come peacefully together in *humor*, in a speculative comedy—which is not just negatively but positively comic—and which relates to irony just as depth of mind relates to sharpness of mind. Humor, which belongs exclusively to Christianity, contains not only the whole of irony, the poetic nemesis on the fallen world, but also the fullness of love and reconciliation. It contains all the pain of the world conquered in a deep wealth of joy. Precisely because the perspective of humor observes the whole world not just through a moral medium but also through a metaphysical medium, it sees all contradictions as dialectical. It sees the principle of sinfulness, which is present in evil, also in things considered good and pious. It sees the impress of finitude in things considered to be great and elevated. It is all vanity, and is so on the grounds that it all belongs to this frail world. But it loves this world despite its frailty, its evil, and its depravity, and just as it allows the whole of finitude to perish, and sublates the difference between great and small, so also it rescues and restores the whole of finitude, the least together with the greatest. In a *divina comedia* which has the principle of humor within it, God would not just be depicted as the righteous judge of the world, but as the absolute spirit which not only views people through ethical categories, but just as much through metaphysical categories; not just through tragic categories, but just as much through comic categories. In the end, it accepts them all in grace because they are not only sinful but also finite, not only evil, but tainted, not only condemnable, but ridiculous; they are not only fallen but they belong to a fallen world.[1]

As "negative comedy" in the form of the egocentric ironic consciousness is transfigured into "positive comedy" in the form of the humoristic consciousness, the world of hollowness and the nihilistic perspective

---

[1] Martensen, "*Nye Digte* by J.L. Heiberg," op. cit., column 3212, and cited in Soderquist, *The Isolated Self*, op. cit., p. 186.

accompanying it have been "reconciled" with the subject, and this sort of "transfiguration" receives a complete manifestation in *Christian* humor.[1] During these years Martensen was not merely engaged in writing on aesthetic theory. He did have an actual life and was giving some attention to establishing a home and family. On December 22, 1838, our aspiring leader within Golden Age Denmark was married to Mathilde Helene Hess. He says little about this in his autobiography, except that after nine years of marriage this daughter of a ship captain died, leaving him with two children, Julius and Marie. Besides aesthetic theory and family life, Martensen was thinking about the nature of logic, about the mystics, and about moral philosophy.

In 1839 he published an article on logic that was responding to an article that Bishop Jakob Peter Mynster had written; Mynster's article was itself prompted as a response to a statement that had been made in a review of Martensen's dissertation by Johan Alfred Bornemann, the brother of his old university study-mate F.C. Bornemann.[2] The review endorsed Martensen's mediating theology and included the statement: "In theology both rationalism and supernaturalism are absolute standpoints which belong to a by-gone age."[3] Mynster objected to characterizing supernaturalism as antiquated and at the end of his essay mentioned Aristotle's logical law of excluded middle as an aside in defending the

---

[1] Soderquist, *The Isolated Self*, op. cit., p. 186.
[2] Johan Alfred Bornemann, "*De autonomia conscientiæ sui humanæ, in theologiam dogmaticam nostri temporis introducta,*" *Tidsskrift for Litteratur og Kritik*, I (1930), pp. 1-40. Jakob Peter Mynster, "Rationalisme. Supranaturalisme," *Tidsskrift for Litteratur og Kritik*, no. 1, 1839, pp. 249-267. A complete English translation of Mynster's essay is included in Jon Stewart, "Mynster's "Rationalism, Supernaturalism,"" *Kierkegaard Studies. Yearbook*, 2004, pp. 565-582. Lector Martensen, "Rationalisme, Supranaturalisme og *principium exclusi medii*: (I Anledning af H.H. Biskop Mynsters Afhandling herom i dette Tidsskrifts forrige Heft)," *Tidsskrift for Litteratur og Kritik*, no. 1, 1839, pp. 456-473. A complete English translation of Martensen's essay is included in Jon Stewart, "Martensen's 'Rationalism, Supernaturalism and the *principium exclusi medii*," *Kierkegaard Studies. Yearbook*, 2004, pp. 583-598. J.L. Heiberg also contributed an article in response to Mynster. See his "En logisk Bemærkning i Anledning af Biskop Dr. Mynsters Afhandling om Rationalisme og Supranaturalisme," *Tidsskrift for Litteratur og Kritik*, no. 1, 1839, pp. 441-456.
[3] Bornemann, "*De autonomia conscientiæ sui humanæ, in theologium dogmaticam nostril temporis introducta,*" op cit., p. 3.

*Jakob Peter Mynster (1775-1854)*
(The Royal Library, Copenhagen)

either/or between rationalism and supernaturalism, stating: "one can mediate between opposites but not between contradictions."

Martensen's essay is deferential to Mynster while still managing to disagree with him. He insists that the task of theology "has always been to grasp the identity of what is contradictory for the understanding."[1] Christianity, as a religion centered on the incarnation, surely endorses

---

[1] Martensen, "Rationalisme, Supranaturalisme og *principium exclusi medii*," op. cit., p. 457; Stewart, "Martensen's Rationalism, Supernaturalism and the *principium exclusi medii*," op. cit., p. 588.

mediation, for God's becoming human implies that the opposition between divine and the natural has been overcome, that the significance of the incarnate Christ is absolute rather than relative for understanding God:

> …not only did the new creation come forth in order to set right a disturbed relation or to redress an injury—as is one-sidedly maintained by exclusive supernaturalism—but that, on the contrary, the world's entire development was directed toward the second creation, which negated the first. The revelation of Christ and the community life founded by him thus emerge not merely as something inevitable but as something absolutely necessary, as the central point of the universe, and the goal of the entire teleological development of the world, to which everything else is related only as a midway and transitory point. Another way of expressing it is that the creation exists only for the sake of the incarnation, or that God created the world only as the negative of Himself in order to objectify Himself through it, a proposition which, when fully developed, leads to the doctrine of the Trinity as Christian speculation's solution to the task of thinking God as the identity of subject and object.[1]

Martensen's speculative theology views "Christianity as the *immanent* determination of God's essence and the divine world order."[2] Theological mediation is required because the very foundation of the Christian religion itself is established by the mediating activity of God. "The *copula* of the living dialectic" that animates theological construction to be alive for new times is grounded in the divine consciousness enlivening human consciousness and inspires an "immanent thinking" that "finds no rest until it knows the mystery as revelation."[3] Theological results of the Hegelian system, as in Martensen's other assessments of Hegel and things Hegelian, are here again recognized as being inadequate. But even the left Hegelian "Straussian Christology," he urges, "should be absorbed as a sublated ideality," because he sees it as having "a cleansing influence on

---

[1] Ibid., pp. 462-463; ibid., p. 591.
[2] Ibid., p. 463; ibid.
[3] Ibid., p. 465; ibid., pp. 592-593.

theology since it has dealt a certain finite theological empiricism its mortal wound and compelled theologians to enter into questions of principle."[1] Theology, as with all scientific endeavors in the new age carried forward in the wake of Hegel, will engage in speculative, dialectical thinking; this means that a single consciousness, in functioning as the universal human self-consciousness, is both rational and supernatural insofar as it is both divine and human, and all the contradictory images and representations it entertains in its thinking are relative and able to be sublated.[2] This "identity of the subjective and the objective, of self-consciousness and revelation is the presupposition of all speculative theology," and "the immanence which is thought through is transcendence, because the divine thought, which is the immanent principle in human thought cannot itself be without subject or without spirit."[3]

In 1840 Martensen was promoted to the rank of *Professor Extraordinarius* or Associate Professor at Copenhagen University. That year he published a work on medieval mysticism,[4] one of the earliest serious academic treatments of the subject and one that is still relevant to contemporary considerations of mysticism. The book gives a phenomenological description of the mystical consciousness. Three moments—mystery, revelation, and the Highest Good—are analyzed as the interrelated aspects of the mystic's spirit. Life's deepest mystery is located in the Godhead, the divine substance grounding all reality and lying beyond the God of conventional religion. Becoming united with the God beyond God, or the Godhead that is the mysterious ground and possibility of the divine personality, requires entering into relation with revelation. The divine essence separates itself from itself in order for the self-disclosing divine personality to take shape out of the immediate mystery of substance. The mediation of these two, Godhead and the God disclosing the Godhead, is revelation. Through revelation the soul ecstatically is united with God. Martensen, whose inner turmoil

---

[1] Ibid., p. 467; ibid., 594.
[2] Ibid., pp. 469-470; ibid., p. 596.
[3] Ibid., pp. 471-473; ibid., pp. 596-598
[4] Dr. Martensen, *Mester Eckart. Et Bidrag til at oplyse Middelalderens Mystik*, Copenhagen: C.A. Reitzel 1840 (*ASKB* 649). English translation: *Meister Eckhart: A Study in Speculative Theology* in *BHK*, op. cit., pp. 149-243.

on his study trip ended in his preference for personality over pantheism, departs from the mystics on their favoring of divine mystery over divine revelation. But he appreciates their ethical seriousness, including their endorsement of the inner process of Christification that culminates in the imitation of Christ. The third moment of the mystical consciousness is concerned with being united with God in Christ in such a way that one's practical existence fulfills its appropriate destination to reveal God through love. In this moving into union with God, knowledge is very important. Mysticism at its best produced some of the most profound expressions of Christian speculation in the history of religious reflection. One such thinker was Meister Eckhart, the "patriarch of German speculation." For instance, Eckhart says that only in the soul can God be God, for only there is God able to install God's whole essence so perfectly:

> The reason for the gloriousness of the soul lies in the ideal nature of self-consciousness and freedom, in thinking, which is the soul's substance. In knowledge the soul is made participatory in God's nature. For God's knowledge, in which also human beings know, is God's substance and essence; and when God's substance is my substance, then I am God's son.[1]

The mystic is not afraid to affirm the radical immanence of God within the world and especially within the human. As we saw in Martensen's essay on Heiberg's logic course, he is not afraid of making the same affirmation, because that immanence, fully comprehended, is transcendence.

*Outline to a System of Moral Philosophy* was published the next year, 1841.[2] Thirty-nine years later, in 1880, four years before Martensen's death, when Friedrich Nietzsche was attempting to strike upon a locale and climate that suited him, he spent July and August in Marienbad, and one of the books on his summer reading list that he read was H.L. Martensen's *Grundriß des Systems der Moralphilosophie*, the German

---

[1] Martensen, *Mester Eckart*, op. cit., p. 90; Martensen, *Meister Eckart*, BHK, p. 207.
[2] Martensen, *Grundrids til Moralphilosophiens System*, Copenhagen: C.A. Reitzel 1841 (*ASKB* 650). English translation: *Outline to a System of Moral Philosophy* in BHK, op. cit., pp. 245-313.

translation of this book.[1] The book articulates a system of freedom that bears some similarities to Hegel's *Philosophy of Right*. The Preface argues that Hegel is a rich resource for ethics and that criticisms of him for not having an ethics are unfounded:

> Everyone who has studied attentively the *Philosophy of Religion* and the *Aesthetics* will have had ample opportunity to be persuaded that Hegel has known a higher morality than that whose end is absorbed in the state. These works contain the clearest indications of a higher ethical knowledge and especially the *Aesthetics* contains significant contributions to knowledge of the purely ideal meaning of the moral personality.[2]

Hegel has not been given his due in this area because the times necessitated his emphasizing objectivity over subjectivity:

> That Hegel has *not* given a comprehensive ethics can only have its basis in the fact that he, who was called to supplant the one-sided systems of subjectivity and thereby also contentless morality, had to become absorbed most intensely in the theoretical knowledge of objectivity, of the historically concluded forms of the state and religion, of science and art, and necessarily had to place the emphasis on the proposition that "the actual is the rational," while this proposition's practical complement, that we ourselves must produce the rational actually, he less vigorously accentuated. He necessarily had to emphasize more strenuously the moment of substantiality than that of individuality and personality, for the empty, formal personality first had to be destroyed before the true personality could be posited. But surely more people on the whole are accustomed to considering this philosophy as a finished, concluded result, so that it is often misunderstood by friends and

---

[1] See the account of Nietzsche's Chronicle for the year 1880 at http://www.dartmouth.edu/~fnchron/1880.html. A few years later he wrote his 1877 *Genealogy of Morals* in which he is so critical of particular Christian moral philosophers. One wonders if Martensen's text in moral philosophy contributed to Nietzsche's rage over moral philosophers or served to mollify it.

[2] Martensen, *Grundrids til Moralphilosophiens System*, op. cit., p. vii; Martensen, *Outline to a System of Moral Philosophy*, BHK, pp. 247-248.

foes alike, who hereby fly into dead, fatalistic modes of construing. Indeed, the more one realizes that one has only understood the results of philosophy when one in addition has been able to grasp them as living starting points for a new development, then the more it will become manifest that this philosophy has freedom as its principle, the more vividly apparent will become its great ethical views, and the more determinately it will point to the idea of personality as the gravitational point of thinking. Ethics will then arrive at its entire comprehensive meaning as the presentation of the absolutely practical Idea, as the science of the personality's free self-development toward its ideal through the rational necessity of objectivity.[1]

Martensen's primary point here is to insist that the appropriate reading of Hegel regards the system as unfinished until culminating in that practical actualization of the Idea that most would readily acknowledge as the ethical task.

The Hegelian influence is seen in the work's method being designated as "the dialectical or the conceptual method":

In this method every single theorem appears only as part of the totality and is known both on its own and in light of the whole. Since the single understandings appear as *moments* (*movimenta*), they are seen not merely in their repose but in their *movements*; they are considered in their inner-connectedness and mutual limitation, in their contrasts and their unity, in their struggle and reconciliation. Through this discussion, where every relative truth finds its definite place and limit, there results the free, all-embracing and penetrating comprehensive knowledge or *the concept*.[2]

Truth is not grasped within the particular perspective but instead on the other side of the awareness of the relativity of any given viewpoint. Freedom "is and becomes only what it *makes* itself into. The concept of freedom is one with the concept of spirit, self-consciousness, *I*."[3] After discussing human free will as the presupposition of moral philosophy,

---

[1] Ibid., pp. vii-viii; *BHK*, p. 248.
[2] Ibid., p. 5; *BHK*, p. 257.
[3] Ibid., p. 8; *BHK*, p. 258.

Martensen delineates the three-part system as freedom's relation to the Good as law, as ideal, and as kingdom of personality.

The year 1841 also found Martensen serving on Søren Kierkegaard's dissertation committee. Earlier in working on the dissertation, Kierkegaard had paid a visit to Martensen, an encounter that the latter recounts in his autobiography:

> He once came to me in my home and wished to read me part of his treatise on the concept of irony—as far as I remember, a polemic against Friedrich Schlegel's one-sided aestheticism. I let him read, but expressed appreciation only rather coolly. A contributing factor was his language and style, with its intolerable discursiveness. The many tiring repetitions, the unendingly long sentences, and the affected and mannered expressions were unpleasant to me, just as they have always disturbed me when I read his works. But he appears not to have forgotten that I failed to display a greater enthusiasm for his opus.[1]

Martensen ironically ended up giving the decisive vote in favor of approving Kierkegaard's dissertation on the concept of irony.

## II. Dogmatic Theology in Relation to the Church: 1842-1850

Martensen's thinking and writing undergo a shift in the year 1842. From the account of the period 1833 to 1841 it is evident that Martensen's writings on the philosophy of religion are targeted toward the public of the academy. But I have tried to emphasize that during those years a genuine concern for the community of faith or the church can also be discerned. Therefore, the transition that takes place in 1842 should not be understood as one of utter discontinuity that leaves Martensen looking as though he sold out to conservative pressures of the day and abandoned his speculative standpoint altogether. The demands of the time dictated that Martensen emphasize some themes more and others less, but it is not as though he departed completely from the creative,

---
[1] Martensen, *Af mit Levnet*, op. cit., vol. 2, pp. 142-143.

adventurous thinking of his early years. Left Hegelians were gaining prominence within Denmark, and this reality needed to be taken into account. There is a shift in focus, then, but it is not as though keen interest in the church had not been present earlier in the philosophy of religion period, and it is not as though an emancipated spirit does not continue to animate Martensen's thinking and writing.

Five related factors are integral to understanding this transition.[1] Four of these are: (1) the exchange that took place in *The Copenhagen Post* and *The Fatherland* between an anonymous critic and Martensen in January and February of 1840; (2) Copenhagen's version of Fichte's atheism controversy in Jena, namely the Hans Brøchner affair of December 1841 centering around the refusal to let this supporter of left Hegelianism take the theological exam for ordination; (3) two letters received by Martensen in the early 1840s from the German Hegelians Eduard Zeller and Philipp Marheineke inviting him to take part in their continuance of the scientific debate along Hegelian lines, which invitations he declined; and (4) Martensen's relationship with Mynster, who suggested to Martensen that he should combine an ecclesial activity with his activity at the University.[2] The fifth factor in the transition from philosophy of religion to dogmatic theology will receive fuller attention. It is the 1842 essay of Martensen's entitled "The Religious Crisis of the Present" that was published in Heiberg's April 15th *Intelligensblade*.[3]

The crisis centers on the state churches. These churches presuppose "that Christianity is the religion of the world and consequently is able to be a center for the life of the nations and the states, for their moral

---

[1] For treatment of this transition in Martensen's emphasis, see Jens Schjørring, *Teologi og Filosofi. Nogle Analyser og Dokumenter vedrørende Hegelianismen i Dansk Teologi*, Copenhagen: G.E.C.Gad 1974, pp. 27-35. See my discussion of these five factors in *BHK*, pp. 13-14. See also Jon Stewart, "Kierkegaard and Hegelianism in Golden Age Denmark," op. cit., pp. 119-123.

[2] Martensen, *Af mit Levnet*, op. cit., vol. 2, p. 75. Also quite influential at this time was the German theologian Isaak August Dorner (1809-1884), with whom Martensen carried on a correspondence for many decades. See *Briefwechsel zwischen H.L. Martensen und I.A. Dorner, 1839-1881*, vols. 1-2, Berlin: H. Reuter 1888, vol. 1, pp. 50-63. Martensen expresses to Dorner his recognition of the need to give greater emphasis to the objective side of Christianity.

[3] H. Martensen, "Nutidens religiøse Crisis," *Intelligensblade*, no. 3, 1842, pp. 53-73.

and political, artistic and scientific endeavors and aims."[1] The proper functioning of the state churches depends upon a "harmony between the religious consciousness and the world consciousness, between faith and revelation on the one hand and humanity's free self-development on the other hand, between cultus and culture."[2] In modernity this harmony has been disrupted and the discord taking place between these moments is so great that the very existence of these state churches is being challenged.[3]

The challenge to the state churches is posed by two groups, one on the left and one on the right. The group on the left, the left Hegelians such as Strauss and Feuerbach emerging in the middle of Protestant Christianity and speaking on behalf of science, proclaims "in the name of the spirit of the world and modern culture now the time has come to secularize the church and all its spiritual goods."[4] They claim that Christianity itself holds that genuine religion should dissolve itself in the world, as expressed by the parable that says the kingdom of heaven is like a leaven or a ferment that is not to remain in its immediate, solid state, but is intended to penetrate the whole mass and in the process to be transformed and even dissolve in the organism to which it brings its fermenting powers. So too the Christian religion is to give itself to the world and in the process to bring a transformation. That is precisely what has happened: the product of transformation is the secular world that replaces the church, the kingdom of humanity that replaces the kingdom of revelation. And so that this new situation shall not lack religion, a new cultus has taken shape, namely, the culture of the modern world with its art, its philosophy, and its politics, which culture has grown out of the church but now as dissolved in this culture the church belongs to a bygone age; similarly, modernity's saints are now no longer the saints of the church, but the saints of humanity, the highly-talented whom we call geniuses. The cultus or worship of genius, says Strauss, is the only cultus left for cultured people of modernity.[5]

---

[1] Ibid., p. 53.
[2] Ibid.
[3] Ibid., pp. 53-54.
[4] Ibid., p. 55.
[5] Ibid., pp. 55-57.

The other group, on the right, consists of the sectarian Anabaptists together with the pietists who are present in mainline churches. This group proclaims in the spirit of authentic New Testament Christianity "that God's kingdom must be separated from the world." They claim that Christianity demands of true believers that they remain pure from the world's darkness and evil, as expressed by the parable that says "the kingdom of heaven is like a pearl which a merchant found, and when he had found it, he went and sold all his goods in order to get the one pearl."[1] This group wants "to maintain religion in its indissoluble independence and original purity, and so they "fight in discord with the world's life instead of improving it." They become rather innocently "indifferent to the world's interests," which in a sense "is the retaliation for the indifferentism many cultured people exhibit towards religion." These pure disciples understand their discipleship as necessitating being against the world. They insist that the world relinquish its legitimate independence and autonomy and allow itself to be dissolved in religion. "They find in the state church an intolerable confusion of the holy and the profane," and since they doubt that God's kingdom can penetrate the world's hard and cold realities, they develop hard hearts, which abolish the community, with love turning to "fanaticism, which sets itself above the law," and then leads to disquieting activities.[2]

The question becomes how the state churches ought to relate themselves to the crisis, revolving as it does around these two groups? Martensen suggests what is needed is a double task of at once emphasizing religion's independence and eternal difference from the state, and allowing religion to become the all-penetrating world-principle of national endeavors. Both parables need to be heeded, both that of the pearl of great price that is the one thing needful and the ferment or leaven transforming culture. But he adds that "for the proper tolerance and the proper polemic to come forth, it will be necessary for the church not merely to turn its attention *ad extra* [toward the outside], but also *ad intra* [toward the inside]."[3] The state church "must, if it does not want

---

[1] Ibid., p. 58.
[2] Ibid., p. 59.
[3] Ibid., p. 62.

to assume a false position toward its opponents, institute a self-criticism, in order to understand to what extent the church itself must assume a part of the guilt, and to what extent a reformation *ad intra* should be a fundamental condition for a holy polemic *ad extra*."[1] The church needs to listen to both of these groups and learn from them:

> It is a remarkable thing which is everywhere affirmed, that the negative, revolutionary powers, who appear disturbing and bewildering in history, must always be seen under a double standpoint, as on the one hand they must be seen as those who should be judged and prejudged, on the other hand as those who have arrived at a judgment against the established order. That which in the established order is only a liability, a lack, a non-being, and in a sense a secret, here comes to light in a surprising way as a false, destructive activity. These phenomena allow themselves, insofar as they are not merely individual and peculiar, to be construed as a kind of historical concave mirror, which betrays every secret defect in the community by reflecting it back as a false positivity. All sins of omission are here made clear as sins of violation; the outrageous non-knowledge is reflected as an impudent knowledge; the false silence is revealed as a thousand-tongued Hydra. By appearing as though saying: Look in the mirror! these phenomena fulfill their purpose in history; they are indirect revelations of the Idea. From this viewpoint then both the religious sectarianism and the destructive philosophy will be able to allow themselves to be considered. They are the negative expositions of the moments of truth, which have been neglected by the church.[2]

A corrective is required, Martensen is saying, in relation to the established state church.

Religious enthusiasm is on the rise because the state church has been cool religiously. Village parishioners complain "that the established church's sermons do not give the satisfaction which they should," for in

---

[1] Ibid.
[2] Ibid., pp. 62-63. The "thousand-tongued Hydra" mentioned in the quotation refers in Greek mythology to the nine-headed serpent of Lerna, which grew two heads for each one that was cut off.

them "there is too much of the world and too little of God and Christ."[1] People are legitimately seeking and calling for

> a greater primitivity of the religious life, and when they complain about not finding in the church faith's proper intensity and simplicity, then these simple humans in their wisdom say merely the same thing as many cultured people say, who have turned away from the church, because in the religious proclamation they want the Idea's actual presence, because religion appears as merely a derivative reality, as something which is possessed at second hand, and therefore as something seeming to them to be classifiable with the historical, the bygone.[2]

The cultured people can turn to the arts and science as their religious surrogates, but "those simple humans are not acquainted with these surrogates, and are only able to relate to the one thing needful."[3] No, the established church needs to "assume its portion of the guilt" in relation to the Anabaptists.[4]

The same is the case in its relation to "the philosophical Anabaptists, who want to rebaptize the age's intelligence in the Straussian dogmatic, in order thus to wash it clean of Christianity":

> The philosophical awakening in modernity, from within which many a false philosophy has been developed, is connected indirectly or directly with the endeavors that actual philosophy has carried out in order to reform the sciences and with this the whole culture. But a reform of the science of religion will never be able to be implemented with success, when it does not find the proper cooperation within agents of the church and theology, which in this domain are the proper vocations for leading reform. If religion is to be in truth that power in which all the age's moments of culture find their mid-point, in which not merely feeling but also that seeking reflection finds rest—and religion must indeed be able to be everything for all—: then

---

[1] Ibid., p. 64.
[2] Ibid.
[3] Ibid.
[4] Ibid., p. 65.

the church intelligence must also be able to cope with philosophy of the age. But it is an experience, which nearly always recurs, that precisely many of those who want to conserve interest in religion and the church, and who just therefore ought themselves to have entered into living exchanges with philosophy in order to employ the means it offered for renewal and further development of the religious understanding, place themselves in a hostile relation to speculation. Others explained that certainly nothing should be more welcome to them than a reconciliation of religion and speculation, but they spurned the same every actual endeavor for implementing this purpose as quite unsuccessful and as something to which further respect could not be given. They would certainly enter into the reformatory endeavors, but under the condition that everything nevertheless should remain with the old. Still others maintained from the very first a perfect indifferentism and continued to behave as if nothing at all had happened. In this way, then, the guilt is just as much on the churchly side, when the revolutionary party in science obtained the progress which it has obtained, concerning which one can be convinced, namely, by a look at the state in which German literature finds itself at the moment....—And already both believing and unbelieving agree on requesting the state to sublate the state church and to establish a general culture of freedom, since the churchly unity of the body politic is really only a show, when the knowing ones in the community are not in addition able to be the believing ones, when in reality there exist two congregations along side each other, which mutually exclude each other.[1]

Martensen is not simply rejecting what the left Hegelians have to contribute; rather, as in the 1839 response to Mynster's "Rationalism, Supernaturalism" essay, he here again seems to be counseling that these philosophical maverick views "should be absorbed as a sublated ideality." Harmony of religion and culture is not to come about through any sort of powerful intervention of the state, but by the church itself "making an advance in spiritual self-consciousness."[2] The dispute, therefore, must be carried out on the spiritual domain.

---

[1] Ibid., pp. 69-71.
[2] Ibid., p. 72.

The thrust of Martensen's whole essay on "The Religious Crisis of the Present" is to offer reflection on the church in relation to culture. This treatment of Christ and culture continues the next year in Martensen's publication on Christian baptism.[1] This book came in response to the missionary work of Baptists in Denmark in the late 1830s and early '40s.[2] Bishop Mynster, acting in line with Danish law as established by an 1828 order, claimed that all children born in Denmark belong to the religious community of the state or to the Danish Lutheran Church. Mynster maintained that if the Baptists would not allow their children to be baptized, the state was justified in taking care that the baptism of these children was carried out, even if this was done against the will of the parents and even if the children had to be brought to the baptism by police power.[3] Mynster viewed this policy as defending the rights and spiritual freedom of the child. Martensen could sympathize with Mynster's acknowledgement of the right of society as over against a one-sided individualism and subjectivism, but he could not follow him on this matter. He writes: "I assumed that infant baptism ought not to be granted if it could not really be the beginning of the development of a Christian life, that the foundation ought not be laid when there could not be a further building on this, when the parents' opposition, perhaps even ridicule and derision, impeded the appropriation of baptism within the child."[4] Martensen expressed this view in Copenhagen's clergy conference, where the issue was being debated with fervor.[5]

In this 1843 book on baptism Martensen begins in earnest making good on his commitment to give greater emphasis to the objective side of Christianity. The arrival of Baptist missionaries in Denmark occasioned the question of whether infant baptism can be dogmatically

---

[1] Dr. H. Martensen, *Den christelige Daab betragtet med Hensyn paa det baptistiske Spørgsmaal*, Copenhagen: C.A. Reitzel 1843.
[2] For an account of the rise of the Baptist movement in Denmark, see Koch and Kornerup, *Den Danske Kirkes Historie*, op. cit., vol. 6, pp. 302-310.
[3] Martensen, *Af mit Levnet*, op. cit., vol. 2, p. 71.
[4] Ibid., vol. 2, pp. 71-72.
[5] Ibid., vol. 2, p. 72. Martensen informs us that this was a most unpleasant task for him, though he discovered that it did not provoke a break with Mynster.

justified. The Baptists place as the kernel and essence of Christianity "the conscious, personal life of faith, immediately conceived by the effects of the Holy Spirit in the soul, while the sacraments are regarded as symbolic signs and shadows of this."[1] On Martensen's view, this results in a one-sided prominence of the subjective, merely personal Christianity that is common in Reformed communions but in Lutheran congregations as well. In Protestantism of late, he notes, "the meaning of baptism has been handled predominantly with reference to the subjective side, while its objective side, that which is properly sacramental, has been left in the background."[2] The sects' one-sidedness is evidenced in their striving toward free, self-conscious religiosity, while forgetting the conditions and presuppositions of religiosity. This can be seen as being a controversy between mother and daughter in regard to the birth and proper beginning of the Christian life. The question finally becomes: Is faith the first, the original, with baptism the second, the derivation, or is baptism the first and faith the second? Martensen's purpose in this writing is to articulate a "clarification of the fundamental presuppositions of the believing consciousness, the presuppositions, without which no reborn consciousness is possible, and of a knowledge of infant baptism as these presuppositions' fulfillment."[3] He sees infant baptism as closely connected with other aspects of the Christian enterprise. The eternal election of grace or predestination, Christ's revelation, the Spirit's outpouring, and the effects of grace are all moments contributing to a living, organic unity in the concept of the church's constitution. He treats in turn, then, in the five sections of the treatise: baptism as the church-constituting sacrament, infant baptism, predestination, the new birth, and affirmation of faith or confirmation. Our consideration of this text will be limited to a rather careful look at the first of these five sections.[4]

Martensen begins his account of "Baptism, the Church-Constituting Sacrament," with an important statement about the nature of Christianity.

---

[1] Martensen, *Den christelige Daab*, op. cit., p. 1.
[2] Ibid., p. 2.
[3] Ibid., p. 4.
[4] Ibid., p. 5.

> It is faith alone which saves, not the dead but the living faith, not the alien but the personal faith. To have faith is the same thing as to have salvation, to have certainty of eternal life both as a present and a future reality. But precisely because faith carries eternity in itself, it cannot have a temporal, random origin, but must have a divine beginning. The Christian faith must therefore be considered even as a work of divine grace. Divine grace is known not merely in the fact that salvation has come to the world; it is known just as much in the fact that faith in grace is given to a human.[1]

He mentions Luther's words on the meaning of the third article of the Creed in the *Small Catechism*, that a Christian confesses that "I cannot by my own reason or strength come to Jesus Christ or believe in him." There is a priority of grace to faith:

> Hence, although in one respect faith is the freest and most personal of all things, the deepest human reality, it yet does not have its final ground in the human personality and freedom. Therefore the believing personality is also designated in the Holy Scriptures as a new creation, an appellation which expresses that a Christian does not live her life of faith by herself, but that this is a given, a derivative, a communicated reality.[2]

Subjective Christian faith, therefore, is dependent upon an objective dimension of Christian faith.

Christianity is a religion that perpetuates itself through proclamation. As Martensen puts it: "Faith comes by hearing [through preaching]....In order for faith to take root in a human, there only needs to be a preacher, who herself has been grasped by Christ, in whose interior the Christian life of faith moves, and who through her personal expression can thereby awaken the same life in those who are hearing."[3] Christian preaching is not merely the private communication from one individual to another concerning his Christian moods and condition, his inner dispositions and spiritual emotions. Martensen uses the imagery of "organism" from

---

[1] Ibid., p. 5.
[2] Ibid., pp. 5-6.
[3] Ibid., p. 6.

the world of biology to characterize the church. Preachers from most denominations profess that they come not in their own name but in the name of Christ, and preachers are to be conscious of a call. The Christian preacher must, therefore, recognize herself as an organ or instrument of Christ, but she cannot be an "organ" of Christ unless she has previously been incorporated into the "organism" of Christ, that is, the church. The error of the sects, according to Martensen, is that

> they want to unite themselves with Christ without the church: they do not view the church as a *presupposition* for the individuals, but regard it only as a result, as a *product* of their holy endeavors. The sects want to form the whole, by an atomistic composition of the parts, instead of realizing that it is precisely the secret of an organism that the whole precedes the parts, that consequently the *community* of the holy is the presupposition for the holy individuals. Instead of considering the church as the holy mother of the individuals' faith and love, the sects considered it exclusively as a production, an offspring of the individuals' faith and love.[1]

The appropriate understanding of the church carries with it a conviction about God's commitment to it. "That Christ has constituted the church is not merely to say that he has given it an historical beginning in time, but that in time he has given the church an eternal beginning, a beginning which secures the church an eternal life and an eternal youth, a victorious development toward salvation."[2] That Christ has given the church this eternal beginning, in addition is to say, "that he has even made himself the Spirit's principle, that he—the God-Man, the only begotten, in whom the fullness of the Godhead bore flesh—has set himself in an organic relation to his church, to the whole as well as to each individual member."[3] As founder of the church, the Christ is also founder of faith, so "the faith of the church is, therefore, not only faith in Christ, but faith through Christ and faith by means of Christ."[4]

---

[1] Ibid., p. 8.
[2] Ibid., p. 9.
[3] Ibid.
[4] Ibid., p. 10.

To confess as Christians do the two claims, that faith comes from hearing or preaching and that faith comes from baptism, is possible because the two claims are not irreconcilable:

> Everywhere in the world of Spirit, wherever reference is made to spiritual productivity, we are able to discern this twofold beginning, the relative, which is only of a preparatory nature, and the central, the infinite, which is the life-empowering and really creative beginning. In secular language the infinite beginning is called the beginning that bears the hallmark of genius, because it is not the subject who to all intents and purposes moves itself towards the Idea, but the Idea, the ultimate reality itself, which in its indivisible fullness itself takes a life-empowering beginning in the subject, and opens up the source of enthusiasm and the mystery of productivity in this one. The beginning bearing the hallmark of genius consists not in the fact that the individual chooses its own idea, but in the fact that the Idea itself chooses the individual as its agent. The individual which itself wants to choose its idea without being chosen by the Idea, is either a fanatical enthusiast [*Sværmer*] or a rationalist.[1]

The analogy Martensen is making compares nature's spiritual endowment of the genius to the Christ's equipping and endowing of the baptized. The beginning of genius can easily be present without the individual realizing it and this beginning bestows upon the individual a major task along with the communication of special gifts. It is similar in baptism, except that now the sphere is not human life in general but specifically life within the Christian community. However, "it is the Christ himself, the principle, which includes the entire fullness of churchly life, who here makes himself to be the individual's genius."[2] We note that Martensen, with this notion of an infinite beginning, is talking about a moment in time when eternity is gaining entrance within the individual in a unique way.

If one considers the faith of the disciples, one realizes that their faith was not brought about by means of a natural reflection upon his doctrines,

---

[1] Ibid., pp. 12-13.
[2] Ibid., p. 13.

but by means of the divine-human power of Christ's *personality*. It was the Christ's relating to them rather than their relating to the Christ that evoked their faith. Because of this priority of Christ in the faith relationship, Martensen is able to contend that there are no "second-hand disciples":

> This genesis of faith, its foundation by Christ, its development from authoritative to free personal faith, which nevertheless still rests upon the fact of its divine constitution, must in substance repeat itself in all following generations, since the order of salvation cannot be an order essentially other than what it was for the first disciples. It is this continuity in the order of salvation which is effected by means of holy baptism. What Christ's personal election was for the first circle of disciples, baptism is for the subsequent church, the divine fact by which Christ gives his church the true, the eternal beginning in the individual….By means of baptism the church's constitution is continued from generation to generation, so that every new generation which is added to the church is just as primitively appropriated by Christ as were the first disciples. For it results from Christ's kingly office, that he, although he no more goes in a sensible form from Galilee into Judea, nevertheless substantially and personally moves on in the history of the world, from generation to generation, and that he is still, what he was from the beginning, the founder of true faith upon earth.[1]

A few pages later Martensen will write: "It is clear in and for itself that in the period when the essential task was to implant the church in the world, much had to be shaped otherwise than in later times, where the church had established firm roots in the world, where God's kingdom had become just like nature."[2] But he is in no sense saying by this that the later generations are therefore placed at an advantage over the earlier. And preaching rests not upon the apostolic Scriptures, but most directly on the fact that "we are appropriated by Christ in a way that is just as original or primitive as were the apostles, that Christ has given us the same beginning of faith, the same source of faith, if not the same

---

[1] Ibid., pp. 10-12.
[2] Ibid., p. 23.

measure of the Spirit, as he has given them, and with this has qualified us to perpetuate the community with the apostles by means of the holy Scriptures."[1] So "preaching is to be in the apostolic spirit"; otherwise one would have to speak as one without authority.

As far as cultus or worship goes, Martensen affirms: "The Baptist view presupposes that cultus is a relation in which the human posits itself toward God, but it overlooks that cultus just as much is a relation in which God posits Godself toward the human, and that this latter is the deeper relation in which the former is grounded."[2] The Baptists "hold literally that worship means service of God; and therefore they regard God exclusively as object, as an object of the religious acts of humans, without remembering that the human can make God the object of its cultus only insofar as God Godself cultivates the human."[3] Martensen confesses that the Christ "cannot merely be thought of as the object for his church's cultus, but must be thought of as the eternal founder of this cultus, who never ceases to act in his church. There must be talk not merely of an objective Christ, but of a living, eternally present subjective Christ":

> Precisely this is the concept of Christ's kingdom, the fundamental mystery on which the church rests, that the empirical schism between here and the hereafter, between the world on this side and the world on the other side, already is sublated in communion with him, who is the personal center in the whole realm of personality, and who will not be far away from his disciples who only in him are able to be one.[4]

The sacraments are properly understood as acts of this ever-present Christ, "acts that are independent of faith, but through which faith is grounded and developed."[5] A sacrament is a real communication of God's grace. *Historical* presence via remembrance is one thing, *mystical* presence in the depths of the soul is another thing, but these forms of

---

[1] Ibid., p. 14.
[2] Ibid., p. 15.
[3] Ibid.
[4] Ibid., p. 16.
[5] Ibid., p. 17.

presence find their living center and higher unity in the *sacramental* presence, in which Christ himself reproduces his historical presence through his institution.[1]

Martensen does not move fully away from the speculative view in his conception of Christian baptism, but he does distinguish how the speculative and the rationalistic conceptions understand what we today would call the historical Jesus and the biblical Christ or the pre-Easter Jesus and the post-Easter Jesus, and then he opts to bring these two views together:

> In Protestantism there are the rationalistic and the speculative conceptions of the sacraments. In the rationalistic view, the reigning perspective, there is in the Protestant cultus only *an image of Christ*, but no real Christ…. The sacraments are sensual means by which his image is enlivened for the church, and in this way too it exercises a moral influence. On the other hand the newer speculative conception, which will not allow itself to be satisfied with an historical relic, teaches that Christ is in his church as an omnipresent idea of Christ, who lives in the church's thought, in its faith and devotion; and the kingly office is posited in this, that Christ, who as an individuality has vanished, is present in his church as *Spirit*. Furthermore, in this cultus a relation is to take place not merely to Spirit, but a personal relation to the personal Christ, so again this can only become a relation to his image, not to his very self. For as a definite personality he has vanished; he is present only as a universal spirit.[2]

The appropriate view of the Christ as operating within the world involves affirming aspects of both of these views:

> The higher conception of Christ's kingly office, which unites what is here divided, is the primitive Christian conception according to which Christ as head of the body, personal prototype of humanity, cannot be separated from his organism, but brings himself to presence through his image, even works in, with, and under his institution. That the Lord is risen is not to say

---

[1] Ibid., p. 18.
[2] Ibid., pp. 18-19.

that his individuality has evaporated into the universal Spirit, but that he who in his individuality includes the entire fullness of God and the entire fullness of humanity, has sublated the temporal and spatial limits for his works. He is lifted up in order to be able to draw all unto himself, he has ascended in order to be able to fulfill all things, Eph 4. In his church spread throughout the whole world, the risen one himself gives a presence that is no less objective than his sensible presence on earth, although it is a veiled, a mysterious presence. His earthly appearance, his image in the word, his historical institution, he himself posits as means for his mysterious work. His own historical phenomena must become the visible element in which the risen one envelops his invisible presence.[1]

In equipping himself for serious work in dogmatic theology addressed to the public of the church, Martensen it appears had taken up a serious study of the writings of Martin Luther. He finds Luther such a helpful resource because he recognized the need for subjectivity in these matters, and he defended this need over against the interpretations of the Roman Catholic church; but Luther also recognized the need for objectivity, and he defended this need over against the interpretations of the Protestant sectarians.[2]

In the discussions that follow in the next sections on infant baptism, predestination, the new birth, and confession of faith and confirmation, Martensen rounds out his thoughts on the Christian doctrine of baptism in a way that always respects the reality of human freedom. In the process he mentions the paradox, baptism's emphasis on the single individual, the Protestant principle of subjectivity, and of course the concern that faith's objectivity not be forgotten about if one is to have a proper understanding of the sacraments.

In the year 1843 Vilhelm Birchedahl published a little book on the church year.[3] The book is a polemic against Mynster in defense of Grundtvig in the debate over Mynster's suggestion for a new homiletical periscope series as part of his proposal for a new service

---

[1] Ibid., pp. 19-20.
[2] Ibid., pp. 20-23.
[3] Vilhelm Birkedahl, *Kirkeaaret, et Billede paa den christelige Livsudvikling*, Copenhagen: C.A. Reitzel 1843.

book and church liturgy. Martensen had participated in the Theological Faculty's consideration of Mynster's liturgical proposal and finally gave a dissenting vote on whether it should be approved.[1] This controversery brought Martensen into liturgical studies and led to his publication on "The Church Year"[2] that came out in December of 1843. Birchedahl had shown the parallelism between the church year and Christian development of life in the individual. Martensen's essay presents a parallelism of sorts, only his is a parallelism between the astronomical year with its laws of nature and the church year with its higher laws of the Spirit and revelation. Sketching in bold strokes the cosmic significance of Christianity, Martensen develops the meaning of Christmas, Easter, and Pentecost as manifestations of eternity in relation to time. He also entertains some speculative thoughts on astronomy, which he understands as that imaginative thinking about the heavenly bodies, that poetic speculation about the nature of these bodies and their relation to spiritual life. With the rise of the Copernican system and the realization that the earth is not the center of the universe, things have changed for theology; however, this change in situation does not prevent our speculative theologian from writing of the earth as being the center of a divine revelation of extraterrestrial dimensions. He grants the possibility of multiple revelations of the Logos, but insists that one understand these as finding their center in the revelation in Christ.

Martensen became more entrenched in Golden Age Denmark and in the state church when he took on the duties of Court Preacher on May 16, 1845. In that capacity he had the responsibility to proclaim God's word to the king and the queen. From the publishing of his 1843 essay on "The Church Year" to the publication of his *Christian Dogmatics* in the summer of 1849, Martensen is just about completely silent literarily. There are two very minor publications during these years, besides his collection of sermons which would be published regularly from his assumption of duties as Court Preacher to the end of his

---

[1] Martensen, *Af mit Levnet*, op. cit., vol. 2, p. 82.
[2] Martensen, "Kirke-Aaret," *Urania: Aarbog for 1844*, ed. by J.L. Heiberg, Copenhagen: H.I. Bing 1843, pp. 161-188; reprinted in Julius Martensen, *Mindre Skrifter og Taler af Biskop Martensen*, op. cit., pp. 93-109.

life.[1] A brief article in a newspaper appeared on April 29, 1844.[2] It focuses on a book written by the Baptist-oriented theological candidate Magnús Eiríksson.[3] Its purpose is not to enter into an ecclesial or scientific conflict with Eiríksson, but to point out how he is guilty of literary impropriety or abuse. Mr. Eiríksson is before his time, quips Martensen, referring to Eiríksson's quoting of material from his lectures on speculative dogmatics before they had been published. In particular, Eiríksson refers to paragraphs on baptism from the 1839 version of the lectures on dogmatics, while Martensen in the meantime had published his doctrinal statement on baptism in 1843. The theological candidate had ignored the distinction between dictated paragraphs of an oral lecture and the style of a written book, between the university, with its possibility of personal interaction between the lecturer and his listeners, and literature, between the listening public and the reading public. Herein lies his literary abuse. The second minor publication is a Preface to the 1847 second edition of his book on Christian baptism.[4] There he points out how several readers found his doctrine of baptism entered into the magical. This accusation, he responds, depends on a confusion of the concepts of the magical and the mysterious. Something is magical if it presents a false relation between the supernatural and the natural such that the natural is interfered with or interrupted instead of being completed or fulfilled according to its true destiny. "A conception of divine grace which destroys the meaning of human freedom, a conception of the new creation and redemption of human nature by Christ whereby these come to disturb the works of the first creation, would be one which taught that something is communicated to the child which it could not oppose."[5] But any Christian will want to say that the relation between Christ and human nature involves more than can be explained according

---

[1] A chronological list of all of Martensen's published sermons and talks are included in Julius Martensen, *Mindre Skrifter og Taler af Biskop Martensen*, op. cit., pp. 13-24.

[2] H. Martensen, "Litterairt Uvæsen," *Berlingske Tidende*, no. 115, April 29, 1844.

[3] Magnús Eiríksson, *Om Baptister og Barnedaab, samt flere Momenter af den kirkelige og speculative Christendom*, Copenhagen: P.G. Philipsen 1844.

[4] H. Martensen, *Den christelige Daab. Betragtet med Hensyn paa det baptistiske Spørgsmaal*, 2nd ed., Copenhagen: C.A. Reitzel 1847, pp. iii-viii.

[5] Ibid., p. iv.

to empirical psychology. Much superfluous talk about the sacraments could be spared, suggests Martensen, if those entering into theological discussion would state at the outset whether or not they acknowledge a mystery in the sacraments, for opposite answers to this question lead to entirely different views of the essence of Christianity and usually to very different views of the essence of the Christian church. Martensen concludes his Preface by addressing himself to particular comments on his work on baptism made by reviewers.

In 1848, the year after Martensen's first wife died, he was married to Virginie Henriette Constance Bidoulac, the daughter of a French immigrant. At the close of his life Martensen says that after sharing life with her for the past thirty-five years, he is unable to express what she has meant and daily means to him. The testimony he gives to this meaningful relationship is not long, but it communicates some of what he felt for Virginie:

> Only this will I say, that the influence she has exerted on me includes both my activity and myself, my internal humanness. Her sensible counsel has often supported me in my work, and if my sermons have increased in intensity, if they have come to penetrate more into the individual, more into the mystery of the individual human, then it is owed in great part to her. If I have even become more humble, more loving, more tolerant in my opinions, it is owed in great part to her. If my sense for the individual, for the single self, the little person has been developed, while earlier I was only disposed to look at the whole and the great; if, to take an example from a single area, my sense for nature has been developed so that I cannot merely enjoy the great general impression but can also contemplatively take pleasure in the single objects of nature, the individual flower, the individual leaf, it is owed to her. I could continue to express much along this vein, but I know it would not have her approval. I will therefore only express the wish that the grace might be granted me that until my last day she might continue to be my life's good genius![1]

---

[1] Martensen, *Af mit Levnet*, op. cit., vol. 3, pp. 219-220.

Martensen's literary silence from 1843 to 1949 cannot be attributed completely to his changing family circumstances and his new duties as Court Preacher, for during these years he was also preparing his dogmatics. In 1848, while proofreading the galleys of this major work, he shared them with the Swedish poetess Fredrika Bremer who was then staying in Copenhagen.[1] That this work holds importance for its time and even beyond is evidenced by one of Martensen's harshest critics besides Kierkegaard. Danish Kierkegaard scholar Niels Thulstrup was not one to give complements to Martensen very quickly; in fact, he very consistently delivered on his penchant for having always to make Kierkegaard shine, especially in relation to those who had some appreciation for Hegel, like Martensen did. Nevertheless, Thulstrup could write: "If one were to point to a single work as representative of the main trend of Danish theology in the 19th century, one's choice would necessarily fall on Hans Lassen Martensen's *Christian Dogmatics*."[2]

Søren Kierkegaard would surely notice what Martensen wrote in the Preface to his *Christian Dogmatics* and in fact see some of what was included as being directed to him. In this Preface Martensen expressed his "conviction" that

> coherent theological thought, indeed theological speculation, is both possible and necessary.....And those who do not feel the tendency toward coherent thought but are able to satisfy themselves by thinking in random thoughts and aphorisms, sudden discoveries and hints, can also be within their rights in viewing coherent knowledge as unnecessary for themselves. But when, as in recent times, it begins to be put forth as a sort of dogma that *the* believer can have absolutely no interest in seeking coherent knowledge of that which is of greatest importance for him,…that *the* believer must view the concept of systematic knowledge about faith as a self-contradiction that abolishes true Christianity, etc.—then I confess that such statements, even when I have heard and seen them put forth with ingenious paradoxicality, are not

---

[1] Ibid., vol. 2, p. 134.
[2] Niels Thulstrup, "Martensen's Dogmatics and its Reception," *Kierkegaard and the Church in Denmark*, Copenhagen: C.A. Reitzel 1984 (*Bibliotheca Kierkegaardiana*, vol. 13), pp. 169-197, and reprinted in slightly modified form in *Kierkegaard and His Contemporaries*, op. cit., p. 181.

*Fredrika Bremer (1801-1865)*
(The Royal Library, Copenhagen)

capable of convincing me. Indeed, I can see them only as containing a great misunderstanding and a new or, rather, old error....As far as I can see, there is only one person who corresponds perfectly to the concept of *the* believer, namely, the entire Universal Church. As individuals, each of us possesses the faith to only a certain limited degree, and we must certainly be on guard against making our own individual, perhaps rather one-sided, perhaps even rather sickly life of faith into a rule for all believers.[1]

---

[1] Kirmmse, ed., *Encounters with Kierkegaard*, op. cit., p. 324.

In this monograph's second chapter we will note how Kierkegaard regarded this statement as a very personal assault on his writings.

Martensen begins his *Dogmatics* with an eighty-six page "Introduction" in which he deals with issues of theological method. In § 33 of the Introduction, Martensen speaks about the speculative and dialectical character of dogmatic theology's method. This important statement on methodology conveys a sense for how he here is maybe softening the tone by which he endorses theology's speculative nature—from the more unbridled enthusiasm for speculation which characterized his lectures on Speculative Dogmatics of a decade earlier—but nevertheless is still clearly endorsing the place of speculation in theological construction:

> The task of dogmatic theology, consequently, is to present the Christian view in a system of interconnected scientific concepts. The dogmatic concept is most exactly an *explicative* concept, an unfolding of that which is given in intuition, a development of its inner connections within itself. But the explicative concept contains in itself the urge toward the speculative concept, which does not merely rest content with presenting the connection between the elements, but also inquires about possibility and ground; which does not merely talk of the *ita* but the *quare*. The fundamental explication will not be able to avoid developing such contradictions of thought, such antinomies, which require a *mediation* in the concept; for as it is said in Sirach's Wisdom (33, 17): "The works of the Highest are always two, one against the other"; and the speculative depends precisely on grasping the contradictions in the unity of the Idea. A speculative *view* must always be presupposed, if the presentation is not to lose itself in an external understanding, or only confine itself to comprehending the Christian symbols in their practical, merely utilitarian meaning. However many doubts, for instance in an Irenaeus and a Luther, have been entertained against a speculative conceiving, yet we always encounter in their works that contemplative eye which grasps all singular realities in the light of the fundamental Idea. But although we grant to Luther that the fundamental form for dogmatics as the thetical theology is *ita*, not *quare* (Luther often complains about the curiosity of the scholastic sophists with their constant *quare* and exhorts remaining content with *ita*): yet it will not be possible to separate the explicative and the speculative concept by a firm and unmovable limit. Every *ita* contains

a hidden *quare*, which under careful explication cannot do otherwise than come forth and invite that higher sort of conceiving. Certainly we must always maintain that conceptual comprehension is the fragmentary in our knowledge, while the whole lies in the fullness of intuition, which is not exhausted by any conceptual development. But just as they have always been put to shame who pretended to have conceived everything; so have they no less been put to shame who have thought once and for all to be able to mark out the limits for all human conceiving, to be able to establish a *non plus ultra* [no more going beyond], by which it is to have its continuation. For afterwards it appeared constantly that there yet was given a "*plus ultra* [more going beyond]," and the supposedly firm limits revealed their movable nature by moving. Healthy reflection will therefore know that speculative conceiving itself is a greatly movable and dialectical concept, which does not allow itself to be disposed of by a dry yes or no, does not allow itself to be dismissed by the assertion that it must either be perfect or not be, for it is only as becoming; every conclusion in the concept will therefore always only be relative, every solution to the problem will in addition be a new sharpening of the problem; the concluded in knowledge will in addition contain the divinatory, which points toward another and still higher solution.[1]

In his Prize Essay of 1833 Martensen had affirmed the creative tension between the intuition of faith and the concept of speculation. Here we find him in 1849 continuing to affirm this tension as the creative conflictual milieu in which genuine theological construction is carried out.

Martensen's "Introduction" is followed by a fifty-page articulation of "The Christian Concept of God" in which he discusses "God's Essence," "God's Attributes," and "The Triune God." God is Spirit: "As Spirit

---

[1] H. Martensen, *Den christelige Dogmatik*, Copenhagen: C.A. Reitzel 1849, pp. 79-80. English translation: *Christian Dogmatics*, translated from the 1856 German edition by W. Urwick, Edinburgh: T. & T. Clark 1878, pp. 64-66. This is my translation from the Danish. At the close of this statement Martensen offers a footnote referencing Sibbern's *Bidrag til Besvarelsen af det Spørgsmaal: Hvad er Dogmatik?* for the distinction between the explicatory and the speculative methods of development, and concerning what is merely relative and transitory in this distinction.

God reveals Godself most precisely as "The Lord"; but according to the entire truth of God's essence, God is not merely the Lord who separates Godself from God's world, but the eternal "Love," which reconciles the world with Godself."[1] The Christian theologian is able to speak about more of reality than human reason relying merely on its own resources is able to do, because a more expansive world is available to "human reason as enlightened by God's word and Spirit."[2] Divine love leads to divine self-limitation and this is clearly affirmed by our dogmatician:

> God limits God's power, as God from the depths of God's eternal life calls forth a world of created beings, which God produces in a derivative sense to have life in themselves; but exactly by this fact that God is the power in a free world, God reveals the inner greatness in God's power. For that power is not the true power, which does not tolerate any free movement outside itself, because it itself will immediately be everything and do everything; but that power is the true power, which creates freedom, and which nevertheless is able to make itself all in all.[3]

On this topic of divine power, then, Martensen stresses "the concept of inner infinitude" and "the intensive, the central absolute" over against the Pantheists' "concept of external infinitude" and "the extensive absolute."[4]

Very important for Martensen's understanding of God is the reality of possibilities. "Only the very self of God has a perfect knowledge of the eternal *possibilities* of God's revelation."[5] Humans attempt to grasp the divine mystery, which means grasping the eternal possibilities, but even the highest speculative comprehension is going to be but a beginning, and "even the highest speculative knowledge is inseparable from a believing ignorance."[6] "God's essence is revealed in God's attributes."[7] Possibilities

---

[1] Ibid., p. 89; ibid., p. 73.
[2] Ibid., p. 106; ibid., p. 89.
[3] Ibid., p. 98; ibid., p. 81.
[4] Ibid., p. 99; ibid.
[5] Ibid., p. 108; ibid., p. 89.
[6] Ibid.; ibid.
[7] Ibid., p. 109; ibid., p. 91.

are the critical element in a number of attributes. "In the eternal God are all the possibilities of existence, the sources of the entire creation."[1] "In the depths of eternity is the creation as *possibility*, in the omnipresent One stirs the *actual* creation, which is released to an existence that is differentiated from God. Everything is filled by God, but that which is filled is different from that which fills. The omnipresent God is the inmost fundamental being in all the existing realities, the life in all the living, the Spirit in all spirits."[2] Although the creation is contained in God, God is yet not contained in God's creation"; for as transcending all creatures, "whose possibilities of existence God governs," God is free in relation to them.[3] Martensen cites the biblical declaration, "For God nothing is impossible" (Luke i 37, Matt, xix 26).[4] God's creative power has not been expended in the laws and powers of nature, but "in God's depths there is an inexhaustible fountain of possibilities for new beginnings, new revelations, new signs."[5]

Possibilities are the lifeblood of freedom and provide the lure to move freedom forward. Concerning providence, "what speculation calls the Idea, the world-forming thought, is designated in the Holy Scriptures as Wisdom," and as "the divine Sophia, the heavenly maiden."[6] A complete revelation of the attribute of righteousness can only be revealed in the world of freedom.[7] Since it is the nature of goodness to be able to possess its fullness only through communication, it is clear why describing the goodness of God leads to affirming God as *Communicativum* Sui [self-communicating].[8] In Martensen's vision, the human needs God and this is the human's highest perfection: "Receptivitity for the communication of the divine life is developed at all stages of creation, but only in the human does it appear as the perfect receptivity, as receptivity for the very

---

[1] Ibid., p. 112; ibid., p. 93.
[2] Ibid., p. 112; ibid., pp. 93-94.
[3] Ibid., p. 113; ibid., p. 94.
[4] Ibid.; ibid., p. 95.
[5] Ibid.; ibid., p. 96.
[6] Ibid., p. 116; ibid.
[7] Ibid., p. 117; ibid., p. 97.
[8] Ibid., p. 119; ibid., p. 99.

self of God, and precisely therefore is the human the most perfect creation, because it stands in absolute *need* of God. Only in the human can God's goodness reveal itself as love."[1] "Insofar as the divine communication of life is considered from the standpoint of the universe, it is goodness, insofar as it is considered from that of personality, it is love."[2] The divine attributes find "their concluding unity in love, which does not express a single aspect but the whole divine essence, since all other attributes are only more precisely determinations of love."[3] "All the divine attributes are combined in love, as in their center and life-principle."[4] The divine love "makes those who believe partakers of God's own divine *nature* (2 Peter i 4)."[5] Love is "a community of persons."[6] And finally, Martensen understands God as being a dipolar reality: "God lives a double life, a life in itself in undarkened peace and self-sufficiency and a life in and with God's creation, in which God submits Godself to the conditions of finitude, even allows God's power to be limited by the human's sinful will."[7]

After his discussion of theological method in his *Dogmatics*, Martensen offers his reflections upon the seven central Christian symbols or representations of Creation, Fall, Providence, Incarnation, Soteriology, Ecclesiology, and Eschatology. We will learn a little more about Martensen's *Christian Dogmatics*, however, by examining his next book that clarifies certain elements of the dogmatics in response to critics.

It is indeed in response to the critics of his dogmatics and in particular to the criticism of Rasmus Nielsen that Martensen wrote his *Dogmatic Elucidations* in 1850.[8] Nielsen's publication of his lengthy polemical work, *Mag. S. Kierkegaard's "Johannes Climacus" and Dr. H. Martensen's "Christian Dogmatics": An Investigative Review*, came as a surprise to

---

[1] Ibid.; ibid.
[2] Ibid.; ibid.
[3] Ibid., p. 123; ibid., p. 102.
[4] Ibid., p. 119; ibid., p. 99.
[5] Ibid., p. 120; ibid.
[6] Ibid., p. 121; ibid., p. 100.
[7] Ibid., p. 122; ibid., p. 101.
[8] Martensen, *Dogmatiske Oplysninger. Et Leilighedsskrift*, Copenhagen: C.A. Reitzel 1850 (*ASKB* 654).

*Rasmus Nielsen (1809-1884)*
(The Royal Library, Copenhagen)

Martensen.[1] Nielsen, a professor of philosophy at the University of Copenhagen who had been very much a Hegelian until his intellectual conversion through the writings of Kierkegaard, had been friendly and sympathetic towards Martensen. In fact, Martensen says he was pleased to have such a brilliant co-worker who was working for the same cause. He had even shared several parts of the work in dogmatics with Nielsen

---

[1] R. Nielsen, *Mag. S. Kierkegaards "Johannes Climacus" og Dr. H. Martensens "christelige Dogmatik". En undersøgende Anmeldelse*, Copenhagen: P.G. Philipsen 1849. See Martensen, *Af mit Levnet*, op. cit., vol. 2, p. 137.

prior to its publication and had received his complete approval; but now suddenly Nielsen declared the whole dogmatics as a totally unsuccessful product because the problem of faith and knowledge had been completely misunderstood.[1] Martensen states in his autobiography:

> Against me he sought to argue that Christianity in no way is to be an object of objective knowledge, that the highest truth is the paradox, that the absurd is the only thing which can be believed, and that we can only believe in a power of the absurd; that faith is an infinite passion of intensity, and other assertions of this sort which are all well-known from the Kierkegaardian literature but about which I have to say that I have no use for them.[2]

In Martensen's rejoinder of 1850, the year in which he was promoted to the rank of *Professor Ordinarius* or Full Professor, he sought to elucidate Nielsen's misunderstandings and to clarify his own standpoint.[3] Nielsen, for his part, continued his criticism of Martensen, just about making a literary career out of his polemics against the Dane who saw more than a disjunctive relation between faith and knowledge.

Martensen points to the difficulty of the situation at hand at the outset, that is, a situation in which one can no longer assume agreement on even the most basic dogmatic presuppositions, for opposing opinions have their bases in different standpoints, fundamental views, and comprehensive scientific outlooks. Even the dissertation defense at the universities is now a thing of the past because it only had meaning as long as one proceeded from a common, presupposed metaphysic and employed the syllogistic method by which one argued for knowledge of a single truth. Now it is realized that knowledge of a single truth has to be advanced along with a comprehensive framework of thought and can only be justified insofar as it is seen as being a necessary part in a whole organism of knowledge. Instead of squabbling on endlessly because of holding different presuppositions, Martensen believes it is better if each person presents his or her view of life as completely, pointedly, and concretely as possible, setting it in relation to the opposing views, and

---

[1] Martensen, *Af mit Levnet*, op. cit., vol. 2, p. 137.
[2] Ibid., vol. 2, p. 138.
[3] Martensen, *Dogmatiske Oplysninger*, op. cit., p. 2.

then leaves it for the work itself to gain a hearing and effect what it is able. This, he says, is what he has sought to do with the publication of his dogmatics.[1]

Martensen's biggest complaint about his critics is that they have focused just about exclusively on introductory matters, or matters of method, whereas Martensen made a concerted effort in his dogmatics to get beyond the merely preliminary matters to the doctrines themselves; indeed, he says that method can only be fully understood in its application. He feels that the scrutinizing investigation of the religious view he presented has been placed in the background as the general question of principles which were treated in the Introduction has been discussed by his critics in an abstract and formalistic way.[2] Martensen, now in his dogmatic period, is addressing himself to the public of the church, and it becomes clear that he views his own shift in interest and concern towards dogmatics as reflecting the mood of the time:

> This mode of procedure [abstract and formalistic] has surprised me not a little; for it certainly must still be vividly recollected how in a recently expired period we became tired and bored with the theological and philosophical questions of introduction, how for a great part the theological and philosophical literature consisted only of introductions and provisional preparations towards a construction of a system, how every scientific dilettante generally believed he ought to communicate his thoughts about faith and knowledge and how a system *should* look: plus how then eventually the insight developed that these general investigations could not really be conducted with any genuine fruit when they have not been treated in connection with the actual knowledge, the actual presentation of the subject matter in question. I think that there was a reason for assuming that this superior insight had taken hold. Now since I wanted to produce a thorough dogmatic view, I certainly endeavored in the Introduction to present the principles I wanted to follow in the working out of the whole; but by no means have I given the Introduction that completeness I would have given it if I had written only an Introduction to dogmatics. Indeed, I chose here intentionally the condensed presentation; for it should be considered as

---

[1] Ibid., pp. 2-3.
[2] Ibid., pp. 4-5.

only a part of the whole and should not stand independently outside of this....Nevertheless I see now that the critics again have taken the old, wide path, which in a simple remark can be designated as the *German*, namely, where one romps in nothing but propædeutical investigations, raises clouds of dust, but never quite gets to the subject matter.[1]

The critics are behind the times in that they are still absorbed in methodological issues instead of concentrating on the substance of the dogmatics.

There is one extended passage in which Martensen criticizes Nielsen for being incongruous with the Kierkegaardian corpus he is promoting, and that concerns Nielsen's use of direct as opposed to indirect communication. I quote the passage in full because of its relevance to Kierkegaard:

A famous dogmatician (the old Daub) on several occasions said: Blessed are those who will not foist their wisdom onto others. This word I must reluctantly be mindful of when I see the impetuousness by which Professor Nielsen wants to foist on me the wisdom that he seems to have found in Master Kierkegaard's writings. We should indeed certainly seek to instruct each other and to correct each other's mistakes; but it is well known that when one wants to teach and instruct an other, then it depends so very much on *the mode*, and in respect to the mode Professor Nielsen appears to me to have been highly unsuccessful. When he compares me with another author and tells us that by the study of Johannes Climacus and the other related pseudonyms he was brought to a changed standpoint, then this certainly is something he is free to decide; but when then in addition he is annoyed that I do not also have a changed standpoint, and with a fanaticism bordering on violence wants to give me a view of "the problem": then this seems to me by no means to be the right mode. Indeed, that is to say the more he himself must acknowledge that by a stroke of good luck he has arrived at the new standpoint, with the greater slowness ought he really go to work against the others, who only with terrific difficulty are able to give up the conviction which has been certified for them through

---

[1] Ibid., pp. 5-6.

a continuous trial. I shall at the same time not dwell on the form and tone in his review, not least because this already has often been the subject of [10] public conversation and he himself still gives new demonstrations of his writing mode. Only one remark must I make with respect to the form, because it is related to the subject matter. Namely, he acknowledges that he has borrowed his thoughts from writings which, in the presentation of truth, employ the "indirect communication," operate by means of irony and wittiness; he acknowledges that his thoughts have been extracted from "a humorous context" (p. 7). But when he then on the other hand—in order by this to help me gain a view of the problem—himself wants to employ the direct, straightforward form of communication of the truth, consequently does not want to talk gymnastically, experimentally, and sparklingly, but in a didactic lecture format (not γαμναστικῶς but δογματικῶς): so I had hoped that he then also would have actually translated the pseudonyms' thoughts from the indirect mode of communication into the direct. I had expected that he then also would have reproduced for me these thoughts in a new, self-created form by which it would have been possible for me to see the whole with a fresh eye. But unfortunately he has only summarized and for the most part made a word-for-word reprint of various passages from the pseudonymous writings, such that through it all he only talks in the pseudonyms' words, in their well-known parables and manners of speaking about fortunate and unfortunate lovers, about matrimonial love, about faith's passion in ultimate concern, these ways of speaking whose inner truth-content I precisely had expected that he would then open up for [11] me. He adds to be sure the assurance that all this is to be understood as a "direct communication" and that he now has deprived the pseudonym of his brilliant weapon, namely, that of irony and wittiness, and forced him into a didactic lecture's stiff form, in order thus to allow him to continue fighting with objective knowledge. Presumably I must at a certain point admit that, by tearing these propositions out from "the humorous context," he has deprived the pseudonym of the brilliant weapons. However, I wish that he would have done it far more thoroughly, of course, in order to give him a weapon of a completely different nature, by, as said, conceiving his thoughts in an actually new form, which really would be the single condition for a proper dogmatic debate. I could then do not other than find that the reviewer had not really himself stayed properly at home in his new standpoint, and that has happened to him which has happened to beginners who adopt a new philosophical teaching, that they do not merely think with their master's thoughts but also speak in this one's words and for a time lose the use of their own tongue. But then I came to realize that another thought had occurred to me. The reviewer, I thought, wants to invite me to a changed standpoint, wants to give me a view of the problem and the new standpoint's splendors; he wants from this new standpoint to be able to issue a critical judgment not merely over the dogmatic's present condition but also over introductory science, hermeneutics, etc.; and he himself is still so wrapped up in the baby clothes of the new wisdom, he still moves so awkwardly, so starry-eyed disciple-like in this wisdom's first elements, that not once is he able to lecture me on his [12] doctrines with his own words! Then I wondered whether I yet had not been right, since in the Preface to my *Dogmatics* I said that just as there was a time when we had not a few among us who all too early had been absolute in knowledge, so too not lacking now are those among us who all too early have become absolute in faith and all too early have become faith's defenders. – I must consequently give up on an independent presentation from Professor Nielsen's hand and be content with the assurance that everything that was taken up in "the investigative review" is taken as a "direct communication."

Now concerning Johannes Climacus and the other pseudonyms, these are in the present context of no business of mine. Certainly I admit that of these writings I have had a completely other conception than the reviewer. Namely, I have not presumed that it was these writings' intention to give us a new system or to establish any kind of philosophical school. Least of all have I presumed that it was their intention to give the grounds for a reform of dogmatics. From the scant acquaintance I have of these writings, I had rather come to suspect that the meaning was in a Socratic way to set a deeper skepticism in motion within the reader in order thereby to awaken him or her to seek the problem, which is higher and more than all theological and philosophical academic problems, namely, the personal problem of life, which no system can give us or solve for us, but which only the individual human is itself able to place before itself and is itself able to solve from its own God-given peculiarity. Consequently, I have presumed that these writings travel in a completely other direction than the one taken by Professor Nielsen. For Professor [13] Nielsen travels manifestly in a scholastic direction and wants to lead us to a new doctrine of knowledge and on this to establish a new treatment of theology. At the same time I attach no importance to this my conception of the pseudonyms, for my acquaintance with this diffuse literature is, as I said, only very scant and fragmentary, because among other reasons in following both my course of study and my individual spirit's direction I am less receptive to an experimenting presentation of the highest truths, and chiefly seek my instruction concerning these truths among those authors who employ direct communication. Fortunately, indeed, Christianity also made use not of the experimenting but the direct communication, with which of old has come humanity's desire towards it.—Consequently I consider those writings as to me, in the present context, quite irrelevant. The propositions the reviewer puts forward against me, I consider as propositions for which nobody except he himself is responsible. Whether those propositions perhaps have an entirely other meaning in the humoristic context among the pseudonyms, whether the reviewer is here in understanding, or in not-understanding, or in misunderstanding, all this lies outside of the circumference of my investigation. I shall here only limit myself to the far smaller and more modest task of sweeping before my own door, by showing that I have absolutely no use for the doctrinal propositions the reviewer with such great obtrusiveness has wanted to communicate to me, since on these I must apply the old saying that the true in this is not new and the new not true; just as I also shall show that whatever is supposed to be the position as regards his understanding of the pseudonyms, so is there irrefutably shown that he has not understood me, but in the most arbitrary way misunderstood and misconstrued my thoughts.[1]

This statement will provide fodder for Kierkegaard's ruminations, which disclose that he largely agrees with Martensen's criticisms of Nielsen.

The response to Nielsen occupies a major portion of the elucidation's 104 pages. Martensen notes that in the dogmatics he has developed the thesis that "nobody can know the truth if he has not placed himself in a personal relation to the truth."[2] So, of course, Christianity cannot be

---
[1] Ibid., pp. 9-14.
[2] Ibid., p. 14.

appropriated along the speculative way, if by speculation one means a disinterested, impersonal thinking, or a thinking that is altogether in the realm of the natural human: nobody can become a Christian by speculating.[1] But Martensen stands by his distinction between *fides, quæ creditor* and *fides, qua creditur*, or "the faith which is believed" and "the faith through which one believes," or the objectivity and subjectivity of faith; the truth of Christianity is independent of the faith of the individual.[2] Nielsen has claimed that the divine things are incomprehensible; Martensen questions whether they are *absolutely* incomprehensible, or whether in their incomprehensibility they are not *relatively* incomprehensible, so that Christianity, although it is a communication of and about existence, is also the communication of a doctrine, in the presentation of which is entailed a certain comprehensibility.[3] The Christian thinker must surely strive to unfold what he or she experiences in life.[4] But when one takes a single element of life, as Nielsen does, namely the experience of the paradox, and seeks to make it the fundamental basis for theology, then the approach is mistaken, for it only designates the divine truth from one side of the matter, only expresses the relation of contrast and the repulsive relation of the human consciousness but not the relation of union and the relation of attraction.[5]

Nielsen had investigated to see whether there could not be a different sort of objective knowledge, and that gives occasion for Martensen to offer some reflections on the nature of objective knowledge. By objective knowledge Martensen means "a knowledge in which there is truth, a knowledge in which there is an agreement between thought and its object, so that the thinking is a true image of the matter."[6] Now one can certainly imagine an objective knowledge that is impersonal and indifferent, although one can hardly imagine an absolutely disinterested knowledge; on the other hand, one can also imagine an objective knowledge which is conditioned by the most intense, most personal relation to the object, and

---

[1] Ibid., p. 15.
[2] Ibid., p. 16.
[3] Ibid., pp. 20-21.
[4] Ibid., p. 24.
[5] Ibid., p. 26.
[6] Ibid., p. 27.

so, Martensen asks, why should there not be a true knowledge of God conditioned by faith? Faith is ultimately concerned. In genuine faith the subjective and objective concern is indissolubly united, although these certainly do not appear without an alteration of attitudes.[1] But theology is not faith. Therefore, to the charge that in his dogmatics Martensen has not repeated the Christian representations or symbols in their practical, applicatory meaning, he appropriately responds that "it is not the task of dogmatics to *preach reconciliation* but to present it as knowledge, to search the *content of revelation* contained in the reconciliation, to scientifically develop the contemplative moment of faith, which by no means excludes but includes the practical, namely, insofar as this becomes an object of the universal consideration of faith."[2] It is for this reason that Martensen maintains that the concept of revelation is the all-embracing concept in the dogmatics.[3]

Martensen claims that being able to take part in a dogmatic treatment requires being more than an amateur in logic, for it also requires positive facts and an acquaintance with the truths of revelation as grounded in the experience of religious life, as well as some ability for an immediate and living intuition of the Idea so that reflection shall not come to hang in an empty space.[4] Martensen's logic, the logic of theonomy, needs the positivity of faith, an experience of faith, and an ability for reflecting on this faith. And his theological method demands that one not stop at the subjective side of faith, with Schleiermacher likely his target in this statement:

> In my theological works and not least in my dogmatics, I have striven to show that faith is not merely a practical God-relation, but also a contemplative relation, which includes a comprehensive view of the world and human life in its relation to God, a view of heaven and earth, nature and history, heaven and hell (*Dogm.* § 8); and that I therefore have not been able to be satisfied

---

[1] Ibid., p. 35.
[2] Ibid., pp. 39-40.
[3] Ibid., p. 40. Martensen views the thought that faith is not merely a consciousness of reconciliation but a consciousness of revelation as being a fundamental thought in all modern theology.
[4] Ibid., p. 8.

with a dogmatics which only wanted to give a doctrine of the religious subject, of piety, instead of a doctrine of God and God's revelation, only wanted to describe the human's experiences of the *effects* of Christianity, but not provide a doctrine of Christianity itself, as in its eternal truth it is addressed to the human and wants to be taken up by the human (*Dogm.* § 32).[1]

The dogmatic task, Martensen reiterates, is to develop scientifically the contemplative moment of faith. This surely entails "the *existential* thinking" Nielsen wants to emphasize, "that thinking which is one with the religious life itself, that thinking concerning the divine things that we have in the immediate religious experience, in the conscience, in devotion, in the moment of prayer, in the moment of worship, and in the moment of religious action," or as he has certainly emphasized, "in the moment of passion."[2] Martensen believes this is the same as what he, with Daub and Mynster, has called knowledge *in* religion as distinguished from knowledge *about* religion, which when it is completely developed becomes theology. Our Danish dogmatician refers to this latter sort of knowledge as a knowledge of reflection or an ideal knowledge, as opposed to the original, existential type of knowledge.[3] Nielsen has suggested that Martensen's whole project has the effect of stripping faith of its "risk." Martensen's response is that in by-passing critical reflection on the content of faith, one runs the real risk of believing that which is not true. For religion is not an isolated moment in the self, set off in a place of its own apart from the influences of other thoughts and representations: no believer is secure against delusions with respect to her faith.[4] Therefore the church has regarded it as important to have the doctrines of the faith presented in their coherence, the most convincing of which have been those having their deepest roots in an existential grasping of the truth, which are yet conditioned by a reflective thinking. Thus speculative reflection as a reflective or ideal second type of thinking

---

[1] Ibid., pp. 40-41.
[2] Ibid., pp. 41-42.
[3] Ibid., p. 43.
[4] Ibid.

serves to condition that existential, immediately religious thinking that provides the final principle for theological formation. Speculative thinking, therefore, is a second-order, reflective type of thinking that conditions the first-order religious, existential type of thinking that provides the final basis for theology's constructive statements.[1]

Professor Nielsen, Martensen notes, presents the relation between faith and knowledge in such a way that one of these must always be on the descendent when the other is on the rise, so that one of these makes the other superfluous. In response to this Martensen gives one of his clearer statements of the relation between faith and knowledge:

> But if knowledge should make faith superfluous, then faith itself must be only a knowledge, a lower, vague and confused knowledge which deservedly becomes replaced by the higher. Now faith is of course also a knowledge, but mind you an *existential* knowledge, that is, a knowledge which is one with the religious life itself, a knowledge of religious experience, while theology is an ideal knowledge and must incessantly draw its nourishment from the former. A theology which understands itself will therefore never posit itself in the place of faith, since this would be the same as thinking that the river could make the source superfluous, by which it has its living origin, or that the top of the tree could make the roots superfluous. A theology which wants to posit itself in the place of faith would not merely misunderstand the meaning of faith's existential knowledge, but would also overlook the fact that faith is far more than a knowledge, namely, it is a life in God which not merely moves in thoughts but also in feelings and affections, in a holy relation of the will to God, so it assuredly cannot realize how any theology which knows faith from experience would be able to render itself guilty of such a misunderstanding. For true theology faith is absolutely irreplaceable, and to posit theological knowledge in the place of faith would be, as Sibbern has so strikingly expressed it, the same as thinking that one could warm oneself by an astronomical theory about the sun instead of warming oneself by the sunlight itself.[2]

---

[1] Ibid.
[2] Ibid., p. 48.

Faith and knowledge need to be carefully distinguished but not separated.

The Middle Ages differentiated between a twofold certainty. On the one hand there is that certainty of religious experience which is given with faith, and on the other hand there is the certainty of ideal knowledge which is to be striven for in theology: *certitudo experientiæ* and *certitudo speculativa*.[1] The one of these by no means makes the other superfluous, because they are each of a different nature. The theologian or any Christian, declares Martensen, can have the experience where states in our internal life are such that we do not believe what we know, that is to say, where we do not really believe it to be the case that there is real power in what is known; the work of knowledge, therefore, in no way makes the struggle of faith superfluous for theology: "The more perfectly the truth is presented as knowledge, the more earnestly does knowledge again put to us the question whether we now also possess the corresponding repose in faith, whether we now also perceive the corresponding certainty of experience—*certitudo*, not merely *per intellectuam* but also *per affectum*."[2] Theological knowledge thus leads one back to that other kind of work than the work of knowledge, namely, the work of faith which is the one thing needful both for the wise and the simple.

Martensen is convinced that part of Nielsen's difficulty with his use of the speculative method is that the reviewer is operating with a completely different concept of speculation than Martensen acknowledges in his dogmatics. The notion of speculation is understood by Martensen as having its roots in the intuition of faith and as striving in faith after a relative rather than absolute comprehension of the divine things, acknowledging that faith is far richer than knowledge and intuition far richer than the concept.[3] One does not have to say either with Kant that God is absolutely incomprehensible or with Hegel that God is absolutely comprehensible in order to be a systematic thinker:[4]

---

[1] Ibid., p. 49.
[2] Ibid., p. 51.
[3] Ibid., pp. 51-52.
[4] Ibid., p. 52.

*Martensen and His Literary Production* 67

The knowledge I have described and had in view is not the purely philosophical, but that theological or dogmatic speculation which proceeds from the presuppositions of the revelation of faith and seeks to clarify its intuition of revelation through the concept, although it certainly acknowledges that the conceptualization is the piecemeal in our knowledge, while the totality lies in the fullness of intuition which is not exhausted by any conceptual development.[1]

It is this type of speculation, Martensen claims, that is found in the most profound teachers of the church such as Origen, Irenaeus, Athanasius, the Gregorys, Augustine, Anselm, and Thomas. Martensen maintains that even in Luther one finds essential features of an all-embracing speculative view and insights into a great coherent Idea which sheds light on the whole of existence, even as his writings invite the one who wants to seriously penetrate into them to a continuous pursuit of thought and dialectic.[2] The concern is not simply to defend "speculation" as a mere name. Martensen is agreeable to describing the sort of knowledge in question as "a union of *contemplatio* and *meditatio*," as with Bonaventura and the Victors, where *contemplatio* is taken to mean that free intuitive overview of the whole and *meditatio* is taken to mean that discursive dialectical thinking which seeks to clarify the overview through the concept; nor does he mind if someone wants with the Fathers of the early church to designate this sort of knowledge as Christian *gnosis*.[3] At the same time, Martensen does not understand why one should not dare denominate it as speculative, since speculation designates an absorption in the ideas, a beholding in the mirror of the Idea. Nielsen has merely adopted the concept of speculation from the systems of modern philosophy instead of from church history; dogmatic inquiry, as over against philosophical speculation, "has its own principle which is independent of philosophy, and therefore ought to be judged according to its own standard."[4]

---

[1] Ibid., p. 66.
[2] Ibid., pp. 66-67.
[3] Ibid., p. 67.
[4] Ibid., p. 68.

Martensen, in the course of responding to Rasmus Nielsen's review,[1] addresses the question about a change in view from his early lectures and from his theonomic standpoint:

> With this point I posit another connected one, which certainly is less essential. The reviewer seems in several places to want to express that I formerly have had another view of speculation than the one I now acknowledge. I call this point less essential, because it only concerns my own historical development, but not the works I now have made available to the public. At the same time I presume that nobody will be able to show me a *principal* contradiction between my now published dogmatics and my first dogmatic work on the autonomy of human self-consciousness (1837); or to show me that in my later writings I have given up the concept of the theonomic and with this the attending contesting of autonomic speculation, which is expressed in that writing, as well as in a treatise about "The Idea of Faust," which I published about the same time and which is found printed in Heiberg's *Perseus*. The conflict, which a couple years later was conducted concerning rationalism and supernaturalism—a conflict which unfortunately did not receive the carry-through among us that had been desired, but which has certainly not been without repercussions among us, namely, through that "Either—Or" expressed and so powerfully accentuated by Mynster—which from my involvement regarded only the concept of mediation, concerning which I by no means denied but demanded that mediation should be sought from the standpoint of *believing* knowledge. But it would surely be deplorable, if in more than ten years, which is the time that has elapsed, I should not have worked myself forth to greater clarity and, under a continuous study of the philosophical systems of the ages, namely, the Hegelian and the movements proceeding from this, should not have arrived at a more determinate knowledge and a sharper criticism of the relation of these to the problems of Christian theology. And it would be strange if I should not have a right to a continuous development, a right, which however a few people seem to want to deny me, as they seem to think ill of me that the dogmatics, I now have published, is not a stereotypical copy of my first lectures. Moreover, I would regard it as a lack of moderation to write in a

---

[1] See ibid., pp. 9-76.

more detailed way about my own historical development and to demand the public pay attention to an elaborate account of the preliminaries to my dogmatics and the transformations and modifications that I have carried out in giving repeated university lectures. I confine myself to the desire that the work I now have set forth in literature as the result of the development I have undergone up to this point, in some way might deserve the attention of the experts.[1]

Martensen makes this same point in his memoirs, namely, that he continued to maintain a theonomic standpoint throughout his career. But it is important to see that he is stating the same in 1850.

In this work Martensen also responds to the criticisms of Jens Paludan-Müller.[2] The main point Martensen deals with in response to Paludan-Müller concerns "that old theologoumenon, that even if sin had not entered the world, Christ would still have come."[3] Martensen is not Protestant enough, the charge runs, in the way he places a one-sided emphasis on the Incarnation over against Redemption. In Martensen's view it is permissible to speak of "Christ's eternal, metaphysical relation to the human race, and not merely to the human race, but to all of creation, whose head he is."[4] He writes:

> God's Son has allowed himself to become incarnate, has reduced himself in order to become the world's Redeemer; but I cannot admit that *only* for that reason has he allowed himself to become incarnate, since he just as well has allowed himself to become incarnate in order to become the world's Perfecter. When the Scriptures designate Christ as Alpha and Omega, as the Firstborn of all Creation, in whom and to whom all things are created, under whom all things shall be gathered as under the head, then I do not see how one can be correct *only* to allow that his coming be conditioned by sin.[5]

---

[1] Ibid., pp. 68-69.
[2] J. Paludan-Müller, *Om Dr. Martensens christelige Dogmatik*, Copenhagen: C.A. Reitzel 1850.
[3] Ibid., p. 87.
[4] Ibid., p. 89.
[5] Ibid.

*Jens Paludan-Müller (1813-1893)*
(The Royal Library, Copenhagen)

Martensen makes the case, then, for the scriptural character of this Christological claim. Furthermore, he disagrees with his reviewer's charge that this Christological claim is impractical, having no point of contact in the religious consciousness, except in the consciousness of sin. Martensen responds that there is indeed a point of contact in the human consciousness: "in the urge toward God's kingdom, which proclaims itself in the conscience and certainly has not resulted from sin; in the longing of the creation after the perfect community of love with God, which [longing] cannot be stilled, if God does not Godself assume the creation's nature in order by this to enable the creation to participate in God's nature."[1]

Martensen makes an interesting strategic point at the conclusion of his book that deserves comment. Martensen believes the Lutheran church has much to offer because it contains at least in principle the ecumenical church in its fullness.[2] The striving after ecclesial universality must be given expression in Christian dogmatics, but what form ought modern dogmatics take in relation to the forms which have appeared in church history? The Protestant Reformation stressed the theme of reconciliation, but this in-and-of-itself is not sufficient for the modern era. The first few centuries of Christianity stressed the theme of revelation, and this theme was re-emphasized in the dogmatics of the Middle Ages, but neither is this in-and-of-itself sufficient for a modern dogmatics. What the church needs at present is rather a presentation of the faith which in a new form reproduces the consciousness of reconciliation as well as reproducing the consciousness of revelation, or put more correctly, which *recapitulates both in a higher synthesis*, a synthesis which recapitulates that which was legitimate in the medieval dogmatics, although now developed for an entirely different context, so that the objective side of revelation may be given its due.[3] Martensen believes that a modern dogmatics, which does not set this return to the revelation of the early church as its task but only wants to limit itself to reproducing the Augustinian element of Protestantism, will not find itself on the path of progress but on the contrary will disclose that it has misunderstood the present state of the church.[4] This is not to say that the present time is not also in need of the pungent word of Augustinianism, but that the current situation clearly is more comparable to that situation of the church in the second and third centuries than to that of the sixteenth. The enemy against which the church has to defend itself is not as in the sixteenth century, a religiosity fossilized in externality, not a church law with a spiritless belief in authority

---

[1] Ibid., p. 90.
[2] Ibid., p. 97.
[3] Ibid., pp. 97-98.
[4] Ibid., p. 98.

and a dedication to the dead letter; the real danger now as Martensen reads the times is "a pagan cultural consciousness, a false spirituality," which, just as in the second and third centuries was expressed through a series of gnostic systems, is now in modernity expressed among the masses as a pantheistic and atheistic way of thinking that denies the foundation of the Christian view of the world and now just as then is joined with a false antinomianism, a doctrine of freedom that wants to liberate humanity from justice, wants to emancipate it even from the unwritten law of conscience.[1] He writes:

> In contrast to this pagan cultural consciousness, this false gnosis which we encounter sometimes in a scientific, sometimes in a popular form, the church needs the true gnosis, a Christian enlightenment, in order to be able to say in a meaningful way amidst the genuine confusions of the time: "I know what I believe." In contrast to this false gnosis the church ought also now as before to bring itself to an awareness that true reason and true science do not lie with unbelief, but that it [the church] itself possesses true wisdom when in faith it will envision reality in God's light [*vil se Lys i Guds Lys*].[2]

So for Martensen the period of the Reformation and the period of the first three centuries of Christianity are the great church-historical points of orientation which ought to be kept in mind when working out a dogmatics.

And this point of view finds support within Protestantism itself. The Reformation by no means wanted to sever itself from the true Catholic church, but wanted to preserve continuity with the ecumenical tradition, a fact that is demonstrated by the way the Augsburg Confession has placed the dogma of the Trinity at the head of its doctrines of the faith.[3] By this, as Martensen understands it, "our church has clearly intimated that it conceives Christianity not only as a consciousness of reconciliation but also as a consciousness of revelation. For the dogma of the Trinity is not

---

[1] Ibid., pp. 98-99.
[2] Ibid., p. 99.
[3] Ibid., p. 100.

primarily a dogma of reconciliation but a dogma of revelation and allows the light of revelation to pour out over all dogmas of reconciliation."[1] But the doctrine of the Trinity was only appropriated in a traditional way by the Reformers; it does not receive a living development and in later Protestantism was even placed in the background.[2] Martensen is not interested in appropriating the doctrine of the Trinity in the shape in which it lies in the Nicene statement of the fourth century, for there it seems as if it were only a metaphysical and ontological interest which produced this doctrine.[3] It may well be that modern speculation in Germany has conceived the determinations of Nicea predominately in this way and has made use of the doctrine for developing an idealism which dissolved and weakened the historical content of Christianity into an abstract metaphysic. But in Martensen's view, the doctrine of the Trinity does not have its roots in an abstract metaphysical interest:

> One misunderstands the ecclesiastical doctrine of the Trinity when one does not see it as the delineation of the *Logos*-doctrine of the second and third centuries, which latter by no means aimed at dissolving the historical into the metaphysical, but whose fundamental idea was that the metaphysical has become historical, that *Logos* has become flesh, and whose leading concern was to view the historical facts in the light of revelation.[4]

Martensen's final elucidation clarifies that it is from "this point of view of the intuition of historical revelation" that he has sought to treat the doctrine of the Trinity in his dogmatics. For him, although the immanent Trinity certainly is a presupposition for the economic Trinity, the abstract development of the former is not the main thing; the primary matter is "the development of the latter, the economic Trinity, by which it is known how God's essence is vividly reflected in the word of reconciliation, in the facts of sacred history and the life of the church, and by whose delineation and development the required synthesis of *reconciliation* and *revelation*

---

[1] Ibid.
[2] Ibid., pp. 100-101.
[3] Ibid., p. 102.
[4] Ibid., p. 101.

is accomplished."[1] In this sense, claims Martensen, the doctrine of the Trinity is of a very practical nature.[2] And we fittingly turn now to the practical period of Martensen's career.

### *III. Practical Theology Directed to Society: 1851-1884*

During roughly the last three-and-a-half decades of his life, the primary public to which Martensen directs his theological thought and writing comes to be society. Occupying him most of these years is his involvement as bishop of Sjælland. Martensen's interest in the public of society grows out of the concern to allow the theology, which he addressed to the academy and to the church, now to elucidate particular difficulties arising within a Christianity attempting to relate itself to modern culture. Many works were produced by Martensen during this period extending roughly from 1850 to his death in 1884. The monumental *Christian Ethics* appeared in the 1870s, but we will be unable to discuss that work here. Neither will we be able to look in detail at any of the other books addressed primarily to the public of society.

We have seen that in his *Dogmatic Elucidations* of 1850 Martensen was addressing himself explicitly to the public of the church. Defending his systematic presentation of the imaginative representations or symbols of the Christian faith, that work can be seen as contributing indirectly to the proclamation of the gospel, since Martensen understands the enterprise of dogmatic theology to be carried out in the service of preaching, or on behalf of the *kerygma* or message. But this is not to say that by 1850 Martensen was not already existentially engaged by another public, namely, that of society. For two years had already passed since the Revolution of 1848, and that event, it seems, jolted Martensen into a new social and political consciousness. The Berlin crisis of 1835 had confronted our budding theologian with the options of pantheism and theism. The crisis of the early '40s was less clearly defined, but it can be viewed as one in which our successful young professor had

---

[1] Ibid., pp. 101-102.
[2] Ibid., p. 102.

been confronted with the options of left or right Hegelianism. Now at the close of the '40s our established ecclesial spokesperson is faced with a new crisis: How will he relate to the new situation created by the Revolution?

In his *Levnet* Martensen reflects back on these times, and there is no reason to question the overall soundness of his observations. He writes: "At the beginning of this year (1848) Christian the Eighth died, and shortly thereafter the February Revolution broke out, which spread like an earthquake to the rest of Europe and everywhere an upheaval was produced."[1] The Revolution brought about a rise in religious consciousness, especially those forms of religion in which the prophetic and apocalyptic elements played a major role.[2] But, most of all, 1848 was a year of awakening in the whole arena of the social:

> For this is the world-historical meaning of the February Revolution, that it was not merely a political-liberal revolution as the July Revolution, but in addition was a social revolution. *The fourth estate* [class] and its demands is the innermost feature of the February Revolution. The social problem is the question of rich and poor, of work and capital, of the destitution of society and of a more equitable and just distribution of the goods of the earthly life. It was this problem that fermented and turbidly stirred at the bottom of the February Revolution.[3]

Martensen's interpretation of the Revolution is that at the heart of it one finds that which is in contrast to liberalism, and that when this is finally realized, a fight is inevitable: "For liberalism wants individualism, socialism wants society and solidarity." Liberalism is insensitive to the needs of the poor and opposes their requests in a fanatical way

> ...because it does not want to deprive itself of its control of capital, its free competition, its stock market speculations and swindles, etc. It is confirmed more and more that liberalism wants to dissolve society into nothing but individuals with their individual concerns, which for a great majority is

---

[1] Martensen, *Af mit Levnet*, op. cit., vol. 2, p. 120.
[2] Ibid., vol. 2, pp. 123-124.
[3] Ibid., vol. 2, p. 127.

merely the concerns of money; socialism, when it is understood according to its true meaning, wants to hold society together in solidarity, wants to subordinate the individual to society.[1]

Martensen notes that all that he has said about the social side of the Revolution dawned on him in 1848. He received a feeling at that time, he says, that if a person did not consider and grasp the social side of a matter, one would be unable to come to a full understanding of it. It seems that not a great deal has changed in the six score years that have passed since Martensen wrote his autobiography:

> I had to remember [in 1848] what Fr. Baader had said several years back about the disrelation between the haves and the have-nots. I had to be reminded of his word that our present social culture resembles not a tree which spreads out its branches to all sides, but a pyramid at whose little top there is found some few favored people, while its broad base forms an infinite swarm of possessionless and destitute which is entrusted completely to itself and therefore relegated to every sort of self-help, because neither by heart nor stomach, neither by duty nor honor is it tied to the state, to which it is related with indifference if not hatred.[2]

Martensen's practical theology addresses itself to society, to this social problem. But he felt little support and sympathy for his concerns. This leads him to suggest: "Perhaps a new revolution, a new 1848, is necessary in order to bring humanity back to understanding what one cannot convey to them along the way of reflection."[3] He continues: "Time will tell whether we have a right to say: when the new 1848 comes, when liberalism and socialism stand struggling against each other in full consciousness, then will a new era break out in world history and society will take on a new shape."[4] He is confident that when that day comes, socialism will win the day.[5] So that, if liberalism seems to be prevailing

---

[1] Ibid., vol. 2, pp. 128-129.
[2] Ibid., vol. 2, pp. 129-130.
[3] Ibid., vol. 2, pp. 130-131.
[4] Ibid., vol. 2, p. 131.
[5] Ibid., vol. 2, p. 129.

*Ditlev Gothard Monrad (1811-1887)*
(The Royal Library, Copenhagen)

at the present, socialism clearly has the future; liberalism is destined to become a subordinate moment.

While the Revolution led to an awakening in the areas of the religious, the political, and the social, this remarkable year also led to an ecclesiastical awakening. The old, pre-revolutionary order included the established church, now suddenly thought had to be given to a new church constitution and to the whole matter of the relation of church and state and how this relation should be patterned in the new order of things. D.G. Monrad (1811-87), the first Minister of Ecclesiastical Affairs and Public Instruction, in a letter to bishops and theological faculty, expressed the opinion that the recent political changes would exert a radical influence on the Danish church and suggested that a gathering of people representing the church be called to discuss proposals for the shape of the new church polity, so that a recommendation could be presented to the Parliament.[1] This, of course, was an important question, whether church and state should continue to be united, whether there should continue to be an established church, or whether church and state should be completely separated.[2] It seems that Monrad's inquiry was not clear, and this problem prompted an inquiry from the ecclesiastical representatives requesting a more detailed explanation; this inquiry, subscribed to by all concerned, was signed by Martensen, Grundtvig, and Clausen. The reply given to this inquiry was evasive and vague, but the result was that a gathering, representing the church, to discuss this important question never took place.[3]

*Grundlovet* or the Fundamental Law of the Constitution, which was finally passed on June 5, 1849, gave Danes freedom of religion. And it declared the existing Danish Church or the Evangelical Lutheran Church to be the Danish National Church, which was to be supported by the state. The Fundamental Law provided that the constitution of the Folk-Church be settled by law. This issue of the church constitution is one which occupied Martensen during the early part of this third period of his career. His book, *The Danish Folk-Church's Constitution* of 1851, is his contribution to the discussion.[4] To this day, however, legislation laying down a constitution for the church has not been enacted. Martensen, at the end of his life, laments the fact that this determination has stood as an empty promise for so long, "while the church has been at the mercy of a purely secular ministerial regime, and with this been placed under a capriciousness far greater than under Absolutism."[5] Under the influence of liberalism he sees the Danish Folk-church as having stressed excessively the freedom of the individual, while the church as an institution in society has been confined in a most undeserving unfreedom.

Simultaneously with these social, political, and ecclesiastical upheavals, a war was being waged in southern Jutland. In 1848 a

---

[1] Ibid., vol. 2, p. 131.
[2] Ibid., vol. 2, p. 132.
[3] Ibid., vol. 2, p. 133.
[4] H. Martensen, *Den danske Folkekirkes Forfatningsspørgsmaal*, Copenhagen: n.p. 1851.
[5] Martensen, *Af mit Levnet*, op. cit, vol. 2, p. 133.

rebellion in the duchy of Holstein instigated the First Slesvig War with Germany. Martensen, being from that area originally, was asked by the ecclesiastical representative, N. Nielsen, a cousin of his, to express his view of the involvement of the clergy of Schleswig-Holstein in the affair. Should the clergy turn to supporting Germany since they have seemingly been betrayed by King Frederik VII, who is therefore no longer to be regarded as the authorized political ruler to whom they swore an oath of allegiance, or should they continue to recognize Frederik's authority over them? This led to Martensen's first political statement. He published a lengthy letter in 1850, which, in response to the revolutionary activism on the part of German nationalist clergy in the duchies, commends continued allegiance to the King of Denmark as Duke of the duchies.[1]

Having taken a stand on this politico-ecclesiastical matter, Martensen's involvement with the controversy in southern Denmark was far from over. In 1851 the office of General Superintendent in Schleswig, or the bishop's office there, became vacant and it was believed that Martensen who was from there would make the perfect candidate for the position.[2] Martensen's memoirs become confessional as he admits here to "an inconsistency in my mode of action." Martensen was pressured to assume this new responsibility by those who saw it as a duty to his fatherland under the difficult circumstances of the times. The Professor and Court Preacher finally agreed to accept the position and to move to his hometown of Flensborg.[3] But shortly before the time came to move, Martensen had grave self-doubts about his ability to be equal to the task. He recalled Mynster's words to him, "Whatever you do, do with heart!"[4] And, with the approval of his wife, he decided against going to Schleswig. Mynster was very comforting and loving towards Martensen in regard to this decision; most others viewed it as an anti-patriotic act made out of a selfish desire for a better and bigger appointment, namely that of a replacement for Mynster in the office of bishop primate of the Danish church.

---

[1] H. Martensen, *Sendebrev til Hr. Overconsistorialraad Nielsen i Slesvig. Et Ord om Embedseden og den Slesvig-Holsteenske Geistlighed*, Copenhagen: C.A. Reitzel 1850.
[2] Martensen, *Af mit Levnet*, op. cit., vol. 2, p. 150.
[3] Ibid., vol. 2, p. 151.
[4] Ibid.

A last item to be mentioned in Martensen's transition to ecclesiastical representative is the publishing of his 1853 work on *The Establishment of Worship in the Lutheran Church*, which is subtitled *An Essay in Practical Theology*.[1] The occasion for this writing was the celebration of the Reformation at the University of Copenhagen. The work contains some general reflections on the Christian worship of God as well as a characterization of the worship of the Evangelical Lutheran Church in which Martensen discusses "God's Word and the Liturgical Tradition," "Law and Gospel, Sacrifice and Sacrament,""The Reciprocal Community in Worship," "Evangelical Freedom," "The Relation between Cult and Art," and some closing comments on the nature of practical theology which he defines in a much more narrow fashion than is being used here.[2] Martensen begins his treatise with these words: "All divine services, all temples and altars on earth point back to the inclination towards God which is indelibly implanted within human nature; and they all point back to the inclination towards community within human nature which here expresses itself as an inclination to worship in a fellowship and to give this shared worship an external, visible shape."[3] The essay unfolds this presuppositional comment, developing more fully that organic view of church and society which existed in nascent form in earlier writings and which will play such an important role in the practical theology that we must leave largely unaddressed.

---

[1] H. Martensen, *Om Gudstjenestens Indretning i den lutherske Kirke. Et Forsøg i den practiske Theologie*, Copenhagen: C.A. Reitzel 1853.

[2] The fact that Martensen restricts the scope of practical theology to inner-ecclesiastical matters by no means militates against our use of the term in a more general way as including within its scope the whole relation of Christianity to society. There are theologians who are concerned that practical theology not extend its bounds beyond inner-churchly activity. Martensen was definitely far from that mentality. He endorsed wholeheartedly the belief that theology be *praxis*-oriented and directed explicitly to the public of society. The fact that he restricts the term practical theology to the ecclesiastical reflects not a theologically conservative position on the social relevance of the gospel but rather the historical precedent established by Schleiermacher's *Brief Outline on the Study of Theology*, trans. by Terrence N. Tice, Richmond: John Knox 1966. See pp. 91-114 for Schleiermacher's reflections on practical theology.

[3] Martensen, *Om Gudstjenestens Indretning i den lutherske Kirke*, op. cit., p. 1.

Kierkegaard's attack on the church took place in 1854 and 1855. Martensen gives his own account of this in his autobiography:

> I was yet to have an experience of the most unpleasant sort: Søren Kierkegaard's attack on Mynster's posthumous reputation, which was tantamount to an attack on me. Shortly after Mynster's death, I gave a sermon at the Castle Church (where we had so often gathered around his pulpit) in which I included Mynster among the Christian witnesses to the truth that the sermon gave me occasion to discuss. This became the object of a violent attack by Kierkegaard, an attack that would very soon rock the entire country. The blow that was inflicted on me was calculated far in advance, and it was intended to be a mortal blow, to destroy me utterly, and to make it impossible for me to hold the high position that had recently been entrusted to me. If this event is to be understood historically—and in a certain sense its consequences entitle it to be viewed as an event in the ecclesiastical history of our little society—I assume that it may be explained, in part, by the fanatical notion that Kierkegaard had formed about a high mission to which he had been called, and, in part, by simple, personal animosity, not to mention hatred. No matter how much people talk in general about objectivity, about the principle of the thing, and about justice in connection with literary disputes and similar affairs, personal issues nonetheless play an important role, often in the narrowest way, and it is impossible to arrive at an adequate explanation without reference to them. His shamelessness in saying publicly that I had given that sermon about Mynster in order to promote my candidacy for the episcopacy made clear the degree to which there was a personal element involved. One would not have expected that a man of Søren Kierkegaard's spirituality and intelligence would lower himself to that sort of thing, which was appropriate only for scribblers of the lowest and most common sort. Both here and in other cases, however, he has descended to his genre. Sibbern made the very telling comment that S. Kierkegaard had here revealed himself to be a philistine.[1]

---

[1] Martensen, *Af mit Levnet*, op. cit., vol. 3, pp. 12-13; Kirmmse, ed., *Encounters with Kierkegaard*, op. cit., p. 201.

A key difficulty was Martensen's use of the phrase "witness to the truth." He explains his use of the phrase as applied to Mynster:

> I do not intend to make the least excuse for this term—as though it were less than proper, or something that ought to be retracted. I would use the same term today. When taken in the right sense—that is, in context—my expression was completely proper. But S. Kierkegaard had the dishonesty and the effrontery to tear it out of context, to take it to an extreme, and to assign to the term "witness to the truth" the meaning "blood witness" or "martyr." Naturally, neither I nor anyone else had had this in mind. I had included Mynster among the Christian witnesses to the truth because my sermon emphasized his importance to our fatherland, the desolate times in which he appeared, his battle against unbelief and rationalism, and how he had reintroduced the Gospel into many hearts. Anyone who carefully considers the concept of a witness to the truth must come to the realization that the main thing is that a person so characterized must have witnessed to *the truth*, but that suffering and persecution are in no way a sure sign of a witness to the truth, because fanatics and false teachers have also often been subjected to great suffering and have become martyrs. Furthermore, external suffering and martyrdom belong to certain historical epochs and presuppose particular social conditions and circumstances; they cannot appear during all epochs, while witnesses to the truth may be found at all times and under all social conditions.[1]

By June 6, 1854, the day after Martensen had been installed as bishop of Sjælland, he was sending out a pastoral letter to the clergy of the diocese inviting them to join him in working for the unity and solidarity of the church.[2] The attack began in earnest at mid-December of 1854 and extended into September of the next year. By the end of the year, Martensen was making his single response to the attack Kierkegaard had launched against him:[3]

---

[1] Ibid., vol. 3, pp. 13-15; ibid., pp. 201-202.
[2] Bishop Martensen, *Hyrdebrev. Til Geistligheden i Sjællands Stift*, reprinted in *Mindre Skrifter og Taler af Biskop Martensen*, op. cit., pp. 110-112. For Martensen's treatment of his being selected as bishop, see *Af mit Levnet*, op. cit., vol. 3, pp. 1-8.
[3] Bishop Martensen, "I Anledning af Dr. S. Kierkegaards Artikel i Fædrelandet, Nr. 295," *Berlingske Tidende*, no. 302 (December 28, 1854). An English translation of this response is reprinted in *M*, Supplement, 360-366.

*Martensen as Bishop (1808-1884)*
(The Royal Library, Copenhagen)

I myself wrote a reply to Kierkegaard's attack, which I published in *Berlingske Tidende* and which many people thought should have been worded more gently. It is possible that they were right, and the only answer I can give to this is that, at that time at least, I was not capable of writing otherwise than as I did. I had been made indignant by the moral vileness. And I have always accepted the notion that there is a righteous anger, an indignation, which has a right to be expressed. Subsequently, Kierkegaard complained a great deal that after that article I observed complete silence instead of involving myself with him, as he demanded, in a fuller polemical debate.

I really could not do him the service of appearing with him in a theatrical piece performed for idle and curious spectators. I maintained silence. He deserved no answer other than that which was given to him.[1]

A parallel is seen by Martensen between Kierkegaard's attack on the established church and that which had been leveled against it over the years by the sects:

> In *The Moment* (of which I read only the first issues) he unleashed his attack on the established church. He declared that the church and its pastors had deviated entirely from the Christianity of the New Testament, that what was called Christianity in this country was an enormous falsification of Christianity, an enormous lie; and that the best advice which could be given to a person was both from the Word and from the sacraments. Here he addressed himself to the masses—he, who had earlier disdained the masses and had sought only a quiet encounter with the individual. His method differed in no way from that of the sects, which attack the established church because it is not in accord with what they call the Christianity of the New Testament—which they prove with a number of scriptural passages that have been torn our of context. This was precisely Kierkegaard's course of action, and there was no continuity between *The Moment* and his earlier, more profound writings that had been directed at the individual.[2]

Martensen goes on to say that Kierkegaard's attack "produced great results." His supporters were "the sectarians and all those who were hostile to the church and the clergy," together with "the out-and-out atheists and those who deny God, who wanted to have nothing to do with Christianity or religion."[3] Martensen acknowledges that Kierkegaard, in his attack on the church, "wanted to enter into public life actively, as a reformer," but as he observed this reforming activity it "was without aim or purpose," for Kierkegaard was calling for an abandonment of the established church without providing "any direction concerning where

---

[1] Martensen, *Af mit Levnet.*, op. cit., vol. 3, p. 16; Kirmmse, ed., *Encounters with Kierkegaard*, op. cit., p. 202.
[2] Ibid., vol. 3, pp. 16-17; ibid., pp. 202-203.
[3] Ibid., vol. 3, pp. 17-18; ibid., p. 203.

one ought to go."[1] He thinks that if Kierkegaard is viewed ideally, "he comes more and more to resemble an *accusing angel* in his attitude toward the Folkekirke, and it is as such that he is still hailed and invoked by the opponents of the Folkekirke. He himself also seems increasingly to have viewed his mission as that of an accusing angel."[2] Martensen judges, however, that unfortunately "it was a heartless criticism" and surely "not that of the Holy Spirit."[3] At the same time, Martensen clearly affirms Kierkegaard's uniqueness and the tremendous value of his literary production:

> It would be regrettable if the great wealth of spirit and genius that is to be found in Kierkegaard's writings did not yield some fruit for the future. Until now we have seen only flawed preliminary attempts, but there has yet to appear any writer of significance who shows signs of having been genuinely inspired by the many brilliant details in his writings. Even if these details are one-sided, they are nonetheless suited to provide impulses and to produce ferment.[4]

These two large fish in the small pond of Copenhagen, Denmark, could simply never establish a positive relationship; however, here Martensen has been able to offer some appreciative words about Kierkegaard, which we will see Kierkegaard on equally rare occasions is able to do in relation to Martensen.

Kierkegaard died on November 11, 1855. It seems fitting to give Martensen the last word, which we can do by noting that the next month he published a little writing, *In Memory of J.P. Mynster*, which in its original form was written to be read at the Society of the Sciences of which Bishop Mynster had been a member for many years.[5] The work begins with these introductory words:

> Only very few personalities could be said to be as deeply embedded in the history of the Danish church and culture in this century as that of Mynster.

---

[1] Ibid., vol. 2, p. 19; ibid., pp. 203-204.
[2] Ibid., vol. 3, p. 20; ibid., p. 204.
[3] Ibid., vol. 3, pp. 20-21; ibid.
[4] Ibid., vol. 3, p. 22; ibid., p. 205.
[5] H. Martensen, *Til Erindring om J.P. Mynster*, Copenhagen: Gyldendal 1855.

> Not only has he for more than a half century profoundly influenced his nation as a speaker and author, but also in several important official positions participated in the administration of church and school in Denmark, and we are hardly able to be reminded of anything of importance in a spiritual respect that has taken place in his time in Denmark, except that he also in one way or another, directly or indirectly, has participated in it, whether this participation was for or against, promoting or inhibiting. A complete presentation of his life and activity would therefore call in addition for a presentation at the same time of ecclesial, literary and social relations in Denmark, a picture and appraisal at the same time of the spirits and movements, conditions and events in our fatherland. Such a presentation however lies outside the limits we here have had to set for ourselves, to which must be added the fact that the direct biographical sketch for the most part has been taken up previously by Mynster himself in his *Communications* of his life. It is only a single page of his life's *inner* history which shall here rather be told, as here shall be attempted a contribution towards presenting what we could call his way of conviction or the way he has walked in order to arrive at a conviction of that which for him was the seriousness of life.[1]

Martensen states that he will try to accomplish this not by following him on his long spiritual journey, nor by dwelling on the various stages along the way of that journey, but by drawing attention to decisive starting points for Mynster's spiritual journey of life.[2] And the author then proceeds first to underscore the importance of religiosity for Mynster, secondly to consider at length Mynster's relation to his "kindred spirit" Jacobi, and finally to ask how Mynster understood the relation of Christianity to modernity.

It is this last consideration of the relation of Christianity to the modern age in which Martensen later says the roots or fundamentals of his own ethics can be found.[3] The age of modernity is designated as the age of humanity, and this humanity can be related in a positive way to Christianity:

---

[1] Ibid., pp. 5-6.
[2] Ibid., p. 6.
[3] Martensen, *Af mit Levnet*, op. cit., vol. 3, p. 203.

For humanity, which includes everything that belongs to human existence and human culture, *can* also envelop the free, heart-felt relation to Christianity, since Christianity is the religion of humanity designed for satisfying the deepest necessities in human nature; since the human is created in God's image and Christ is the Son of Man come to redeem and complete human nature to its original destiny; since it is precisely the purpose of Christianity to restore genuine human existence.[1]

But Martensen notes how humanity can also designate a view and tendency of life which allows all things divine to be destroyed in the human.[2] Then human freedom and independence is so glorified that it looks back to positive religion as to the times of immaturity, dissolves positive Christianity in a so-called universal human religion and morality, or even sets itself free from all fear of God and does not acknowledge any other deity than that which becomes conscious of itself in the human and reveals itself in the powerful works of human genius. Mynster protested against this humanity that refuses to seek the reception and completion of the human in Christianity; but Martensen emphasizes how Mynster just as much protested against a Christianity that suppressed the human instead of emancipating and fulfilling it.[3]

In attempting to isolate out the forms of that humanity which turned away from Christianity, Martensen wants to further specify the form of humanity (*l'humanité*) that arose with the French Revolution.[4] Two figures from the literature of that time are focused upon by the new bishop because in a symbolic way they characterize the ideal of humanity which spoke to the majority of deeper and more serious intellects and exercised a profound influence on culture. The one is Goethe's Prometheus and the other is Lessing's Nathan the Wise.[5] For Mynster it is certainly enough to be a human, there is nothing higher one could want to be; however, one cannot be an abstract human, but can only become a human in concrete relations.[6] And for Mynster the true human ideal, human nature in its

---
[1] Martensen, *Til Erindring om J.P. Mynster*, op., cit., p. 44.
[2] Ibid., p. 45.
[3] Ibid., pp. 45-46.
[4] Ibid., p. 46.
[5] See the discussion of these two figures, ibid., pp. 46-48.
[6] Ibid., p. 48.

purity, is found in the Christ; so nobody can arrive at a true and complete human existence except by a life lived in imitation of the pattern of Christ. At the same time, Mynster "never has been able to sympathize with any pietistic tendency which wants to isolate Christianity from the greater context of human life, from science and art, from fatherland and people, and which does not want to acknowledge the same revelation of God in the kingdom of nature and in the kingdom of grace, in reason and in the gospel."[1] In protesting against both a godless humanity and a humanless Christianity, Mynster with the abilities and gifts given to him, worked for the proper union of the Christian and the human. In that sense it can be said that Mynster was an influential proponent of Martensen's logic of theonomy in its practical theological expression.

Over the next years Martensen wrote much more, but these writings fall beyond the years of Kierkegaard's life. He continued his correspondence with his friend Gude until February 7, 1883, about a year before his death.[2] Johanne Luise Heiberg, who had been Martensen's friend for over forty years, tells in her memoirs of the death of this man who "did not allow himself to be overwhelmed by his feelings."[3] She writes how near the end his body became weaker and weaker, and yet he was full of thanksgiving.[4] Fru Heiberg relates how Martensen faced the end:

> When I sadly expressed my sorrow over this to Martensen, he said: "All this I am able to lay behind me and I have nothing to do with this. I abide by Christ's words, and he has said after his resurrection: *'I live, and you shall live.'*" Generally and mildly he said all this. All of us who loved him rejoiced over the spirit of peace which had spread over his whole being,...rejoiced over the fact that he should tranquilly and blissfully fall into a slumber.[5]

---

[1] Ibid., p. 52.
[2] Martensen, *Biskop H. Martensens Breve*, vols. 1-3, ed. by Bjørn Kornerup, Copenhagen: G.E.C. Gads Forlag 1955-1957, vol. 2, p. 145.
[3] Johanne Luise Heiberg, *Et liv genoplevet i erindringen*, op. cit., vol. 4, p. 293.
[4] Ibid., vol. 4, p. 294.
[5] Ibid., vol. 4, p. 295.

*Ludvig Jacob Mendel Gude (1820-1895)*
(The Royal Library, Copenhagen)

According to Ms. Heiberg, Martensen was prepared to die, and he did so in tranquility, in humility, and in cheerful, hopeful faith.[1] Upon his death, an English critic bestowed on him a very lofty place in nineteenth-century Protestant theology: "He was a great man, a man who did honour to Denmark. It is not the critics of his own country only, it is the more

---

[1] Ibid., vol. 4, p. 296.

impartial Germans who have declared Hans Lassen Martensen to be the greatest Protestant theologian of the present century."[1]

After the death of Hans Lassen on February 3, 1884, two volumes of the correspondence between Martensen and Dorner were published as well as the equivalent of a volume of correspondence with Bishop Otto Laub. Decades later three volumes of his letters to L. Gude were published. In all, Martensen's public theology had been given expression in no less than twenty books, eight essays and review articles, six volumes of correspondence, not to mention his many hundreds of sermons which were published. It is now time to turn to an analysis of how Kierkegaard made use of these as a source for his thinking and writing.

---

[1] Edmund Gosse, "Bishop Martensen," *The Expositor*, series 3, no. 1, 1885, p. 68.

# Chapter 2

# Martensen in Kierkegaard's Writings

We have seen that Martensen's literary production during Kierkegaard's lifetime was significant. He was definitely the leading theological voice in Denmark and Kierkegaard had a multi-faceted relationship with him. Therefore, identifying Martensen as a contemporary Danish source for Kierkegaard's writing is a complex matter. Kierkegaard was privately tutored by Martensen. He was taught by Martensen both in lecture courses he attended and via those from which lecture notes were obtained from others. He engaged in a few conversations with Martensen over the years. He had his eyes and ears set on what Martensen was up to as a public figure in Copenhagen life. At the end of his life he related to Martensen as an aspirant to the bishop's seat and then as the bishop of Sjælland who succeeded Mynster. Kierkegaard owned and read the writings Martensen had published. Kierkegaard declares in his journals and notebooks that he has not criticized Martensen in his published writings. While this is the case that Martensen is not mentioned by name, it is not reflective of the degree to which Kierkegaard is intending to counter Martensen's approach and emphases in his writings. On occasion Kierkegaard incorporates a journal entry, which had referred explicitly to Martensen, into the text of a published work and then speaks of "the docent" or "the professor" instead of mentioning Martensen in particular. So Martensen might not be explicitly mentioned in some works and yet he is the original intended target. This relates to what Jon Stewart identifies as "code words" that Kierkegaard uses, that is, words that Copenhagen insiders could decode but others could not, allowing for a certain level of civility in criticizing other intellectuals within the restricted, rather "small town" confines of the Danish capital.

To account for every reference to Martensen in Kierkegaard's writings is no small task, and an absolutely thorough execution of that endeavor cannot be accomplished within the space limits of this monograph. We will, however, attempt to execute that task in a relatively thorough fashion in this chapter. References in both Kierkegaard's published works and his notebooks and journals will be cited in this endeavor to execute the noble intention of providing exhaustive, comprehensive coverage of Kierkegaard's references to Martensen in his writings. A best effort will also be given to identify allusions that Kierkegaard seems to be making to Martensen.

In his book that reconsiders Kierkegaard's relations to Hegel, Jon Stewart has identified three periods of Kierkegaard's authorship in which, upon close investigation, one finds a quite differentiated and complex development in his relation to Hegel.[1] The first period runs from 1834 to 1843 and here Kierkegaard is depicted as being infatuated with Hegel and positively influenced by him. In the second period from 1843 to 1846 Kierkegaard is regarded as being most critical of Hegelian forms of thinking, but Stewart contends that these strictures are directed against Danish Hegelians rather than Hegel himself. In the final period from 1847 to 1855 Kierkegaard is viewed as dropping his polemic against Hegelians but as openly using Hegelian concepts and methodologies. In considering Martensen as a source for Kierkegaard, it will be convenient to make use of these three periods. However, with the focus on Martensen it is better for the cutoff between the first and second periods to come at 1841 rather than 1843, so the periods to be considered are 1834-1841, 1842-1846, and 1847-1855.

*I. The Early University Years: 1834-1841*

Kierkegaard makes many hundreds of references to Martensen in his journals and notebooks. In his youthful years at the university from 1834 through the writing of his dissertation on irony of 1841, the budding

---

[1] Jon Stewart, *Kierkegaard's Relations to Hegel Reconsidered*, Cambridge and New York: Cambridge University Press 2003, pp. 597-618.

intellectual records a number of journal entries relating to this intriguing figure five years his senior. In the 1834 context of being privately tutored by Martensen in Schleiermacher's *Glaubenslehre*, Kierkegaard makes observations on various excerpts, translated into Danish, from that watershed work in modern theological reflection.[1] Sometime during 1836-1837 journal entries were made in reference to Martensen's review of J.L. Heiberg's introductory lecture to Hegel's logic.[2] The year 1837 also finds the young student making entries on Martensen's 1836 German writing *Ueber Lenau's Faust* and on his Danish reworking of that writing as "Betragtninger over Ideen af Faust. Med Hensyn paa Lenaus Faust."[3] In relation to the Danish version of Martensen's writing on Faust, Kierkegaard expresses vivid disappointment because Martensen published his work before Kierkegaard could complete his: "How unhappy I am—Martensen has written an essay on Lenau's *Faust!*"[4] Joakim Garff pinpoints the reason for the disappointment:

> In his introduction Martensen subjected the entire idea of Faust to a careful examination, placing it in a larger intellectual-historical context which—alas!—included the most important of Kierkegaard's own points, namely that the medieval Faust is the genuine one, while Goethe's is a falsification that lowers the stakes, bearing as it does the imprint of the pantheism of the times, et cetera.[5]

On comedy Kierkegaard learns from Martensen as well as from Heiberg, and yet he notes that there is "mimicry" of Hegel at work in Martensen's view.[6]

---

[1] *Pap.* I C 20; *JP* 1, 3843.
[2] *SKS* 17, 198-202, CC:12; *JP* 5, 5181. *SKS* 17, 121-122, BB:32; *JP* 5, 5200. Then Kierkegaard later, likely in 1843, makes reference to a phrase Martensen used in this article, *De omnibus dubitandum est* [Everything must be doubted], as the subtitle to the completed manuscript entitled *Johannes Climacus*, *Pap.* IV B 1; *JP* 5, 5621.
[3] *SKS* 17, 49, AA:38; *JP* 3, 1183. *Pap.* II A 597; *JP* 5, 5225. *SKS* 18, 83, FF:38; *JP* 5, 5226.
[4] *Pap.* II A 597; *JP* 5, 5225.
[5] Joakim Garff, *Søren Kierkegaard: A Biography*, trans. by Bruce H. Kirmmse, Princeton and Oxford: Princeton University Press 2005, p. 78.
[6] *SKS* 19, 375, Not12:7; *PJ* 179.

In 1837 Kierkegaard is already poking fun at Martensen as "someone with a master's degree who during his foreign travels has drunk tea with this or that great scholar,"[1] referring of course to Martensen's two-year study trip from 1834 to 1836. Kierkegaard did not appreciate Martensen's attempts to benefit from Hegel's brilliance. In 1838 he pens these words: "Those who have gone beyond Hegel are like country people who must always give their addresses as via a larger city; thus the addresses in this case read—John Doe via Hegel."[2] Kierkegaard also had in his possession notes from Martensen's lecture courses, either that he had taken or that he had procured from another student. These include his "Introductory Lectures to Speculative Dogmatics" of 1837-1838,[3] his "Lectures on the History of Modern Philosophy from Kant to Hegel" of 1838-1839,[4] and some of his "Lectures on Speculative Dogmatics" of 1838-1839.[5] It appears that the lectures on German idealism from Kant to Hegel, for instance, were drawn on in later work: "the organization for his never published *De omnibus dubitandum est*, for example, almost follows the syllabus of Martensen's lectures."[6] Kierkegaard in addition comments on other writings of Martensen from these early years, namely, Martensen's dissertation on autonomy,[7] his review of J.L. Heiberg's *New Poems*,[8] and years later on his 1840 writing on medieval mysticism[9] and his 1841 *Outline to a System of Moral Philosophy*.[10] Kierkegaard remembers a decade after the fact what a sensation Martensen's lectures made among the

---

[1] *SKS* 17, 50, AA:40; *JP* 2, 1570.
[2] *SKS* 18, 109, FF:176; *JP* 2, 1572. Kierkegaard also writes, likely from 1836: "The Hegelian cud-chewing involving three stomachs—first, immediacy—then it is regurgitated—then down once more; perhaps a successor master-mind could continue this with four stomachs etc., down again and then up again. I do not know whether the master-mind understands what I mean." *Pap.* I A 229; *JP* 2, 1566.
[3] *SKS* 19, 125-143, Not 4.3-4.12; *JP* 5, 5277.
[4] *Pap.* II C 12-24, in *Pap.* XII, pp. 280-331; *JP* 5, 5353.
[5] *SKS* 18, 374-386, KK:11. *Pap.* II C 26-27 are included in *Pap.* XIII, pp. 3-43, and II C 28 is in *Pap.* XIII pp. 44-116; *JP* 5, 5299.
[6] Ronald M. Green, *Kierkegaard and Kant: The Hidden Debt*, Albany: State University of New York Press 1992, p. 6.
[7] *Pap.* IV B 1; *JP* 5, 5621. *SKS* 18, 203, JJ:196; *JP* 2, 1111. *Pap.* V B 49,5.
[8] *Pap.* IV B 46. *SKS* 19, 375, Not12:7; *JP* 2, 1738.
[9] *Pap.* VII-2 B 235. The reference is to "brothers and sisters of the Free Spirit." See H. Martensen, *Mester Eckart*, op. cit., pp. 12f.; *BHK*, pp. 158-160.
[10] *SKS* 18, 362, JJ:368; *JP* 1, 921. *Pap.* VI A 92. *Pap.* X-3 A 567.

students at the University.[1] On the matter of mysticism, Marie Thulstrup concluded that "there were only two points on which" Martensen and Kierkegaard "were agreed, both seeing the doctrine of sin as the main difference between Platonism and Christianity, and both using the term 'mystical consciousness.' It is possible that Kierkegaard borrowed the term from Martensen."[2]

A culminating experience in the theological studies program at the University of Copenhagen was a major examination. While Martensen was not present at the critical oral portion of Kierkegaard's theological examination, testing his proficiency in biblical exegesis and Christian dogmatics, which took place on July 3, 1840, it has been suggested that the questions put by the Hebrew Bible specialist C.T. Engelstoft (1805-1889) "seem to have come from Martensen."[3] The other large hurdle is the dissertation. In considering Kierkegaard's dissertation, *The Concept of Irony, with Continual Reference to Socrates*, submitted in 1841 to obtain the degree of Master of Arts, we remember how Kierkegaard had read portions of it to Martensen and that Martensen had served as a reader and examiner. In the dissertation, of course, Martensen had been mentioned by name in the very last sentence of the work:

> Finally, insofar as there may be a question concerning irony's "eternal validity," this question can be answered only by entering into the realm of humor. Humor has a far more profound skepticism than irony, because here the focus is on sinfulness, not on finitude. The skepticism of humor is related to the skepticism of irony as ignorance is related to the old thesis: *credo quia absurdum* [I believe because it is absurd], but it also has a far

---

[1] *Pap.* X-2 A 135, *PF*, Supplement, 226-227. See Stewart, *Kierkegaard's Relations to Hegel Reconsidered*, op. cit., p. 107.

[2] Marie Mikulová Thulstrup, "Plato's Vision and its Interpretation," *Kierkegaard's Classical Inspiration*, ed. by Niels Thulstrup and Marie Mikulová Thulstrup, Copenhagen: C.A. Reitzel 1982 (*Bibliotheca Kierkegaardiana*, vol. 14), p. 85.

[3] Ronald M. Green, *Kierkegaard and Kant*, op. cit., pp. 6-7. Green includes, pp. 7-8, the fifteen questions Kierkegaard was asked on ethics and the philosophy of religion. On the role of the theological examination in the preparation of a theological candidate at this time, see Skat Arildsen, "His Theological Examination," *Kierkegaard as a Person*, ed. by Niels Thulstrup and Marie Mikulová Thulstrup, Copenhagen: C.A. Reitzel 1983 (*Bibliotheca Kierkegaardiana*, vol. 12), pp. 63-71.

*Christian Thorning Engelstoft (1805-1889)*
(The Royal Library, Copenhagen)

deeper positivity, since it moves not in human but in theanthropological categories; it finds rest not by making man man but by making man Godman. Yet all this lies beyond the scope of this study, and if anyone should wish food for thought, I recommend Prof. Martensen's review of Heiberg's *Nye Digte*.[1]

The commentary on this reference to Martensen notes that in Martensen's extensive review of Heiberg's *Nye Digte* filling nineteen newspaper columns, he develops his view of Christian humor.[2] Other

---

[1] *SKS* 1, 357; *CI* 329.
[2] *SKS* K1, 376.

examiners "seemed to feel that the dissertation on irony lacked all respect for authority," and Martensen did not offer comment on the work.[1] However, Roger Poole points out the irony in the fact that it turns out to be Martensen himself "who has the final decision as to whether to pass or fail his young opponent."[2] And Poole is one of the few scholars to acknowledge, at least in this instance, that there are some features in Martensen that ought to be appreciated:

> Although Martensen has had a bad press, due largely to our knowing him mainly through Kierkegaard's own eyes, he was a man of high principle. He could very easily, things being as they were, have sunk the young Søren without trace. His dissertation could have been turned down out of hand. Kierkegaard had no allies on the faculty, except perhaps Sibbern. Martensen could have deprived Kierkegaard of his Magister Artium degree, hence of a career and a living, and have made impossible that support from the rear during his writing career that the high academic qualification afforded him.
>
> He could also have taken revenge on Kierkegaard for what must have been seven grueling years of being put to the test by his talented pupil. Many academics, alas, would have taken this opportunity of revenge. To Martensen's credit, however, he allowed the dissertation, of which he no doubt disapproved both the contents and the style, to pass to acceptance without comment. Neither was he present at the defense on 20 September. It was a high and grand gesture, and one that up to now has gone unappreciated.[3]

Howard and Edna Hong have suggested that Kierkegaard could be making an allusion to Martensen in *The Concept of Irony* when he speaks of the abstract dialectical method taking one "beyond" in a couple of senses.[4] The thought is that Martensen's language of "going beyond" or "going further" than Hegel—which is employed in the review of

---

[1] Roger Poole, *Kierkegaard: The Indirect Communication*, Charlottesville and London: The University Press of Virginia 1993, p. 36, p. 38.
[2] Ibid., p. 38.
[3] Ibid., pp. 40-41.
[4] *SKS* 1, 176; *CI* 124.

Heiberg's *Indledningsforedrag* or introductory lecture on Hegel's logic, where Martensen also states that "the objective point of departure of philosophy would have gone beyond the abstract category"[1]—might be being referenced here in a discussion of dialogue that can lead to "abstractly dialectical" positions. However, the two instances of "beyond" are translations of *"Hiinsides"* and *"ude over"* respectively, and these are not usual formulations that Martensen uses in speaking of "going beyond." On the other hand the mentioning of "the fly sheet" in *The Concept of Irony*, in speaking of the Sophists' wisdom as being " *'ein fliegendes Blatt* [a fly sheet,]' which was not kept from flapping about either by a prominent public figure or by integration into a coherent system of knowledge,"[2] was surely a reference to Martensen, since he is mentioned in the comparable journal entry.[3] When Kierkegaard in this work compares the Sophists "to the capsule information that a tutor tries to convey to those being tutored,"[4] he again is likely thinking of his tutor Martensen. Another example of poking fun at his younger professor in the work on irony is when he writes: "But it is by no means my intention to reel off every possible view or by way of a kind of historical survey to follow the pattern of the youngest followers of a fairy tale as a model by always rehearsing the whole lesson at the beginning of each new part."[5]

Another early work of Kierkegaard, this one never published, was *The Battle between the Old and the New Soap-Cellars*. With the introduction of Hegel to university students, there was an onslaught of the disease of Hegelese, and this dramatic satire strikes out against the sort of blind following of a fad that underlay this commandeering of language within the academic arena. Garff thinks "displeasure over the mechanical use of Hegelian phrases by intellectuals and by the deification of philosophy" had reached its "nauseating zenith in Martensen's review of Heiberg's *Introductory Lecture*, which Kierkegaard presumably had immediately read following its publication in January 1837."[6] The second act of this

---

[1] Kierkegaard, *CI* 510, note 302.
[2] *SKS* 1, 247-248; *CI* 201-202.
[3] *SKS* 17, 121-122 BB:32; *JP* 5, 5200. See also *SKS* 17, 91 BB:9; *JP* 5, 5150 and *CI* 526-627, note 477.
[4] *SKS* 1, 249; *CI* 204.
[5] *SKS* 1, 263; *CI* 218.
[6] Garff, *Søren Kierkegaard*, op. cit., p. 81.

comedy takes place at "the Prytaneum," where philosophical discussions are conducted. There is little doubt that Martensen is a target of this farce; the only question concerns which of the play's characters is intended as a caricature of him. On the one hand, Niels Thulstrup, Jens Holger Schjørring, and Joakim Garff have argued that the character "Mr. Phrase, an adventurer, member of several learned societies, and contributor to numerous journals," is taken to be Martensen; on the other hand, Henning Fenger and Jon Stewart have contended that it is rather the character "Mr. von Jumping-Jack, a philosopher," who is the play's intended counterpart to Martensen.[1] The editor-translator of this work, Julia Watkin, gives some support to both sides, noting that "Mr. von Jumping Jack, as the caricature of a philosophizing esthete, may be based on Johan Ludwig Heiberg, although he talks like Hans Lassen Martensen,"[2] and that Mr. Phrase, "as one who has studied Hegel but has now gone farther…may be a figure poking fun at Hans Lassen Martesen."[3] For our source-research purposes, it is more important to realize that Martensen lies behind the scenes of the writing of this play as instigator of much of this Hegelian bemusement and thus is serving as a source of Kierkegaard's activities as a playwright, than it is to nail down exactly which of these two characters is intended to represent the theological-philosophical personage who is establishing the intellectual agenda for at least one young academic within the quaint confines of Copenhagen in the last half of the 1830s. Ms. Watkin also identifies a couple of Latin phrases used in the play as related to the *de omnibus dubitandum est* ["everything must be doubted"] phrase that Martensen had emphasized in his review of Heiberg's Introductory Lecture and elsewhere.[4]

---

[1] See ibid., pp. 80-86, Stewart, *Kierkegaard's Relations to Hegel Reconsidered*, op.cit., pp. 105-114, Jens Holger Schjørring, "Martensen," op. cit., p. 200, Henning Fenger, *Kierkegaard: The Myths and their Origins*, trans. by George C. Schoolfield, New Haven: Yale University Press 1980, pp. 141-142, and Niels Thulstrup, *Kierkegaard's Relation to Hegel*, trans. by George L. Stengren, Princeton: Princeton University Press 1980, p. 188.
[2] *EPW* 261, note 9.
[3] *EPW* 262, note 11.
[4] See *EPW* 114 and note 48 on 264.

## II. Establishing the Authorship: 1842-1846

The years 1842 to 1846 were amazingly productive for Kierkegaard, who produced during this time *Either/Or*, *Repetition*, *Fear and Trembling*, *Philosophical Fragments*, *The Concept of Anxiety*, *Prefaces*, *Stages on Life's Way*, *Concluding Unscientific Postscript*, *Two Ages*, and eighteen *Edifying Discourses* plus the manuscript *Johannes Climacus* and other discourses. During these creative years, though, Kierkegaard was tending to the activities of Martensen. Copenhagen University's theological professor had published his piece on Christian baptism and Kierkegaard entered comments on it in his journals.[1] It is a possible source for Kierkegaard's thinking and writing that has not yet been investigated with any care by Kierkegaard scholars but needs to be.

Kierkegaard's first two upbuilding or edifying discourses were published on May 16, 1843 and four more came out in December of that year, with more to regularly follow. It is interesting that Martensen's small book on Christian baptism also came out in May of 1843. In that book, as we have seen, Martensen places great emphasis on Christian proclamation and thereby on the Christian preacher, who through his or her call and participation in the church has been appropriated by Christ and therefore is able to preach "in the apostolic spirit." In the Danish Lutheran church the apparatus for becoming such an authoritative preacher is ordination into the ministry. Of course, no causal relation between these thoughts of Martensen and Kierkegaard's idea of upbuilding discourses can be established. George Pattison writes about these "works of his right hand": "The discourses are akin to sermons in form, but although Kierkegaard does on occasion refer to them in his own drafts as sermons he repeatedly draws attention in the published Forewords to each set of discourses that they are *not* sermons, giving as a reason that they are written by one who, because he is not ordained, does not have legal authority to preach."[2] Pattison indicates that Bishop

---

[1] *Pap.* IV B 59; *JP* 5, 5710. *SKS* 18, 205, JJ:205.1. *Pap.* VI B 24,1. *Pap.* VI B 98,15. *Pap.* V C 10; *JP* 1, 452.

[2] George Pattison, *Kierkegaard's Upbuilding Discourses: Philosophy, Theology, Literature*, London and New York: Routledge 2002, pp. 12-13.

J.P. Mynster dismissed this whole distinction, and stated "that they were *sermons*,"[1] so in this he also dismissed himself as a source of the distinction for Kierkegaard. If Kierkegaard agrees with Martensen's claim about the centrality of proclamation to the vitality of the Christian religion, which is surely feasible if not likely, and if proclamation in the form of sermons were open only to the ordained, then it might well occur to one who wanted to be contributing to the furtherance of genuine Christianity to do so through writing discourses that functioned as a "poor person's" proclamation in that they were written by one without the authority of ordination. To be sure, this line of influence is a possibility to be winsomely pondered rather than an actuality to be firmly proven. There need have been no connection whatsoever between Kierkegaard's understanding of the role his discourses of direct communication were to play and Martensen's articulation of these thoughts on the importance of proclamation and preaching to the church. And yet, the timings of these two are proximate and the idea of a possible dependency comes powerfully to mind in reading Martensen's words in the baptism book. To the extent that this connection is plausible, it points to the legitimacy of Kiekegaard's claim for an intentional twofold authorship—the pseudonymous and the upbuilding, the unsigned and the signed, the indirect and the direct, the aesthetic and the religious. It minimizes the need to be overly rigorous in applying the Cartesian motto *de omnibus dubitandum est* ("everything must be doubted") to Kierkegaard's claims about the consistently two-natured or dual character of his authorship.[2] Still, one could cling to the thought that at this early stage of 1843 Kierkegaard did not possess full comprehension of the meaning of this twofold productivity and that a keener discerning of this would have to unfold over time as he gradually gained a clearer vision of his vocation as utilizing his unique powers of observation, analysis, and turning a phrase for addressing the needs of the day.

The work *Johannes Climacus, or De omnibus dubitandum est* was begun by Kierkegaard on November 11, 1843, the same day his brother Peter Christian was ordained. This writing contains no explicit reference to

---

[1] Ibid., p. 13.
[2] Ibid., p. 14.

Martensen but his lectures on the history of philosophy and speculative dogmatics stand in the background, for in those lectures, and elsewhere in published writings, he discussed Descartes and his principle that "everything must be doubted." Simply that this phrase, which at this time Kierkegaard strictly identified with Copenhagen's fast-climbing theologian, is included in the title,[1] indicates that it should be read over against the dynamic intellectual context of the day, in which the relation between faith and reason, theology and philosophy had captured the imagination of many, and in which, amidst the confusions resulting from this new fermenting, many—if not Kierkegaard himself—were looking to Martensen as the guiding light and living hope that some theological clarity might be made of it all.

In Kierkegaard's first major pseudonymous work, *Either/Or*, Martensen is again not mentioned by name. However, the Supplement to *Either/Or: Part I* includes a journal entry which identifies Martensen as not having seen the deeper significance in Lenau's *Faust* of Mephistopheles starting the music at the moment Faust begins to portray Don Juan, namely, that the Don Juanian life is really musical.[2] In this volume another selected entry from the journals discusses Martensen's consideration of Faust's killing himself and then deliberates on why that is an inappropriate ending to the piece.[3] In the Supplement to *Either/Or: Part II* is Martensen's description of J.L. Heiberg as Denmark's Dante,[4]

---

[1] See Jon Stewart's consideration of the allusion to Martensen in the title, *Kierkegaard's Relations to Hegel Reconsidered*, op. cit., pp. 242-249.

[2] *EO1*, Supplement, 480. *SKS* 18, 83, FF:38; *JP* 5, 5226. The reference is to the work by Nicolaus Niembsch's pseudonym Nicolaus Lenau's *Faust*, Stuttgart: Verlag der J.G. Cotta'schen Buchhandlung 1836, pp. 49-51. Martensen discusses this work in *Ueber Lenau's Faust* and in the Danish rewriting of that work, "Betragtninger over Ideen af Faust, med Hensyn paa Lenaus Faust," op. cit., pp. 91-165.

[3] *EO1*, Supplement, 478-479. *SKS*, 17, 49, AA:38; *JP* 2, 1183.

[4] *EO2*, Supplement, 404. *Pap.* IV B 46. The sentence reads, "It will soon be two years since Herr Professor [Heiberg] changed from being the witty, jesting, hilarious vaudeville playwright who yet at times seemed somewhat astray in the faith, the victorious polemicist, the measured esthetician, and became Denmark's Dante, the musing genius who in his apocalyptic poem peered into the secrets of eternal life, became the Church's dutiful son from whom the esteemed clergy of the diocese expected everything for the good of the 'parish.'"

referring to his review of Heiberg's *En Sjæl efter Døden. En apocalyptisk Comedie, Nye Digte*.[1] In a "Post-Scriptum to *Either/Or*" by Victor Eremita written in March of 1844, Kierkegaard added the following lines to the text and then crossed them out: "From the point of view of the public good and the friend of the masses, are not the efforts of the Anabaptists [*Gjendøber*, rebaptizers] just as corrupt as from the point of view of dogmatics—!"[2] The translators suggest Martensen's writing on baptism as one example discussing the Anabaptist dogmatic view to which Kierkegaard was referring, pointing thus to this Martensenian writing as a likely source for Kierkegaard, a claim that will be demonstrated in looking at other Kierkegaardian writings.[3]

The single point of possible connection in Constantin Constantius's *Repetition* is the mention of "an apocalyptic author," which likely refers to Martensen, who wrote the review of the book arguing for the Johannine authorship of the Apocalypse and also had written on apocalyptic poetry.[4] It is quite a different matter, however in the writing *Fear and Trembling*. In the Preface Johannes de Silentio mentions "going further" a number of times. He writes that "every assistant professor, tutor, and student, every rural outsider and tenant incumbent in philosophy is unwilling to stop with doubting everything but goes further [*gaaer viderer*]."[5] He notes: "In our age, everyone is unwilling to stop with faith that goes further [*gaaer videre*]."[6] The translators point out that these statements likely refer to Heiberg and Martensen and that " 'going further' refers to the system building attempted by Hegelians along the lines of Hegel's *Encyclopädie der philosophischen Wissenschaften*, titled *System der Philosophie* after the third edition."[7] With the inclusion of the Descartes and the doubt theme, it seems more likely that this is a reference to Martensen than to Heiberg. I would suggest that the "going further" refers instead

---

[1] Heiberg's work, *Nye Digte*, was published in Copenhagen, 1841, and Martensen's review was printed in *Fædrelandet*, 398, January 10, 1841, columns 3209-3211.
[2] *EO2*, Supplement, 419.
[3] *EO2*, Supplement, 504, note 108.
[4] *SKS* 4, 53; *R* 182.
[5] *SKS* 4, 101; *FT* 5.
[6] *SKS* 4, 102; *FT* 7.
[7] See *FT* 340, note 1.

to the need to be critical of Hegel's philosophy and to go beyond it because it does not advance fully beyond the autonomous perspective to the theonomous. In this work we read that "that man [Abraham] was not a thinker. He did not feel any need to go beyond faith."[1] Martensen, of course, makes the case that one engages in theological reflection in order to grasp the cognitive content of faith, but, as we have seen, he does not say that such a move in arriving at a truthful understanding of the faith can then leave faith behind since one has gone beyond it. The reality of faith ever holds the riches, and cognitive inquiry ever needs to return to the origin of truth. In this sense Johannes [Latin for Hans] Martensen agrees with Johannes de Silentio that Abraham "got no further than faith."[2] The latter Johannes charges theology with wanting to court philosophy, which "goes further," and even "going beyond Hegel," thinking it can comprehend things without much difficulty; but it cannot think about Abraham in this way because of "the prodigious paradox that is the content of Abraham's life."[3] The current "generation does not stop with faith, does not stop with the miracle of faith, turning water into wine—it goes further and turns wine into water."[4] These various indirect references to Martensen are a way to criticize him as one who is complicitous with the age in furthering the leveling process that negates freedom, individuality, and responsibility.

Kierkegaard recognized that because of the chasm separating the human from the divine, attempts to gain knowledge of the divine mystery transcending human reach are going to be fragmentary or piecemeal at best. In the Preface to *Philosophical Fragments*, Johannes Climacus warns against being deluded "into thinking that now a new era, a new epoch, etc. was beginning" and that much commotion has been made over the system.[5] Lauritz Vilhelm Petersen had translated Martensen's Latin dissertation into Danish. In his extremely brief Preface he had stated in reference to this writing, "It was the first writing that came out in Denmark in the modern speculative direction and heralded the era in

---

[1] *SKS* 4, 105; *FT* 9.
[2] *SKS* 4, 119; *FT* 23.
[3] *SKS* 4, 129; *FT* 32-33.
[4] *SKS* 4, 132; *FT* 37.
[5] *SKS* 4, 216; *PF* 6.

theology from which people have now already begun to mark time."[1] Martensen is also at least one important figure in the background for understanding the full significance of the statement that "the concept, like a juggler in this carnival time, has to keep doing those continual flip-flopping tricks—until the man himself flips over."[2] This is a reference to the dialectical character of the concept in Hegel's philosophy, which results in given realities flipping over into their opposites. The mediating capacity of thinking possesses this power of *aufheben* or *ophæve*, and in Denmark Martensen was the leading proponent of the importance of such mediating in theological work. It can also be pointed out that Thulstrup believes the last paragraph of *Fragments*—that mentions dealing with the relations between philosophy and Christianity, discovering the principle of mediation, and waiting for one to bring the System—also likely has Martensen in mind.[3]

Jon Stewart has established that "Kierkegaard sees the *Fragments* as a criticism of speculative thought," and especially a criticism of the principle of mediation; it "is primarily a polemic against Martensen's claim for the use of mediation in speculative theology."[4] Stewart has identified other places in *Fragments* where Martensen is likely being alluded to. For instance, "in Chapter I Climacus refers to the doctrine of mediation with the familiar formulation 'to a certain degree,'" indicating by this phrase "that mediation leads to a position half-way, which ultimately says nothing."[5] In the "Interlude" of this work in speaking of skeptical doubt Kierkegaard's Climacus again alludes to Martensen when he writes: "Yet it is not so difficult to understand this or to understand how this casts light on belief, provided one is not utterly confused by the Hegelian doubt about everything, against which there is really no need to preach, for what the Hegelians say about it is of such a nature that it seems rather to favor

---

[1] *BHK*, op. cit., p. 74. See also *PF* 275, note 10.
[2] *SKS* 4, 216; *PF* 6. See Thulstrup's comments on this passage in Søren Kierkegaard, *Philosophical Fragments*, trans. by David Swenson, introduction and commentary by Niels Thulstrup, translation revised and commentary trans. by Howard V. Hong, Princeton: Princeton University Press 1962 [1936], pp. 158-160.
[3] Søren Kierkegaard, *Philosophical Fragments*, op. cit., p. 260.
[4] Jon Stewart, *Hegel's Relations to Hegel Reconsidered*, op. cit., pp. 337-338.
[5] Ibid., p. 346. The passage Stewart is referring to is located at *SKS* 4, 220; *PF* 11.

a modest doubt as to whether there really is anything to their having doubted something."[1] Since this statement is made in the context of also having used "*de omnibus dubitandum est*," a phrase Kierkegaard identified with Martensen, it is clear which particular Hegelian is being targeted. A final indicator of the link between Martensen and the category of mediation is Kierkegaard's 1850 notebook entry that critically states in reference to Martensen: "mediation is his existence-category."[2] Stewart makes the case that Martensen's article "Rationalism, Supernaturalism and the *principium exclusi medii*" "is the main target of the criticism of mediation in the *Fragments*."[3]

Martensen functions as a source of information for Kierkegaard's thinking in having Johannes Climacus pen this work in more than the area of mediation. One reference in *Fragments* refers explicitly to Martensen's writing on Christian baptism. In his Chapter V on the follower or disciple at second hand, Climacus is surely bouncing off ideas that we have seen expressed in Martensen's baptism piece. Climacus speaks of the advantages of Christianity's consequences that build up over the centuries and putatively make it easier for one situated later in time to believe.[4] These advantages are denied by Climacus, but the reference to being "naturalized little by little" has been identified as referring to the baptism book, where Martensen writes: "It is clear in and for itself that in the period when the essential task was to implant the church in the world, much had to be shaped otherwise than in later times, where the church had established firm roots in the world, where God's kingdom had become just like nature."[5] An undated 1844 entry in his JJ journal discloses Kierkegaard's reflection on this theme of "naturalization" and likely predates the publication of *Fragments* on June 13 of that year:

---

[1] *SKS* 4, 281; *PF* 82. See ibid.
[2] *Pap.* X-6 B 137; *JP* 6, 6636. See Stewart, *Kierkegaard's Relations to Hegel Reconsidered*, op. cit., p. 347.
[3] See ibid., pp. 347-355. See also the article by Arild Waaler and Christian Fink Tolstrup, "*Philosophical Fragments*—in Response to the Debate between Mynster and Martensen," *Kierkegaard Studies. Yearbook,* 2004, pp. 208-234.
[4] *SKS* 4, 291-296; *PF* 94-99.
[5] Martensen, *Den christelige Daab*, op. cit., p. 23.

If Christianity could become naturalized in the world, then every child need not be baptized, since the child who is born of Christian parents would already be a Christian by birth. The consciousness of sin is and continues to be the condition *sine qua non* for all Christianity, and if one could somehow be released from this, he could not be a Christian. And this is the very proof of Christianity's being the highest religion, that none other has given such a profound and lofty expression of man's significance—that he is a sinner. It is this consciousness which paganism lacks.[1]

In a note Kierkegaard states that this affirming of naturalization is what he thinks Martensen's "famous theory of baptism" is saying, even if this meaning is unknown to the author. Martensen surely did say in this statement that the early church, which engaged in implanting and spreading Christianity, had to be shaped differently from how the later church—that was well-established and possessed a character more akin to nature—could be shaped. To Kierkegaard's criticism, it must be said, that to suggest that Martensen is endorsing a naturalization of Christianity in the world—by which baptism would become an unnecessary sacrament since every child would by birth already be a natural Christian—is obviously not in keeping with what he intends to be communicating about there being no second-hand disciples or followers. It is precisely his claims about the sacrament of baptism that justify the claim about the essential continuity of the order of salvation from one generation to the next.

Having established, though, this Martensen writing on baptism as one of Kierkegaard's sources, it is interesting in the spirit of Martensen himself to pursue a couple more speculative and significant possibilities of dependency. On the title page of *Philosophical Fragments* is the question: "Can a historical point of departure be given for an eternal consciousness; how can such a point of departure be of more than historical interest; can an eternal happiness be built on historical knowledge?"[2] In the opening paragraph of his discussion of "Baptism, the Church-Constituting Sacrament," Martensen writes about eternal happiness, if we translate

---

[1] *SKS* 18, JJ:205; *JP* 1, 452.
[2] *SKS* 4, 213; *PF* 1.

"*Salighed*" as "Happiness" as the translators have done. Martensen's statement then reads:

> To have faith is the same thing as to have happiness, to have certainty of eternal life both as a present and a future reality. But precisely because faith carries eternity in itself, it cannot have a temporal, random origin, but must have a divine beginning. The Christian faith must therefore be considered even as a work of divine grace. Divine grace is known not merely in the fact that happiness has come to the world; it is known just as much in the fact that faith in grace is given to a human.[1]

The divine beginning, we have also learned, is absolute in character. For in that same work on baptism we have seen how Martensen distinguishes between two sorts of beginning, one temporal and finite, and the other eternal and infinite. Kierkegaard will distinguish sharply between faith and history. Martensen does not do this as sharply, but he does make the distinction. He affirms, as we saw above, that a historical presence and a mystical presence find their higher unity in a sacramental presence. And we recall his distinction between the rationalist and the speculative views of Jesus as the Christ, with the first stressing the historical Jesus, the pre-Easter Jesus, who as a particular personage of the past is remembered and as such inspires Christians in their lives of moral action, and the second stressing the biblical Christ, the post-Easter Jesus, who as a universal spirit of the present is experienced and as such empowers Christians in their lives of faith. This is not probing the issue of faith and history with Kierkegaard's penetrating insight, but it is laying out the general categories that can lead another to a more profound understanding.

*The Concept of Anxiety: A Simple Psychologically Orienting Deliberation on the Dogmatic Issue of Hereditary Sin* was published in 1844. As one comes to expect, no explicit reference is made to Martensen in this book. The dispute centers more on another Danish Hegelian, Adolph Peter Adler (1812-1869) than on Martensen. There are, however, a few indirect references to our professor. In the Preface, Vigilius Haufniensis

---

[1] Martensen, *Den christelige Daab*, op. cit., p. 5.

mentions not needing to "assume that era and epoch" begin with the publishing of one's book,[1] again alluding to the translator's Preface to Martensen's dissertation on the autonomy of modern thinking. A few pages later we read in the "Introduction": "Thus when in dogmatics *faith* is called the *immediate* without any further clarification, there is gained the advantage that everybody is convinced of the necessity of not stopping with faith."[2] In draft form a note was added to this statement, namely: "and this happens every day before our eyes."[3] The editors and translators are confident that this "polemic is not directed primarily against Hegel himself but against the Danish Hegelians Rasmus Nielsen and H.L. Martensen."[4] Also, near the end of the work in discussing those who "bend eternity into time for the imagination," he notes: "Some envision eternity apocalyptically, pretend to be Dante, while Dante, no matter how much he conceded to the view of imagination, did not suspend the effect of ethical judgment."[5] This alludes "to J.L. Heiberg's apocalyptic comedy, *En Sjæl efter Døden* (1841), and Martensen's review of it in the daily paper *Fædrelandet*."[6] It has been suggested that when Kierkegaard, via Vigilius Haufniensis, discussed the conception of eternity in time in *The Concept of Anxiety*, Martensen's comparison of Heiberg to Dante was helpful to him. In his *Fatherland* review, Martensen had concluded that "in art the human has eternal life"; this comparison "enabled Kierkegaard to formulate a contrast between a kind of purely imaginative poetry, like Heiberg's, …and Dante's, where he found the application of ethical criteria to the imaginative creation, the aesthetic material," which Dantian view asserts that "art is an anticipation of eternal life."[7] In the context of this discussion Sylvia Walsh has also identified Martensen as a target of Vigilius because of his "Hegelian tendency to give superiority

---

[1] *SKS* 4, 313; *CA* 7.
[2] *SKS* 4, 318; *CA* 10.
[3] *Pap.* V B 49:2; *CA* 180.
[4] *CA* 224, note 15.
[5] *SKS* 5, 452; *CA* 153.
[6] *CA* 253, note 62.
[7] Alessandro Cortese, "Dante," in *Kierkegaard Literary Miscellany*, ed. by Niels Thulstrup and Marie Mikulová Thulstrup (*Bibliotheca Kierkegaardiana*, vol. 9), pp. 151-152. See *CA* 153.

to the comic in an aesthetic-metaphysical viewpoint that swallows up the temporal in the eternal."[1]

A closer study of the relation between Kierkegaard and Martensen could in addition examine this work in relation to Martensen's doctrine of the Fall in his *Lectures on Speculative Dogmatics*, and this would likely bear interesting results. Also relevant is a trenchant passage dealing with original sin, namely, § 36 of Martensen's *Outline to a System of Moral Philosophy*. His approach to this doctrine and the particular language used to articulate it provide a rich background against which to read *The Concept of Anxiety*. In a long note Martensen gives further explanation to "the religious teaching on original sinfulness, which states that the subjective will prior to every free choice or by *nature* is evil."[2] He writes:

> Just because Christianity emphasizes free choice so pointedly, it also emphasizes the opposite side or the teaching that both good and evil in the human are independent of its free choice. The first side expresses, namely, the moment of *individuality*, the second that of the *race*. In a more restricted sense the one is the moral viewpoint, the other the religious viewpoint. In a moral respect Christianity requires "actions" instead of the old world's "deeds," emancipates the individual from its entire environment, and places its fate as it were into its own hands. But through this moral standpoint it leads the individual to the religious standpoint, as it teaches that the human's most intrinsic worth depends not on what one does but on what one *is*, and that the quality of the fruit depends on the tree's roots. The individual is hereby enabled to gain an insight into its *nature* and trace this back to its unity with *the race*, to the universality of sin and reconciliation, which are conditioned by the fact that that *the individual has become sharply differentiated from the race*. Only the self-subsisting individuality who is

---

[1] *CA*, Supplement, 207. See also, Sylvia Walsh, *Living Poetically: Kierkegaard's Essential Writings*, University Park, PA: The Pennsylvania State University Press 1994, p. 160 and note 35, where she clarifies that "inwardness is further identified by Vigilius…as the factor of the eternal in human beings."

[2] H. Martensen, *Grundrids til Moralphilosophiens System*, op. cit., p. 39; *Outline to a System of Moral Philosophy*, *BHK*, op. cit., p. 275.

entrusted to its personal self-determination will be able in the struggle of temptation to experience sin and grace as *universal* powers which stir in the innermost quarters of the soul, and place it in indissoluble connection with the entire race. The antinomy between Pelagius and Augustine is this contrast between the individual and the race, between the abstract moral consideration and the religious consideration of sin and responsibility. The Pelagian *thesis* states: "Only the free action can be sin, and I allow nothing else to be reckoned to me as guilt than what I myself have resolved and carried out." Augustine's *thesis* states: "We have all sinned in Adam and his offense is reckoned to us as guilt." Consequently, it is not the individual self which sins, but the race, the universal nature, which sins in the individual.—Both propositions are true only in their unity and reciprocal transition into each other. The ancient world does not know this antinomy. Just as it does not know the idea of a comprehensive human *race* but only the idea of various folk-races, so neither does it know the free, personal *individual*. Personal freedom is never presented in an unadulterated differentiation because the individual is only considered as a link in the mass of people and state. It knows only the righteousness of deeds or civil righteousness, but moral righteousness of duty-consciousness as well as religious righteousness or righteousness before God is unknown.[1]

To the careful reader of *The Concept of Anxiety* it should be apparent that Kierkegaard had thought long and hard on that particular passage.

Published on June 17, 1844 along with *The Concept of Anxiety* was *Prefaces*. In this work, by the pseudonym Nicolaus Notabene, the primary target is Heiberg. In Preface VII, however, the primary concern is mediation. In later correspondence betweem Kierkegaard and Rasmus Nielsen, Martensen would sometimes be referred to as simply "the Mediation."[2] Therefore, although Hegel himself is mentioned in the piece, we should heed Stewart's contention that the polemical tone of

---

[1] Ibid., pp. 39-41; ibid., pp. 275-276.
[2] For instance, see *LD* 315, where in Letter 225 written to Kierkegaard on August 28, 1849, Nielsen writes: "Last Sunday there was a grand dinner party out here. His Excellency and retinue were present, including 'the Mediation.'" The notes, *LD* 487, indicate that "Excellency" refers to J.P. Mynster and "the Mediation" refers to Martensen.

the piece supports reading it as targeting Danish Hegelians rather than Hegel himself.[1] It had been intended as the Preface for *The Concept of Anxiety*, but Kierkegaard decided against using it since it would "distract attention from the matter at hand."[2] In this preface there are allusions to a number of Hegelians, and a main purpose is to criticize their lack of originality, and this is a charge Kierkegaard levels elsewhere against Martensen; so he should here be counted among the Hegelians Nicolaus is critiquing.

*Stages on Life's Way*, edited by Hilarius Bookbinder and published on April 30, 1845, is another pseudonymous writing that has very few obvious connections to Martensen. Relatively early in the book there is the statement: "This cannot seem strange to anyone, inasmuch as everyone, after all, has doubted everything...."[3] "Everyone has doubted everything," of course, refers to that famous proposition from the history of philosophy which we have already discussed above, namely, *De omnibus dubitandum est*, set forth by René Descartes in his 1644 major systematic work, *Principles of Philosophy*.[4] Hegel had cited this proposition in his lectures on the history of philosophy, but more important for our purposes is Martensen's citing of it in a number of his publications, so that for Kierkegaard it became a phrase associated with Martensen.[5]

We also encounter in *Stages* the words: "I do imagine my readers to be among these [those who are "satisfied with following the honest path of ordinary common sense" and who easily understand "that the religious is a new immediacy"], since I am far from wanting to instruct the admired ones who make systematic discoveries *à la* Niels Klim, who have left their good skin [*Skind*] in order to put on the 'real appearance [*virkelige Skin*].'"[6] This very likely refers to Martensen in a couple of ways. The "make systematic discoveries *à la* Niels Klim" comment points to chapter 1 of Ludvig Holberg's 1741 philosophical novel *Niels Klim's Underworld*

---

[1] Stewart, *Kierkegaard's Relations with Hegel Reconsidered*, op. cit., pp. 337-341. Hegel is mentioned near the end of the Preface VII, *SKS* 4, 506.
[2] *Pap.* V B 71; *P*, Supplement, 118.
[3] *SKS* 6, 38; *SL* 34.
[4] *SKS* K 6, 111-112.
[5] *SKS* K 6, 112; *SL* 681, note 97.
[6] *SL* 163.

*Trip*,[1] written originally in Latin (*Nicolai Klimii Iter Subterraneum*) and published anonymously in Leipzig in 1741.[2] The *SKS* commentary informs us that, at the beginning of this satirical fantasy novel by the Danish-Norwegian dramatist, historian, and essayist, he depicts Klim as unemployed, penniless, and turning toward his hometown of Bergen, where he explores the mountains. Soon he falls from a mountain cavern into the earth's interior and discovers unknown worlds. The commentary goes on to explain that Kierkegaard refers to the following passage from the novel in Jens Baggesen's translation:

> Although in this way I lived as a kind of beggar, I yet did not waste time in idleness; for in order to expand my knowledge in physics, which I had begun to pursue, I investigated carefully the external character of the land and mountains, and for that purpose roamed all around to the far corners of the provinces. There was no rock too steep for me to attempt climbing up it, no cavern too deep and scary for me to venture down into it, in hope of finding one thing or another that was worth a nature expert's attention and investigation.[3]

The "admired ones" referred to here undoubtedly includes first and foremost our cultured public's chosen one who is relentless in pursuit of truth and whose speculative discoveries bear a striking resemblance to those of Niels Klim. The other reference is to the way these admired ones leave "their good skin" to put on the "real appearance." This is most surely tied to an expression in Martensen's article "Betragtningen over Ideen af Faust," published in Heiberg's *Perseus* in 1837. Martensen there develops how art in the Protestant epoch shall free itself from religion and take the temporal or finite life up into itself, lending life infinity's splendor by taking it up in its heaven.[4] Then Martensen states, "Here the reborn life arises from the spirit of beauty, and we are delighted with the *true* appearance."[5] "Real appearance" in our quote, therefore, is a version

---

[1] *SL* 703, note 121.
[2] *SKS* K6, 199.
[3] Ibid.
[4] Ibid.
[5] "Betragtninger over Ideen af Faust," p. 120m cited in *SKS* K6, 199; *SL* 703, note 122.

of the expression "true appearance ("*sande* Skin") used by Martensen in the Danish version of his *Faust* writing.

Another possible allusion to Martensen is present in *Stages on Life's Way*:

> Someone who pins his hope on speculative drama serves poetry only insofar as he serves the comic. If a witch or a wizard succeeds in bringing about such a thing, if by means of a speculative thaumaturgist [a performer of miracles or a magician] (for a dramaturgist [one versed in the art of the theater, especially the writing of plays] would not suffice) it would satisfy the requirement of the age as a *poetic* work, this event would certainly be a good motif for a comedy, even though it would achieve the comic effect through so many propositions that it could not become popular.[1]

This alludes presumably to Martensen's review of Heiberg's *Nye Digte*, whose importance he stresses "as an expression of 'the spirit of the new age' and of the teachings of speculative philosophy."[2] The *SKS* commentary on this passage[3] points out that the demand for a speculative poetry was introduced by J.L. Heiberg in his 1833 book, *On the Significance of Philosophy for the Present Age*.[4] Heiberg tried his hand at this genre with his 1838 *Fata Morgana. Eventyr-Comedie*, which without great success was performed at the Royal Theater on January 29, 1838, and only a total of five times during the season. Martensen's review of this piece develops a theory of this symbolic poetry of ideas and concludes with the expectation that this genre, which contains the possibility of fulfilling the most important poetic demands of the present, i.e., ideality and universality, will also be epoch-making on the stage. The *SKS* commentary also states that Heiberg's later apocalyptic comedy, "A Soul After Death" in *New Poems*, which was not intended for the stage, can be considered as a further development of the speculative genre. It too was reviewed by Martensen, who, we recall, had earlier developed the concept of apocalyptic poetry. The cultured public's chosen one's

---

[1] *SL* 412.
[2] *SL* 732, note 460.
[3] *SKS* 6 K, 343-344.
[4] *OSP*, 38ff.

review was able to place a positive spin on this genre for the public, which to that point had not seemed to have completely acknowledged the genre.[1] Martensen proclaims that Heiberg's poetic verses had been composed under the inspirations of the spirit of the new age, and that it is this spirit, with its stimulating view of existence, which has here arrived at a poetic breakthrough and holds the Day of Judgment over its deniers. What philosophy already for a long time has whispered in the ear of its disciple, poetry now begins to proclaim from the rooftops.[2] In his review Martensen acknowledges the difficulties of dealing with speculative thinking in the dramatic form and the theatrical performance as compared to in poetry, admits that his intention is not to develop the poetic beauties in Heiberg's new poems or to write a through aesthetic criticism of them but to confine himself to their philosophical or moral aspects, and then proceeds to develop a concept of the comical as the fundamental category of the age, and shows how Heiberg has expressed this.[3] The commentary helpfully adds that Heiberg's and Martensen's endeavors before long were made the object of satirical attack, for instance, in *Johan Ludvig Heiberg efter Døden, Apocalyptisk Komedie i fire Acter*, 1842, authored by the pseudonym Adam Howitz (no doubt C.K.F. Molbech and C. Ploug).[4]

The next work is a huge book that develops most fully the Kierkegaardian critique of Hegel and the Hegelians. Yet, in this analysis we cannot do more than indicate a few ways in which Martensen has served as a source for Kierkegaard's creative labors in this book that was at one point to terminate his activity as an author. Johannes Climacus' 1846 *Concluding Unscientific Postscript* can be understood humorously as a little addendum, of a mere 630 pages in the English version, to his *Philosophical Fragments*. It continues consideration of the *Fragments'* stated question concerning "eternal happiness," which we examined in relation to Martensen's baptism book; we can continue our consideration of this writing as a possible source. An 1845 journal entry is relevant:

---

[1] *SKS* 6 K, 343.
[2] *SKS* 6 K, 343-344.
[3] *SKS*, 6 K, 344.
[4] Ibid.

In a little pamphlet about Baptism, Prof. Martensen, otherwise equipped with fortunate qualifications for becoming a dogmatic thinker, has not exactly legitimized himself as such. The professor establishes Baptism as decisive for salvation, but for the sake of caution** he still adds that if anyone has not been baptized he also can be saved. It is scientific in every way to be of service with fine sand and coarse sand. The only thing lacking, something I most respectfully do not doubt, is that many a person has been reassured about the matter of his salvation by reading this pamphlet.\*\*\* This can be called satisfying the demands of the times and being understood by the age. Without infinitely interested passion the whole question and all the talk about an eternal happiness is coquetry, but God help the infinitely interested person in passion who would be set aside in a lonely cubicle with dogmatic guidance such as that.

*In margin*: \*\*he naively seems to assume and without making use of the dialectical means of caution.

*In margin*: \*\*\*(Strangely enough, in our day it is not at all difficult to reassure people about the matter of their salvation; rather, it is more difficult to alarm them about it)[1]

The fact that Kierkegaard is disagreeing with Martensen is worth noting, but more important for our purposes here is that this establishes without a doubt that he had indeed spent time in this work, so that it was functioning as a source for him. In response to Kierkegaard, we can clarify that Martensen's stance is to affirm the proposition that "baptism is necessary for salvation," but to recognize that, as with any proposition, its truth has its limitations.[2] He explains what he means in a rather long paragraph:

> The sacramental revelation is indeed a free revelation of will, not a process of nature. Christ's royal will surely *gives itself* a presence in and under the visible acts. The visible acts as such indeed are only the creaturely element, which grace employs as means for its self-communication. Herein lies the reason why the divine will cannot be bound only in the outer forms,

---

[1] *Pap.* VI B 98; *CUP2*, Supplement, 29-30.
[2] Martensen, *Den christelige Daab*, op. cit., p. 66.

which are posited by it; but as the divine will has freely couched itself in these, so must it also *stretch beyond* these. If Christ were captured in the sacrament, then the sacrament would cease being a means of grace, and the sacramental presence would only be the expression for an immediate natural necessity, as pantheistic sects have thought of their Christ of nature in the whole visible universe. The sacrament is means of grace only as the expression for an immanence of the divine will. The sacrament's efficacy therefore has its inner purpose and its inner limit in the divine will, but the divine will is not exhausted and delimited by the sacrament. The divine will cannot have exhausted its possibilities in any of its outer forms of actuality. But as it *must* reveal itself according to its essence, and cannot do other than will its kingdom, it must by virtue of its inner infinity, be inexhaustible in possibilities, in new means, new ways to procure its kingdom entrance and progress in the world. Since not merely the single points of actuality, but all of actuality is permeable for the divine will, it must be said that God can change everything into a sacrament, can make everything into a means of grace. This is the truth, which one-sidedly has been taught in speculative mysticism, which in several ways has been repeated in modernity's speculation, and which says that all of actuality can be sacramental. Therefore, it will not have the human spirit bound to a couple of determinate forms of the sacramental presence. The divine center is indeed everywhere and consequently can everywhere come to a presence; every revival can become a baptism, every pure and holy consumption can become a Eucharist. Insofar as one is looking exclusively at the divine possibilities, this has its correctness. But mysticism overlooks that the divine will is not a formless will but an *economic* will, a will that is only satisfied in an economy of revelation. It is an all-ordering will, which wants to imprint its eternal fundamental form in a total organization, a kingdom of redemption in history. The concept of the dispensability of the historically instituted means of grace can therefore only have validity under a presupposition of their *necessity*. The concept of the *possibility* of infinitely many and other means of grace can only have dialectical validity within the ordered *actuality* of the economy of revelation. But within this limit and under this presupposition it has its relative truth. For then it views only the invisible source's primitivity before the actual; the invisible principle's over-arching power over each of its visible forms. In all historical organizations it holds true that it belongs precisely to the given order of things that something will sometimes happen which is outside the given order. This proposition does not contain any defense for the principle of formlessness and empty arbitrariness; for what happens outside the order must only serve to show the reality of the all-organizing, truly royal principle, which does not need to exclude the accidental and the arbitrary from its state, because it has possibilities enough to conserve and reorganize it towards its eternal fundamental forms. Free irregularity does not destroy the positive rule, but establishes it. In this sense we say then that baptism is both necessary and dispensable to salvation. Namely, if we place ourselves at the standpoint of the *given organization*, then we must say that baptism is necessary; for the church is bound to the Lord's historical institution; it must receive the divine gift thus as it is given; it is directed to seek the Lord where he himself has willed to allow himself to be found by it. If we considered the question to the contrary under the standpoint of the *organizing will*, under the infinite point of view of Christ and the Spirit, then we must say that the empirical act is relatively dispensable, because that which makes the baptism, baptism, can also be given without the empirical element. Now if one would from this take occasion to look down on water baptism, then this would only be a self-deception. For it is one thing for a person willfully to place oneself into an irregular relation to the church's institutions, and another to be placed in an irregular relation to them, by the general tremors and crises which occur in history no less than in natural life, and temporarily disrupt the developmental progress of the spiritual organization. Now while mysticism and with it all one-sided idealism exclusively gazes at the Idea's infinite possibilities, the crass orthodox realism confines itself only to the positive given churchly organization, without turning an eye toward the organization's infinite *source*. For this viewpoint the divine grace has as good as been crystallized in baptism, and we arrive at the outrageous consequence that everyone who has not received the church's baptism is irrevocably lost. Since unbaptized children are not able to be saved, it here becomes an unforgivable requirement in all necessary instances to resort to emergency baptism. The teaching on emergency baptism's unconditional necessity is the extreme opposite of the teaching on the free spiritual baptism, which considers every determinate outer form superfluous. Insofar as these opposites exclude each other, they are both equally untrue. The concept of emergency baptism has validity only insofar as it in addition recognizes the possibility of the free spiritual baptism. Only then does the requirement concerning emergency baptism originate not from a fatalistic view of salvation, but from a conscientious faith, which feels itself bound to Christ's institution and command. The concept of the mystical spiritual baptism to the contrary only has validity insofar as this is thought of as acting in place of the churchly baptism, and as an irregularity in the economy of historical revelation can itself be considered as a sort of emergency baptism, which consequently points to the church's baptism, as its canonical model.[1]

This statement can be ignored as the wild speculative thinking of a theologian who is unwilling to take a definite stand on any theological doctrine, including this central one of baptism. From another perspective it can be seen as a theologian who is attempting to affirm the deliverances of the Christian faith while also seeking to honor the context and to recognize the limits of theological reflection and the presumptuousness of limiting what God might be able to accomplish in working through the possibilities of life. Therefore, he affirms a given, an established structure that is to be respected and honored, i.e., the beliefs attending the initiation rite of the Christian religion. But he also wants to affirm that this structure and its churchly endorsement is a theological perspective that ought not be absolutized. So he makes bold to affirm as well another perspective which acknowledges the possibility that God might well choose to work outside of the means of grace established by the church.

Another way in which the piece on Christian baptism stands in the background of the *Postscript* is in its development of the discussion of Christianity in terms of objectivity and subjectivity. Martensen acknowledges the importance of subjectivity and of the single individual, but he also stresses the significant place of objectivity, and in the context of the time he thinks an emphasis on objectivity is needed to offset the overemphasis on subjectivity. Johannes Climacus likewise frames his discussion of Christianity in terms of subjectivity and objectivity. He makes many of the same points Martensen does in embracing

---

[1] Ibid., pp. 68-71.

subjectivity, but leaves any acknowledgement of such a common ground out of his account. Instead, the Hegelian philosophers are presented by him as stressing Christianity understood only in terms of objectivity.

The *Postscript* stands in a very complex relation to Martensen. Niels Thulstrup writes: "In the original manuscript of the *Concluding Unscientific Postscript*, Martensen was mentioned by name in a number of passages, but before publication these were altered to read 'lecturer' or 'a Hegelian.'"[1] Kierkegaard notes that this book "has not mentioned or discussed Prof. Martensen with one single word."[2] Some of the references to a *Privatdocent* have as their target Rasmus Nielsen, another Hegelian at Copenhagen University whom we have encountered already, but Martensen is frequently the intended referent.[3] There are a host of these locations in the text that could but will not be identified here. We will mention, though, an uncharacteristically positive comment that Kierkegaard makes about Martensen in 1846 in the context of discussing the *Postscript*. In a journal entry dealing with the suggestion that Martensen should be dismissed from his teaching position, Kierkegaard writes what appear to be serious words about the strengths of his opponent:

> How can someone be found to take Prof. Martensen's place?...It is absolutely certain that Prof. Martensen, at the time he was appointed, was unconditionally not only the best qualified one, for there was no one else at all who could be considered, but also that he was absolutely qualified, in possession of talent and knowledge. It is also well known what a sensation he made at the time. Perhaps a little exaggeration slipped in—well, it can happen so easily, but nevertheless it is certain that he is a distinguished lecturer, and just as he cannot be said to have had a rival at the time, it still cannot be said that he has one...Prof. Martensen is an excellent lecturer, indeed so excellent that he, without reservation, must at any moment be

---

[1] Niels Thulstrup, "Martensen's Dogmatics and its Reception," op. cit., pp. 169-197, and reprinted in slightly modified form in *Kierkegaard and His Contemporaries*, op. cit., pp. 181-202.
[2] *Pap.* VII-1 B 88; *EO2*, Supplement, 129.
[3] See *Pap.* VII-1 B 88; *CUP2*, Supplement, 133-134, and Stewart, *Kierkegaard's Relations to Hegel Reconsidered*, op. cit., p. 463.

able to obtain an appointment at the most famous university in Germany.... Prof. Martensen's worth remains unchanged.[1]

These are important words to lift up, because they actually help one better understand all the negative words about Martensen as being owed, at least in part, to a deep resentment that Kierkegaard had in relation to him. In other words, Martensen would not have received so much criticism from Kierkegaard and consumed so much of the energies of his negative dialectic if he had not been a thinker, and maybe even a person, of some substance.

A serious probing into the *Postscript* and Martensen would need to turn to the thorough research of Jon Stewart, who concludes that its main target is not so much Hegel himself as Danish Hegelians, and most particularly Martensen.[2] He also shows that the position taken by Martensen in his review of Heiberg's *Introductory Lecture*—affirming that there is "something inexplicable" in both poetry and religion that "can only be understood by faith, a freedom, which to be sure contains necessity in itself, but is infinitely more than this"—essentially provides an outline of the view Johannes Climacus takes in this book.[3] Stewart establishes Martensen's relevance to Climacus' development of such themes as speculative philosophy leading to forgetting oneself and the need to live an ethical existence, his criticism of the presuppositionless beginning, his criticism of the unity of thought and being, his discussion of speculative philosophy in relation to the law of excluded middle, and his treatment of the absence of an ethics in the system.[4] We can close our consideration of the *Postscript* with Stewart's insightful statement "that Martensen is not the uncritical Hegelian he is portrayed as being and, moreover, that Climacus in fact uses Martensen's criticism of Hegel": "Perhaps what irritated Kierkegaard the most was not that Martensen's position contradicted his own but rather that they held views on some issues that were all too similar."[5] We see that here, as in many other of

---

[1] *Pap.* VII-1 B 88; *CUP2*, Supplement, 131-132.
[2] Stewart, *Kierkegaard's Relations to Hegel Reconsidered*, op. cit., pp. 453-466. In his consideration of the *Postscript*, pp. 466-523, Martensen figures predominantly.
[3] Ibid., p. 480.
[4] Ibid.
[5] Ibid., p. 517.

Kierkegaard's writings, Martensen was shaping his agenda more than has hitherto been acknowledged. Kierkegaard was following the chosen one. During these years Martensen's success in relation to the established order of Golden Age Denmark provided occasion for Kierkegaard's ongoing criticisms. He chides Martensen for his parroting of Hegel's development of the comical.[1] He sets forth a question to Professor Martensen regarding the Aristotelian doctrine of virtue.[2] He notes that Martensen has not legitimated himself as a dogmatic thinker in the little piece on baptism.[3] Anticipating his later attack on the established order, Kierkegaard in 1846 registers his contempt for Martensen and others who "live cowardly and effeminately at a fashionable distance in select groups, guarded by illusion (that the masses seldom see them and therefore imagine them to be something)."[4] Kierkegaard is always ready to offer a critique of Martensen's preaching, his life and work.[5]

### III. Criticizing the Established Order: 1847-1855

One of the contributions I hope this monograph will make to Kierkegaard scholarship is to point out that the theme of "the church" had been a major part of Martensen's theological perspective really from the beginning of his writing and became even more central after 1841. Therefore, Kierkegaard's criticisms of Martensen during the 1840s can be understood as being in some ways directed against the church, at least in an indirect sense. The "Attack on the Church" represents a change in strategy for Kierkegaard, but it is not a complete departure from his earlier protests. To the extent that he had been critiquing Martensen, a theologian who had identified himself with the church and understood the church as the foundation of his theological constructive labors,

---

[1] *SKS* 19, 375, Not 12:7; *JP* 2, 1738.
[2] *Pap.* V A 100; *JP* 5, 5712.
[3] *Pap.* VI B 98,15.
[4] *SKS* 20, 45, NB:44; *JP* 5, 5941.
[5] *SKS* 21, 271, NB10:28. *SKS* 22, 165, NB12:41, 41a. *Pap.* X-3 A 55. *Pap.* X-3 A 162.

Magister Kierkegaard had been indirectly attacking the church all along. The centrality of the doctrine of the church in Martensen's understanding of Christian baptism, and his articulation of that understanding early on in the 1843 baptism book, is a key piece in grasping Kierkegaard's critical labors and recognizing some level of continuity between his critique of the 1840s and his attack of the '50s. Kierkegaard had also been at least implicitly attacking the church prior to his official Attack.

Criticisms of Martensen as a member of the establishment become more numerous as the years go on. In 1847 Kierkegaard complains about Martensen: "what a display of abjection!...Martensen has a strictly Christian upbringing [which prevents him from enjoying life] and does not have the kind of talent Heiberg has," however, both men "have absolutely no ethical backbone."[1] It irritates Kierkegaard that such men are supposed to be the authorities judging his work.[2] As Court Preacher, Martensen is made to look like a fool in preaching as a man of distinction for the distinguished.[3] Kierkegaard will later bring his typical humor to depicting Martensen, as has been already pointed out in the Preface: "In the splendid cathedral a handsome Royal Chaplain, the cultured public's chosen one, appears before a chosen circle of the chosen, and preaches movingly [*rørt*]—I say 'movingly,' I do not say dryly' [*tørt*]—no, he preaches movingly on the apostle's words: God has chosen the lowly and the despised in the world—and no one laughs."[4] Martensen provides "how one should not preach."[5] By 1848 Kierkegaard includes Martensen along with Mynster and Heiberg as part of "the great clique"[6] or coterie of the established order, and by the next year he depicts Martensen as a good example of a contemporary figure being made into an authority to the detriment of society.[7] Yet, Kierkegaard thinks that he will be able to get on with his relation to Martensen and the others in excellent fashion:

---

[1] *SKS* 20, 187-188, NB2:119; *JP* 5, 6039.
[2] *SKS* 20, 189, NB2:121.
[3] *SKS* 20, 205, NB2:160; *JP* 6, 6052. *SKS* 21, 271, NB10:28. See also other comments of Kierkegaard on Martensen as Court Preacher: *SKS* 22, 325-326, NB13:86. *Pap.* X-3 A 55. *Pap.* X-6 B 135. *Pap.* XI-2 A 310.
[4] *Pap.* X-6 B 253; *JP* 6, 6787.
[5] *SKS* 22, 394-395, NB14:86, 86.a; *JP* 6, 6552.
[6] *SKS* 21, 39-41, NB6:55.
[7] *SKS* 21, 271, NB10:28.

"In their tranquil minds they are yet able to understand a part of me, and therefore it amuses me to cackle them."[1]

Martensen promised the system,[2] and in 1849 Martensen finally published his *Christian Dogmatics*, the work in systematic theology that he had been working on for so long. Prior to its publication Frederike Bremer, the famous Finnish-Swedish writer and traveler who was visiting Denmark at that time, each day read the galleys of the book with Martensen and this prompted journal entries from Kierkegaard, who points out that this connoisseur prophesied "that Martensen's *Dogmatik* will regenerate all scientific scholarship in the North."[3] As the now well-published if not fully accomplished author of inwardness reads through Martensen's major theological work, he makes in his notebooks numerous polemical remarks on the book and on the theological conflict it occasioned.[4] He is very disappointed that Martensen did not refer to his own writings, except for a reference in the Preface to "random thoughts and aphorisms, sudden discoveries and hints" that he rejects without mentioning the author, and this dismissal instigates Kierkegaard to state "that these couple of lines in that Preface were a dialectical

---

[1] *SKS* 20, 319, NB4:68.
[2] *Pap.* X-6 B 137.
[3] *Pap.* X-6 B 105; *JP* 6, 6475. *SKS* 22, 153, NB12:157; *JP* 6493. *SKS* 22, 325, NB13:86.
[4] *SKS* 22, 153, NB12:14; *JP* 6, 6448. *SKS* 22, 153, NB12:15; *JP* 2, 1132. *SKS* 22, 153, NB12:15a, 15b; *JP* 2, 1133. *SKS* 22, 154, NB12:16, 16a; *JP* 6, 6449. *SKS* 22, 154-155, NB12:18; *JP* 1, 508. *SKS* 22, 156, NB12:21; *JP* 3, 3564. *SKS* 22, 165, NB12:41, 41a. *SKS* 22, 167, NB 12:47, 47a; *JP* 6, 6460. *SKS* 22, 176-177, NB12:62, 62a. *SKS* 22, 177-178, NB12:64, 64a. *SKS* 22, 181, NB12:70, 70a. *SKS* 22, 181, NB12:70b. *SKS* 22, 184, NB12:73, 73a; *JP* 6, 6465. *SKS* 22, 185, NB12:75, 75a, 75b. *SKS* 22, 185-186, NB12:76, 76a. *SKS* 22, 186, NB12:77, 77a. *SKS* 22, 187, NB 79, 79a. *SKS* 22, 189-190; NB12:85, 85a; *JP* 3, 3217. *SKS* 22, 239-240, NB12:157; *JP* 6, 6493. *SKS* 22, 304-305, NB13:49. *SKS* 22, 325-326, NB13:86, 86a-86h. *SKS* 22, 411, NB14:111; *JP* 3, 2657. *Pap.* X-2 A 495. *Pap.* X-2 A 580. *Pap.* X-2 A 589. *Pap.* X-2 A 596; *JP* 6, 6595. *Pap.* X-3 A 70. *Pap.* X-3 A 74. *Pap.* X-3 A 95. *Pap.* X-3 A 105. *Pap.* X-3 A 678; *JP* 6, 6707. *Pap.* X-6 B 97. *Pap.* X-6 B 100. *Pap.* X-6 B 83-143, pp. 129-193. Of these entries, the following have been translated by the Hongs and included in their *Journals and Papers*; after each of these is given in brackets the appropriate entry number from *Pap.* X-6 B 83 (*JP* 6, 6403); 84 (*JP* 6, 6404); 85 (*JP* 6, 6405); 86 (*JP* 6, 6406); 93 (*JP* 6, 6663); 105 (*JP* 6, 6475); 121 (*JP* 6, 6574); 127 (*JP* 6, 6566); 128 (*JP* 6, 6596); 130 (*JP* 6, 6558); 131 (*JP* 6, 6559); 137 (*JP* 6, 6636).

indiscretion."[1] Martensen might be able to ignore him, but he could not in the least way enter into competition with him.[2] Kierkegaard makes many other entries in response to this statement in the Preface to *Den christelige Dogmatik*,[3] and then he later makes entries on the Preface to the second edition of this work as well.[4] Kierkegaard concludes, on the whole, that in this work Martensen—who essentially takes his cues from the clergy, who are suspicious of Kierkegaard because he has no livelihood and because he proclaims Christianity without being compensated for it[5]—is "dogmatically stiff,"[6] in part because he shies away from "anything existential."[7] "Let Martensen…read one of Luther's sermons aloud," suggests the Socratic Dane in 1850, and "then there would be no need to write against Martensen."[8]

Kierkegaard had found support from Rasmus Nielsen, who was and had been a colleague of Martensen at the University for a number of years and who wrote the critical response to Martensen's *Dogmatics* entitled *Mag. S. Kierkegaards 'Johannes Climacus' or Dr. Martensens 'Christelige Dogmatik'. En undersøgende Anmeldelse*, to which, as we have seen, Martensen responded in his *Dogmatic Elucidations* of 1850. In that writing Martensen states regarding Kierkegaard's writings that "my acquaintance with this diffuse literature is, as I said, only very scant and fragmentary."[9] In his "dogmatic elucidations" Martensen also dismisses Kierkegaard's pseudonyms as diffuse literature. Kierkegaard's notebooks include numerous polemical remarks on that Martensenian publication.[10] The relation between Nielsen and Martensen became another major topic

---

[1] *Pap.* X-3 A 95.
[2] *Pap.* X-1 A 165.
[3] *Pap.* X-3 A 95. *Pap.* X-6 B 112. *Pap.* X-6 B 116. *Pap* X-6 B 137; *JP* 6, 6636. *Pap.* X-6 B 138. *Pap.* X-6 B 143; *JP* 3, 3350. *Pap.* X-6 B 171; *JP* 6, 6748.
[4] *Pap.* X-3 A 70. *Pap.* X-3 A 74. *Pap* X-3 A 95. *Pap.* X-3 A 105. *Pap.* X-6 B 133; *JP* 4, 4295.
[5] *Pap.* X-3 A 274.
[6] *Pap.* X-3 A 544.
[7] *Pap.* X-3 A 567.
[8] *Pap.* X-3 A 534; *JP* 3, 3515.
[9] Martensen, *Dogmatiske Oplysninger*, op. cit., p. 13.
[10] *Pap.* X-3 A 164; *JP* 6635. *Pap.* X-3 A 196. *Pap.* X-3 A 236. *Pa*p. X-3 A 567. *Pap.* X-5 B 54. *Pap.* X-6 B 135. *Pap.* X-6 B 137; *JP* 6, 6636. *Pap.* X-6 B 138. *Pap.* X-6 B 139.

treated extensively by Kierkegaard in his notebooks, especially during 1849 and 1850.[1] When Søren's older brother Peter gave a lecture to a gathering of clergy on the topic of Martensen, Kierkegaard, and Nielsen, in which he characterized Martensen as "sobriety," and Kierkegaard as "ecstasy," which Kierkegaard rightly regarded as less than complimentary to him, and furthermore when this hastily-prepared statement was eventually published, Kierkegaard expressed his frustrations over this in his notebooks.[2]

Kierkegaard's animosity towards Martensen continues to mount, for Kierkegaard judges that as a philosopher he is not at all dialectical but operates with categories that are purely rhetorical; and as a Christian he calls for a genuinely actual life, but in his own existence he wants merely to be a success in the world.[3] Thus in his notebooks Kierkegaard points out the difference between an essential thinker and a professor

---

[1] *SKS* 22, 219-220, NB12:129, 129a. *SKS* 22, 414, NB14:120, 120a; *JP* 6, 6563. *Pap.* X-2 A 580. *Pap.* X-3 A 2. *Pap.* X-3 A 12; *JP* 6, 6610. *Pap.* X-3 A 188. *Pap.* X-3 A 198. *Pap.* X-3 A 292. *Pap.* X-3 A 681. *Pap.* X-3 A 701. *Pap.* X-4 A 164. *Pap.* X-4 A 363. *Pap.* X-4 A 364. *Pap.* X-5 A 125. *Pap.* X-6 B 91. *Pap.* X-6 B 95. *Pap.* X-6 B 96. *Pap.* X-6 B 97. *Pap.* X-6 B 99. *Pap.* X-6 B 100. *Pap.* X-6 B 101. *Pap.* X-6 B 102. *Pap.* X-6 B 109. *Pap.* X-6 B 111. *Pap.* X-6 B 120. *Pap.* X-6 B 121; *JP* 6, 6574. *Pap.* X-6 B 124. *Pap.* XI-3 B 14. *Pap.* XI-3 B 101. *Pap.* XI-3 B 107. *Pap.* XI-3 B 157.

[2] *SKS* 22, 392, NB14:81, 81.a, 81.b; *JP* 6, 6550. *SKS* 22, 394, NB14:85, 85.a; *JP* 6, 6553. *SKS* 22, 403-404, NB14:97, 97.a-97.d; *JP* 6, 6554. *SKS* 22, 405-406, NB14:102, 102.a; *JP* 6, 6557. *SKS* 22, 409-410, NB14:108. *SKS* 22, 413, NB14:117. *Pap.* X-6 B 130; *JP* 6, 6558. *Pap.* XI-1 A 47; *JP* 6, 6857. *Pap.* XI-2 A 307. Six years later, on July 5, 1855, brother Peter again gave an address on Søren's writings, this time entitled "Remarks on the Famous Pseudonyms of the Day and the Theology of Their Author," in which he called into question the theological appropriateness of this literature. See *M*, Supplement, 633, n. 230. This second talk caused Kierkegaard to reflect on the talk of six years earlier and write: "Yes, he drew a parallel between Martensen and me and made Martensen out to be sobriety. So, I have made sacrifices, renounced earthly reward—and then it is the hearty brother who is so kind, in contrast to this, to represent Martensen, who in every way has profited, as sobriety. Ah! I, the opposite of sobriety, am depicted as representing ecstasy, presumably a kind of lunacy, whereby the past came rather close to agreement with contemptibilitiy's whole attack on me, which continually aims to represent my life as a kind of lunacy."—*Pap.* XI 3 B 155 and included in *M*, Supplement, 582-587.
For an English translation of these two talks by Peter Chrsitian Kierkegaard at the October 30, 1849 and July 5, 1855 Roskilde Ecclesiastical Conventions, see Appendix B of Bruce Kirmmse's *Encounters with Kierkegaard*, op. cit., pp. 256-268.

[3] *SKS* 22, 154-155, NB12:18; *JP* 1, 508. *Pap.* X-3 A 105.

*Peter Christian Kierkegaard (1805-1888)*
(The Royal Library, Copenhagen)

with Martensen being the latter,[1] claims that Martensen can lecture on everything since he is a professor in contrast to a thinker,[2] observes that Martensen is considered to be sound secularly because he has been married twice,[3] charges that Martensen is capable of being cowardly sneaking,[4] thinks that Martensen "has always been more a reporter and correspondent than a primitive thinker,[5] shows that "the highly talented speculative dogmatician as dialectician" cannot compare to Johannes

---

[1] *SKS* 22, 162, NB12:32; *JP* 3, 3565. *SKS* 22, 179, NB12:67; *JP* 3, 3566. *SKS* 22, 184, NB12:73, 73a; *JP* 6, 6465.
[2] *SKS* 22, 184, NB12:73, 73a; *JP* 6, 6465.
[3] *SKS* 22, 185-186, NB12:76, 76a.
[4] *SKS* 22, 208-209, NB12:115, 115a, 115b; *JP* 1, 707.
[5] *SKS* 22, 325-328, NB13:85, 86.a-86.h; *JP* 3, 3034. *Pap.* X-6 B 103.

Climacus because he believes that one can explain the Christian paradox by means of direct communication,[1] insists that Martensen is a sign that it is a confused time,[2] queries whether Martensen's Christianity and Christianity's proclamation "is more than an approximation,"[3] contends that Martensen's productivity is "betraying and abolishing Christianity,"[4] questions whether Martensen's whole life and authorship have been such that it should go without saying that he is a Christian,[5] believes that with the aid of mediocrity Martensen will finally become classical,[6] and articulates his dismay that this celebrity status comes in spite of the fact that Martensen "is a web of untruth and triviality."[7] As Kierkegaard struggled to find receptive readers of his own work, he noticed that Martensen "has nearly as many listeners as the *"Flying Post"* has subscribers."[8] Kierkegaard became bitter and envious of Martensen's success.[9] It maddened him further that "Martensen was the best-paid writer engaged by Reitzel,"[10] C.A. Reitzel being the leading publisher in Copenhagen during this time. A complete interpretation of the Kierkegaard-Martensen relation, which this monograph cannot provide, would have to include an analysis of Kierkegaard's bitterness and envy,

---

[1] *Pap.* X-6 B 143. On Martensen and the paradox see also *Pap.* X-6 B 142. On Martensen's expression that "fortunately Christianity is direct communication," see *Pap.* X-5 B 52; *JP* 2, 2133, *Pap.* X 6 B 135. Under the pseudonym of Johannes Climacus, Kierkegaard makes an entry on "the higher rationality" that differs from the speculative approach of Prof. Martensen: see *Pap.* X-6 B 68; *JP* 6, 6598. As a disciple of Johannes Climacus, Kierkegaard gives expression to "A Theological Point of View" in *Pap.* X-6 B 105; *JP* 6, 6475.
[2] *Pap.* X-6 B 141.
[3] *Pap.* X-6 B 145. In *Pap.* XI-1 A 48 Kierkegaard considers the sense in which he has "triumphed over Martensen" and the sense in which "the Kierkegaardian polemic has annihilated Martensen."
[4] *Pap.* X-3 A 105.
[5] *Pap.* X-3 A 162. In this entry Kierkegaard discusses "The Difference between Prof. Martensen and me."
[6] *SKS* 22, 386, NB14:68; *JP* 6, 6547.
[7] *Pap.* X-2 A 495.
[8] *SKS* 22, 325-328, NB13:85, 86.a-86.h.
[9] *Pap.* II A 597; *JP* 5, 5225. *SKS* 17, 49, AA:38; *JP* 2, 1183. *SKS* 18, 83, FF:38; *JP* 5, 5226.
[10] "Bookstores, Publishers and Antiquarian Shops," *The Copenhagen of Kierkegaard*, ed. by Niels Thulstrup and Marie Mikulová Thulstrup (*Bibiotheca Kierkegaardiana*, vol. 11), p. 49.

*Carl Andreas Reitzel (1789-1853)*
(The Royal Library, Copenhagen)

possibly employing some of René Girard's work on scapegoating to good effect.

Kierkegaard seems intrigued by the relation he has to Martensen. In 1849 he offers a thoughtful assessment of Martensen in an entry entitled "Prof. Martensen's Status."[1] As we have seen, he is obviously deeply distressed by what he takes to be Martensen's public assault in print, namely, the *Dogmatics* Preface, which Kierkegaard regards as a judgment "that my entire productivity is nothing."[2] From Kierkegaard's

---

[1] *SKS* 22, 325-328, NB13:85, 86.a-86.h
[2] *SKS* 22, 304-305, NB13:49. *Pap.* X-2 A 589.

perspective the conflict between the two of them is not over concepts but over the nature of the Christian proclamation: Martensen leads people "deeper and deeper into the flower-strewn, smiling jargon of illusions," whereas Kierkegaard's version of Christianity has no enticements or anything compelling, and that is why Kierkegaard finds himself standing all alone.[1] Martensen's work in dogmatic theology won praise from lay people for its clarity and for communicating in such a way that even non-theological but educated seekers could understand it and grasp its central meanings; Kierkegaard interprets this as Martensen's willingness to indulge in language that is illusory in order to satisfy his customers and win favor with them.[2] In 1850 Kierkegaard characterizes this relation as "curious," curious in the sense that the difference between them is perceived incorrectly as Martensen wanting "to vindicate reflection with respect to faith, reflecting on the faith, and" as Kierkegaard being against such reflection; this is incorrect because his whole pseudonymous literature has been chiefly concerned with illuminating the matter of faith by dialectic, by reflection.[3] Curious it might be, but the relation between them is also infuriating for Kierkegaard, so that he sometimes has to poke fun at Martensen, like when he thinks of a "crazy comedy," with the scene being that of Judgment Day with the characters of "Our Lord" and "A Theological Professor." Our Lord asks, "Have you sought the kingdom of God first and foremost?" The Professor responds, "No, I can't say that I have, but I know how to say 'to seek the kingdom of God first and foremost' in seven languages."[4] During the years 1849-1850 Kierkegaard's notebooks include many other critical references to Martensen.[5]

A few days after Martensen published his *Christian Dogmatics*, Kierkegaard published his *The Sickness Unto Death*. This writing, by Anti-Climacus, gives us Kierkegaard's most mature articulation of his

---

[1] *Pap.* X-3 A 161; *JP* 6, 6655. On the relationship between Kierkegaard and Martensen, see also *SKS* 22, 303, NB13:46-47 and *Pap.* X-3 A 274.
[2] *SKS* 22, 325-328, NB13:85-86.a-86.h.
[3] *Pap.* X-2 A 596; *JP* 6, 6595.
[4] *Pap.*, X-3 A 398; *JP* 3, 3573.
[5] *Pap.* X-6 B 103-193, pp. 129-193. Many of these references have been identified here, but not all of them.

theological anthropology. I have attempted to show elsewhere that a parallelism can be discerned in their views of the human in relation to God.[1] Both Martensen and Kierkegaard gave a relative endorsement of pantheism as a position to be affirmed but sublated; there is a divine substance of all reality that is the source of life's power. But pantheism with its power must yield to pantheism with its personality. God as personality is the divine subject who enlivens human personalities by making room for them to have their own power in a relatively independent sense. Kierkegaard can develop his intricate analysis of despair because of this underlying theological anthropology: despair, in its various forms, results when the human self does not shape her life in accord with its God-grounded structure. Faith is the means by which the self enters into relation to God and allows itself to benefit from the relationship with the divine fountain of possibilities. The self is potentiated because it is open to possibilities. The formula for this, "in relating itself to itself and in willing to be itself, the self rests transparently in the power that established it,"[2] bears striking resemblance to Martensen's definition of virtue or striving freedom in his *Outline to a System of Moral Philosophy*, which reads: "It is virtue, striving freedom, which relates itself to itself as to that which does not exist in its own power," i.e., the human self relates itself to itself, and in relating itself to itself relates itself to another power, the divine Other.[3] *Sickness* does also include a reference to "speculative dogmatics," which could also be referring to Martensen.[4]

George Pattison makes an important argument in his book on Kierkegaard and the crisis of culture, focusing on "the public"—as an outgrowth of modernity as urbanity, as "something that anyone can pick up," as distinguishable from "the people"—"as a phenomenon of urbanity" and thus as "the substitute for" the "lost immediacy of corporate presence" that characterized ancient and pre-modern communal life but is no longer

---

[1] Curtis L. Thompson, "From Presupposing Pantheism's Power to Potentiating Panentheism's Personality: Seeking Parallels between Kierkegaard's and Martensen's Theological Anthropologies," *Journal of Religion*, vol. 82, 2002, pp. 225-251.
[2] *SKS* 11, 130; *SUD*, 14.
[3] H. Martensen, *Grundrids til Moralphilosophiens System*, op. cit., p. 75; *Outline to a System of Moral Philosophy*, BHK, op. cit., p. 295.
[4] *SKS* 11, 209; *SUD* 97, and see p. 179, note 38.

"possible in the large-scale differentiated world of the modern city."[1] "The public" is an abstraction that is closely related to "the press," which Kierkegaard understands as "the evil principle in the modern world"[2] and as being "really designed to make personality impossible."[3] To these two, the public and the press, we can add "the crowd," which Kierkegaard says "is really what I have made my polemical target," because "the crowd has no essential reflection" and ends up blinding people so "they don't really know what they are doing."[4] These three are interconnected realities that combine to bring about a leveling of distinctions and of passionate living. All three of these categories are abstractions that have been spawned by modern culture and leave it in a crisis. These reduce life because they lift up the quantitative and foster sameness. "The public is number."[5] For Kierkegaard, "Eternity does not *count*, it is quality."[6] In fact, we could add to these three "the numerical," and "the church" too. These all emphasize the objective side of reality at the expense of the subjective. It would also be not inappropriate to add another category to the mix: to "the public," "the press," "the crowd," "the numerical," and "the church" I believe we can legitimately add "the professor," to more completely round out Kierkegaard's repertoire of terms that identify constitutive elements of that modern form of culture that is leveling life by shrinking the scope and squelching the intensity of human freedom. Martensen knows the crucial place of subjectivity, but he is attempting to provide a corrective of his own, to what he sees as an overemphasis on subjectivity, by emphasizing objectivity. So Kierkegaard's criticisms are understandable, especially if Martensen's project is considered apart from the context he understood himself to be addressing. Many of Kierkegaard's problems with Martensen are targeted at his emphasis on objectivity as opposed to subjectivity. Martensen, then, is a source for Kierkegaard's analysis of his contemporary cultural configuration, which

---

[1] George Pattison, *Kierkegaard, Religion and the Nineteenth-Century Crisis of Culture*, Cambridge: Cambridge University Press 2002, p. 21, p. 41, p. 66, and p. 67.
[2] *SKS* 20, 152, NB2:29; *JP* 2, 2148. Cited by Pattison in ibid., p. 33.
[3] *Pap.* XI-1 A 25; *PJ* 570.
[4] *SKS* 20, 94-95, NB:137; *PJ* 255-256.
[5] *Pap.* XI-2 A 26; *PJ* 615.
[6] *Pap.* XI-1 A 536; *PJ* 611.

he sensitively and presciently discerns as insidiously shaping human existence in deleterious ways. We are suggesting that Kierkegaard's outrage with "the public" is not unrelated to the role he sees the church playing within that structured cultural system of leveling that robs people of their passion and individuality. In 1850 Kierkegaard notes: "The established order indeed has an atlas [*Atlas*] in Professor Martensen, a man in satin [*Atlask*]."[1] In that same year Kierkegaard published his *Practice in Christianity*. In that work, of course, he does not refer directly to Martensen. But in a draft from 1849-1850 he wrote: "If the scene were in eternity and not in the confusion of established Christendom, then Prof. Martensen would unconditionally be dismissed simply and solely for the little comment (in his *Dogmatiske Oplysninger*) that he drops with almost unbelievable assurance: "Fortunately Christianity is direct communication. That is, unfortunately this remark proves beyond a doubt that Prof. M. has absolutely missed the point in Christianity."[2] Kierkegaard recounted how in a conversation on October 22, 1850 with Bishop Mynster after he had read *Practice*, that Mynster had told him: "Yes, half of the book is an attack on Martensen, the other half on me."[3] Kierkegaard told Martensen that in about two years' time the established order will thank him for having published the book [*Practice in Christianity*].[4] And it is very surprising and important to underscore that in 1851 Kierkegaard evidently still had hope of winning Martensen over to his side. Kierkegaard cites as one of the advantages Mynster gained from his relation to Kierkegaard was that in the area of literature he provided an option to Martensen and his system and thus made it possible for Mynster to choose Martensen.[5] In the context of deliberating on his relation with Mynster, Kierkegaard

---

[1] *Pap.* X-3 A 572.
[2] *Pap.* X-5 B 54. This entry is included in *PC*, Supplement, 330-331. For an essay discussing the relation between Martensen's *Dogmatic Elucidations* and Kierkegaard's *Practice in Christianity*, see Poul Lübcke, "Indirect Communication and Kierkegaard's Transcendental Existential Perspectivism," *Søren Kierkegaard and the Word(s): Essays on Hermeneutics and Communication*, ed. by Poul Houe and Gordon D. Marino, Copenhagen: C.A. Reitzel 2003, pp. 28-38.
[3] *Pap.* X-3 A 563 *JP* 6, 6691. See also *Pap.* X-4 A 604; *JP* 6, 6813.
[4] *Pap.* X-4 A 365. On Kierkegaard's comment about reading *Practice in Christianity* in order to be proven right against Martensen," see *Pap.* X-5 B 111.
[5] *Pap.* XI-2 A 311; *JP* 6, 6847.

states: "And I shall be able to do it [attack Mynster's church leadership] in such a way that I will manage to bring both Martensen and Paulli over to my side."[1] When this does not happen, Kierkegaard likely figured he needed to take more drastic action.

The action he eventually took assumed the form of a corrective. Throughout his authorship Kierkegaard had been presenting the ideal, and in the pseudonyms the presentation had assumed the form of indirect communication. Now it was time for direct communication. The task at hand was to reintroduce Christianity into Christendom, to restore the Christian religion to its New Testament form. "Christianity is praxis, a test of character."[2] "Without imitation, Christianity is mythology, poetry."[3] Many have been disappointed and repulsed by the one-sidedness of Kierkegaard's "Attack." However, he was fully aware of its one-sidedness, but saw that as an essential aspect of a corrective: "The person who is to supply the 'corrective' must make a close and thorough study of the weak side of the established—and then one-sidedly deploy the opposite. That is precisely what the corrective consists in, and also the resignation in the person who is to do it. The corrective is in a sense spent on the established."[4] Kierkegaard was very self-aware and intentional in carrying out his attack; he had by no means lost his mind, as some think had to be the case. The first part of his authorship was dedicated to giving an account of how an individual became a Christian; the primary concern of the second part of his body of writings was to demonstrate how a person lives as a Christian.[5] The attack on Christendom should be understood as the last chapter in carrying out that second concern.

Bishop J.P. Mynster died on January 30, 1854. At a memorial service for Mynster held the Sunday before Mynster's funeral, February 5, 1854, Martensen preached a sermon eulogizing Mynster on the text Hebrews 13:7-8; he referred to Mynster as an authentic witness to the truth in "the holy chain of witnesses to the truth that stretches through the ages

---

[1] *Pap.* X-4 A 382.
[2] *Pap.*, X-5 A 134; *PJ* 557.
[3] *Pap.*, X-4 A 626; *JP* 2, 1915.
[4] *SKS* 22, 254, NB12:97; *JP* 1, 408.
[5] Niels Thulstrup, "The Contemporary Reception of the *Concluding Unscientific Postscript* and the External Circumstances," op. cit., p. 146.

from the days of the apostles." This sermon, delivered in Christiansborg Castle Church on what was the Fifth Sunday of Epiphany, was promptly published.[1] The funeral for Mynster followed shortly thereafter, on February 7, 1854. Well, Kierkegaard had understood the phrase "witness to the truth" to be at the heart of his whole cause as an author and his literary enterprise. His extraordinary task had been to re-present the ideal, and in so doing to counteract those like Mynster who had been robbing Christianity of its rigor, emasculating Christian faith by discounting the place of *imitatio Christi*, and thereby lessening the chance of genuine witnesses to the truth appearing in Denmark. Martensen's published sermon, therefore, calling for the faithful to imitate Mynster as one of the witnesses to the truth, agitated Kierkegaard's caustic pen, resulting in an initial article and other notebook entries, some of which would be used in the public attack.[2]

Mynster and Martensen were the central figures evoking Kierkegaard's attack on the church. And really, as Garff indicates, "[i]t was clear that Martensen merely served as the occasion for all this and that he was not the cause of the attack."[3] But with Mynster's death, Martensen, as "the country's supreme Bishop, the official authority,"[4] becomes the focus, and Kierkegaard can write that Bishop Martensen must bear the responsibility for the confused religious condition of the time.[5] At some points Kierkegaard pronounces that the attack is against Mynster though through Martensen.[6] Yet, it is the former tutor and teacher and now aspiring bishop who catalyzed the twenty-one articles Kierkegaard published in the *Fædrelandet* as well as the series of ten polemical pamphlets entitled *The Moment*. The opening insinuation Kierkegaard made in his first attacking article was that Martensen's memorial address was indeed appropriately so labeled, "since it calls to mind Prof. Martensen for the vacant bishopric."[7] The fact that Martensen had felt support as

---

[1] *Prædiken, holdt i Christiansborg Slotskirke paa 5te Søndag efter Hellig Tre Konger, Søndagen før Biskop Dr. Mynsters Jordefærd (Den 5te Februar)*, Copenhagen 1854. Excerpts of Martensen's sermon are included in *M*, Supplement, 359-360.
[2] *Pap.* XI-3 B 31. *Pap.* XI-3 B 38. *Pap.* XI-3 B 49. *Pap.* XI-3 B 89. *Pap.* XI-3 B 208.
[3] Garff, *Kierkegaard*, op. cit., p. 734.
[4] *Pap.* XI-3 B 134.
[5] *Pap.* XI-3 B 225.
[6] *Pap.* XI-2 A 258.

bishop, Kierkegaard believed, would place Martensen in a mindset that should make everything very easy for Kierkegaard in his attack.[1] The theme of "going further" from Kierkegaard's and Martensen's early days is utilized here near the end of Kierkegaard's life in characterizing the professor's contribution to the process of leveling: "Professor Martensen 'goes further'—that is to be expected of Prof. M.—he goes further in abolishing the ideals and from the pulpit proclaims Bishop M. to be a witness to the truth, one of the authentic witnesses to the truth."[2]

Kierkegaard had his first article finished by the end of February, 1854, but the time was not right for publishing it. He held off on the full onslaught, not wanting to interfere with the process of replacing Mynster. Martensen and H.N. Clausen were the favorites for the prime bishop's chair, among others, but the king finally appointed Martensen on April 15, 1854. He was ordained as bishop on Pentecost, the first Sunday of June. The review of the episcopal ordination sermon Martensen preached on the text John 3:16-21 at that service in which he was elevated to the bishopric, June 5, 1854, was printed in *Berlingske Tidende*, 141, June 21, 1854.[3] The next six months went by with Kierkegaard maintaining his restraint, writing all the while in his notebooks. In the meantime Mynster's autobiography was published, and Kierkegaard learned that Mynster had not mentioned Kierkegaard or any member of his family in the recounting of his life, while Martensen, who seemed always to be the beneficiary of good fortune, received his typical high praise from Mynster. That was yet one more reason for an attack. On December 18, 1854, Kierkegaard's restraint came to an end and his polemic against the established church began in earnest. Not long thereafter more fuel was placed on the fire. Near the end of December, at a service in Our Lady Church on Second Christmas Day, December 26, 1854, at which two bishops were being ordained, Martensen preached on the biblical text Acts 1:9, "But you shall receive power when the Holy Spirit has come upon you; and you shall be my witness."[4] The "witness" theme was

---

[1] "Was Bishop Mynster a 'Witness to the Truth,' One of 'the Authentic Witnesses to the Truth'—Is *This the Truth*?" *M*, 3. See also *Pap*. XI-3 B 197.
[2] *Pap*. XI-1 A 439.
[3] *Pap*. XI-6 B 57; *JP* 6, 6947. Translation modified slightly.
[4] Kierkegaard comments on this review in *Pap*. XI-1 A 142; *JP* 6, 6874.

thus reintroduced, with some of the same phrases that had been used in the initial eulogy for Mynster the previous February being repeated now in this volatile situation of Kierkegaard's attack underway. It should be noted that the liturgical calendar called for the "witness" or "martyr" theme to be dealt with on this day, since it was designated as St. Stephen the Martyr Sunday. But given the contentious context, a decision could have been made to downplay that theme.

With the "witness" theme being raised again, it is no wonder that Kierkegaard's notebooks include so many reflections on this Martensenian declaration concerning Mynster as witness to the truth,[1] a number of which were included as part of the attack on the church. Kierkegaard's attack begins in response to this declaration on December 18, 1854, and it continues through the tenth and last installment of *The Moment*, which was completed by September of 1855. The whole attack is against Martensen, but especially focused on him are the first, second, fourth, and fifth newspaper articles: the first entitled "Was Bishop Mynster a 'Truth-Witness,' One of 'the Authentic Truth-Witnesses'—Is *This the Truth*?"[2]; the second entitled "There the Matter Rests!"[3]; the fourth entitled "The Point at Issue with Bishop Martensen, **as** Christianly Decisive for the, Christianly Viewed, Dubious Previously Established Ecclesiastical Order"[4]; and the fifth entitled "Two New Truth Witnesses."[5] The last mentioned title refers to the two men who were ordained as bishops at the service, just mentioned, held on St. Stephen's the Martyr day; it introduced further irony into an event already fraught with conflictual meanings. In Martensen's sermon, which was published, he refers to these two ordinands as "witnesses to the truth," and Kierkegaard objects

---

[1] See *M* 625, note 57.
[2] *Pap.* IX-2 A 252; *JP* 6, 6930. *Pap.* XI-2 A 307. *Pap.* XI-3 B 31. *Pap.* XI-3 B 49; *JP* 6. 6875. *Pap.* XI-3 B 82. *Pap.* XI-3 B 89. *Pap.* XI-3 B 95. *Pap.* XI-3 B 134. *Pap.* XI-3 B 138. *Pap.* XI-3 B 140. *Pap.* XI-3 B 159. *Pap.* XI-3 B 168. *Pap.* XI-3 B 202. *Pap.* XI-3 B 211.
[3] *M* 3-8. For journal entries on this topic, see *Pap.* XI-2 A 265. *Pap.* XI-2 A 411; *JP* 6, 6964. *Pap.* XI-3 B 57; *JP* 6, 6947. *Pap.* XI-3 B 82. *Pap.* XI-3 B 89. *Pap.* XI-3 B 99. *Pap.* XI-3 B 101. *Pap.* XI-3 B 107. *Pap.* XI-3 B 188. *Pap.* XI-3 B 201.
[4] *M* 9-15.
[5] *M* 19-24.
[6] *M* 25-27.

*The Church of Our Lady*
(Copenhagen City Museum)

to this identification because of how it bastardizes the notion and contributes to and emblemizes that leveling that is going on within all aspects of the culture. One other newspaper article focusing especially on Martensen is the twenty-first entitled "That Bishop Martensen's Silence Is (1) Christianly Indefensible; (2) Ludicrous; (3) Obtuse-Sagacious; (4) in More Than One Regard Contemptible."[1]

Kierkegaard's reason for attacking the church had been larger than Martensen's public reference to Mynster as a witness to the truth, but

---

[1] *M* 79-85. On Martensen's prostituting silence after Kierkegaard's article against him on the occasion of the funeral oration for Mynster, see *Pap*. XI-2 A 285. *Pap*. XI-3 B 9. *Pap*. XI-3 B 82. *Pap*. XI-3 B 107. *Pap*. XI-3 B 134. *Pap*. XI-3 B 164. *Pap*. XI-3 B 251.

that was clearly the instigating event. A journal entry dated March 1855 offering a self-assured assessment of the damage done, however, definitely overestimates the effect of the attack on the new Bishop: "In three articles—a prelude to what would come—I finished with Bishop Martensen, and in such a way that I, if I wanted to avail myself of such things, would have had it in my power to turn the matter so that everything later was a result of the Martensen blunder of representing, from the pulpit, Bishop Mynster as a truth-witness, one of the authentic, one of the holy chain."[1] This sounds more like journal writing to lift one's spirit than an accurate rendering of the situation, for Martensen certainly had not been "finished." The same sort of despondent melancholy hiding behind hoped-for efficacy characterizes another 1855 entry: "I can certainly comprehend that my article against Bishop Martensen must have had, as I intended, a fairly strong effect."[2]

For months of direct attack Martensen remained silent, just as he had in relation to Kierkegaard's indirect attack of him via the pen of Johannes Climacus.[3] Robert Perkins reminds us that "there was an officious silence from the church leadership, most of the clergy, and the cultural elite except for those who, quite unlike Kierkegaard, worked politically for the separation of church and state."[4] As we noted in our account of Martensen above, he eventually published a single statement, "On the Occasion of Dr. S. Kierkegaard's Article in *Fædrelandet*, no. 295"[5] in response to the attack, and this prompted Kierkegaard to inscribe more entries in his notebook.[6] On April 15, 1854, when Martensen was named successor to Mynster as Bishop of Sjælland, Kierkegaard penned a rather long entry on "Martensen on the Bishop's seat."[7]

---

[1] *Pap.* XI-3 B 134; *M*, Supplement, 546.
[2] *Pap.* XI-3 B 99, *M*, Supplement, 505.
[3] *Pap.* XI-3 B 107. This entry is entitled "Bishop Martensen's Silence or a Contribution to a Characteristic of the Witnesses to the Truth."
[4] Robert L. Perkins, "The Authoritarian Symbiosis of Church and Crown in Søren Kierkegaard's 'Attack Upon Christendom,' " *Anthropology and Authority: Essays on Søren Kierkegaard*, ed. by Poul Houe, Gordon D. Marino, and Sven H. Rossel, Amsterdam and Atlanta: Rodopi 2000, p. 139.
[5] Martensen's article is included in *M*, Supplement, 360-366.
[6] *Pap.* XI 3 B 82. *Pap.* XI-3 B 89. *Pap.* XI-3 B 107. *Pap.* XI-3 B 142.
[7] *Pap.* XI-3 B 89. See also *Pap.* XI-3 B 159.

Kierkegaard did not doubt that Martensen occasionally attempted to practice or act in the manner of the deceased Bishop Mynster.[1] However, while Kierkegaard is convinced that Martensen will gladly inherit Mynster's tradition,[2] he holds that the Christian proclamation Bishop Martensen represents is the very lowest, so Martensen will instantly give an exposure of the established order's weak aspects.[3] As Bishop Martensen is no more authentically existing than when he was a professor, it is still clear that Martensen is taking the latter of the two ways: "One way is to suffer, another to become a professor of another's suffering."[4]

The same type of administrative leadership of the church comes from Martensen as came from Mynster, namely, a form of leadership that draws attention away from the real question of the day that Christianity simply does not any longer exist at all.[5] Mynster was more cautious, refraining from passing judgment on Kierkegaard, whereas Martensen is less effective administratively because he "plunges in headfirst."[6] Kierkegaard notes that a characteristic of a demoralized time is that certain pathetic expressions come into use, and one such expression that came into use since Martensen had been made bishop was the term "shepherd" for bishop; this is because the public most appropriately considers him quite an uncreative man in that he is indeed the public's respectful servant and therefore people, for flattery purposes, call him "shepherd."[7] Closely related to "the public" for Kierkegaard is "the numerous." If Martensen is the servant of the public, so too does he do nothing against the abuse of the numerical and in fact even woos numbers.[8] Officiousness and busyness which Martensen seems to want to display is a trick, in order to divert attention away from having to conform to the existential, to

---

[1] *Pap.* XI-3 B 51.
[2] *Pap.* XI-3 B 89.
[3] *Pap.* XI-3 B 89. *Pap.* XI-3 B 107.
[4] *Pap.* XI-1 A 581; *JP* 1, 614.
[5] *Pap.* XI-3 B 49; *JP* 6, 6875. For another comment on the church leadership of Mynster and Martensen in relation to Christianity, see *Pap.* XI-3 B 50.
[6] *Pap.* XI-3 A 257; *JP* 6, 6942.
[7] *Pap.* XI-A 80.
[8] *Pap.* X-4 A 551.

dying.[1] And on the theme of death it irks Kierkegaard to think about the reception Martensen will receive upon his death; he bemoans the fact that when Martensen dies he too will be buried as a witness to the truth.[2]

Kierkegaard can flippantly write that he does not "ascribe to Bishop Martensen as a thinker any other worth apart from being a user of the thoughts of others,"[3] but his preoccupation with Martensen's recognition of him suggests otherwise. Kierkegaard thought enough of Martensen to be deeply troubled by the fact that Martensen had not found occasion to make himself acquainted with Kierkegaard's writings.[4] Very telling for an attempt to articulate Martensen as a source for Kierkegaard is the latter's statement that Martensen "is himself well aware of my knowledge of his whole career." That is why Kierkegaard is so irritated at Martensen's claim that he has not become knowledgeable of Kierkegaard's work, a claim that Kierkegaard finds quite preposterous, as becomes clear from a March 1855 notebook entry:

> But to the more earnest, the ethical point of view! So Bishop Martensen has observed silence; indeed, he is probably even completely ignorant of my whole work! Excellent! It is for this that one is paid thousands by the state, is ranked with councilors of conference—to rule, and then one's ruling means nothing more nor less than that the bishop's farmhand could just as well rule the Church. Bishop Martensen, *a man who is himself well aware of my knowledge of his whole career*, of all this flattery devoid of the idea, all those petty measures that are used—he is now ignorant of S. Kierkegaard's work in the service of the idea. Bishop Martensen perhaps does not even know that I exist! And he is ignorant of a cause that has decisively taken possession of the moment, a cause that, despite the opposition of an entire contemporary public, and although I am doing absolutely nothing to spread it, yet has managed—indeed, there does exist a Governance!—to press through, one does not comprehend how, a cause that occupies the

---

[1] *Pap.* XI-1 A 218.
[2] *Pap.* XI-3 B 49; *JP* 6, 6875.
[3] *Pap.* XI-3 B 134 and included in *M*, Supplement, 544.
[4] *Pap.* XI-3 B 62. *Pap.* XI-3 B 82.

neighboring countries, is read in Norway, translated in Sweden, then in the end the only one who is ignorant of it is the Church's leading ruler, the man salaried with thousands by the state, the councilor of conference adorned in velvet."[1]

Half a decade earlier Kierkegaard expressed similar suspicion over Martensen's putative ignorance of his work and hints that he realizes instead that the theologian has "considerable awareness" of his writings:

> To write a dogmatics in a limited setting like ours, one that even claims to "heed the signs of the times," and then try to ignore completely my work as an author or even try to sweep it away with a few casual words in a preface to a dogmatics which, strangely enough, indirectly bears unmistakable marks that there is considerable awareness of the existence of my work as a writer—yes this is strange. I do not know of anything better to do than to smile, because I have nothing more to say on this occasion.[2]

Addressing Martensen in the personal, direct form of address, Kierkegaard writes as if speaking to another, who is very important to his person and whose acknowledgement and respect he desperately desired and needed:

> We see that you, Herr Professor, are a distinguished man, indeed we all see and know this. But you, Professor Martensen, precisely you, especially since as Christianity's proclaimer you ought to have a much deeper understanding of life, would that you might have seen that I also am a distinguished man.
> Only there is the difference that the signs of distinction that I bear, do not, as yours, sparkle with the brilliance of the moment—but only in historical perspective appear as what they in truth are.[3]

Kierkegaard's life was interestingly entwined with Martensen's. There is a sense that even at death he could not fully get away from the

---

[1] *Pap.* XI-3 B 134 and included in *M*, Supplement, 545. My emphasis.
[2] *Pap.* X-6 B 121; *JP* 6, 6574; See also *Pap.* X-6 B 109.
[3] *Pap.* X-6 B 138.

Martensenian type. Three years before his death Kierkegaard could foresee what his fate was going to be after he died: "I know who is going to inherit me, that figure to whom I am so deeply opposed, he who up to now has inherited all that is best and will continue doing so—namely the *docent*, the professor."[1] We professors are not the only ones to have inherited him but we are among those who have. So he was right. And it is now time for the professor to take even more liberties in what he has inherited.

---

[1] *Pap.* X-4 A 628; *JP* 2, 1915.

## Chapter 3

## A General Interpretation of Kierkegaard's Use of Martensen

In this monograph's first part we introduced Martensen as a thinker. The second part accounted for Kierkegaard's sources of information about Martenen. Now in this third part of the essay the task remains to offer an interpretation of Kierkegaard's use of Martensen as a source for his thinking and writing. I refer the reader to a discussion of "Martensen's Influencing of Kierkegaard" for an earlier interpretive statement I offered on Kierkegaard's use of Martensen as a source.[1] This chapter will be an occasion to examine the tradition of Martensen interpretation and then to draw some points of commonality between Martensen and Kierkegaard on some very large issues, such as their commitment to being engaged in hermeneutical enterprises, their identification of the notion of personality or freedom as the heart of their projects, their according a significant place in the human's growth into deeper passion and intensity to nihilism of a religious type, and their affirmation of a di-polar God who works through possibilities to relate to the world.

### I. The Tradition of Interpreting Kierkegaard's Use of Martensen

This interpretation of Kierkegaard's use of Martensen takes place within what is starting to become a distinguished tradition or history of previous interpretations. What Hans-Georg Gadamer called "effective-history" or "the history of effects" provides the context for the present

---

[1] *BHK*, pp. 58-70.

interpretation of the Kierkegaard-Martensen relation and at least partially sets the parameters for the horizon of meaning or pre-understanding informing that interpretation.[1] We need to acknowledge that what is presented here as an interpretation in this monograph comes out of "the hermeneutical situation," that is, that it has been shaped by a history of effects that includes the tradition of secondary literature on our topic. We can acknowledge this tradition and introduce the reader to it by quickly identifying important figures and works within it.

Within three decades after Martensen's death in 1888, three books had appeared entitled "H.L. Martensen." They were not focused on the Kierkegaard-Martensen relation, but they are relevant for those interested in that relation. V. Nannestad's early work on Martensen sought, he tells us in his Preface, "not so much a characterization of individual sermons as a picture—a portrait of that author-individuality which comes into view through these."[2] The result is an interesting portrait created by drawing on Martensen's sermons as well as on his theological-philosophical writings. The Danish religious thinker is presented as proclaiming an aesthetic Christianity in which the good is identified with the beautiful, so that Martensen's ultimate concern is seen as lying in the unity and harmony of all things. Nannestad depicts Martensen as a spokesperson for "Christianity's own romanticism," in which all the mysteries of the soul are reduced to the mystery of the kingdom of God. A second Danish interpreter of Martensen was his daughter Josepha Martensen.[3] Concentrating on his home and his family, she states in the Preface that the book's purpose "is merely, through a series of more and less eventful incidents, to illuminate his nature and personality in daily life with his wife and children and among friends." As a supplement to Martensen's autobiography, this book gives interesting insights into Martensen's personal life, e.g., his daily routine as marked by order and precision, his love of poetry, music, theater, painting, but the book does not discuss

---

[1] Hans-Georg Gadamer, *Truth and Method*, trans. by Garrett Barden and John Cumming, New York: The Seabury Press 1975, pp. 267-274.
[2] V. Nannestad, *H.L. Martensen. Nyt Bidrag til en Karakteristik af Dansk Prædiken i det nittende Aarhundredes sidste Halvdel*, Copenhagen: Schønberg 1897.
[3] Josepha Martensen, *H.L. Martensen, i sit Hjem og blandt sine Venner*, Copenhagen: J. Frimodt 1918.

Martensen's theology. C.I. Scharling is the primary author of the third of these books and his volume is a good introduction to Martensen's thought.[1] Written by Scharling himself except for three of the essays, it offers the most positive assessment of Martensen to have appeared in book-length form. Like Nannestad, Scharling pictures Martensen as needing to bring all the oppositions of life into a unity.

The next two books to appear in Denmark on Martensen greatly elevated the level of intellectual sophistication informing the interpretation. In 1932 Skat Arildsen published his mammoth book that remains one of the two real highlights of Martensen scholarship.[2] This volume was the first of what was to be two volumes, though the second volume never appeared. Arildsen took up Martensen's relation to various idealist thinkers, but he did this in piecemeal fashion by discussing each particular work of Martensen in terms of its "weft." As a result, even though this study more than any other elaborated the many influences impinging on Martensen, the effect of the elaboration is lost in large part because of its dispersion throughout the treatise. An implicit argument of the work is the division of Martensen's authorship into two periods, a period from 1836 to 1854 that he labeled "Professor Martensen," and a period from 1854 to 1881 that he labeled "Bishop Martensen." More explicitly, Arildsen argued that Martensen's *Den christelige Dogmatik* contains the nucleus of his position and that his later works are merely an outgrowth of that nucleus. This view contradicts Martensen's own view of his work, which regarded the dogmatics and ethics surely as intrinsically related but as relatively independent of one another. Arildsen also appropriately contended that Martensen's position maintained a certain consistency throughout his development. The next year, 1933, J. Oskar Andersen published "Biskop H.L. Martensen's Ungdom,"[3] a long article that responded to Arildsen's dissertation. He argued that Arildsen was too dependent on Martensen's autobiography in giving his account

---

[1] C.I. Scharling, *H.L. Martensen. Hans Tanker og Livssyn*, Copenhagen: P. Haase & Sons 1928.
[2] Arildsen, *H.L. Martensen. His Liv, Udvikling og Arbejde, studier i det 19. Aarhundredes Danske Aandsliv*, op. cit.
[3] J. Oskar Andersen, "Biskop H.L. Martensen's Ungdom," *Kirkehistoriske Samlinger*, series 6, no. 1, 1933, pp. 130-237.

of Martensen's youth with the result "that Martensen was developed so early, that already *before he left school* he had arrived at a clear knowledge not only of his peculiar intellectual system but of his life's scientific vocation, so that both the time as a student and a doctoral candidate have this awareness as a presupposition."[1] And if there was too much use of the *Levnet* for Martensen's youth, there was not enough for his later years. Arildsen did not make use of the autobiographical material after 1836. This was a serious error in Andersen's opinion because Martensen's "works show that he is drawn from an abstract, speculative standpoint to a progressively fuller involvement in personal religious life and his church's confessional teaching."

A furthering of this history of tradition took place with Niels Thulstrup's important work on Kierkegaard's relation to Hegel.[2] There was a breadth to Thulstrup's analysis of this relation, and he realized to some extent that Martensen played a crucial role as one of the two major Danish Hegelians introducing Hegel's thought to Kierkegaard and others. Despite the fact that he was just about never willing to entertain the possibility that Kierkegaard had actually learned something from Hegel and the Hegelians, Thulstrup furthered the knowledge of Kierkegaard's context. And in editing *Bibliotheca Kierkegaardiana* with his wife Marie Mikulová Thulstrup, his labors extended greatly the range of contextual knowledge, some of it trivial and some of it profound, but all of it contributing to a deeper comprehension of Kierkegaard in relation to his times. Leif Grane[3] and Jens Schjørring[4] also both contributed to a fuller understanding of Kierkegaard's context, with Grane's treatment of the theological faculty shedding helpful light on Martensen in the university setting and Schjørring's dealing with 1842 as a critical year for Martensen and then donating his fine essay on "Martensen" in the volume *Kierkegaard's Teachers*.

---

[1] Ibid., pp. 133-134.
[2] Niels Thulstrup, *Kierkegaard's Relation to Hegel*, op. cit.
[3] Leif Grane, "Det teologiske Fakultet 1830-1925," op. cit, pp. 325-495, and especially pp. 328-382, which is on "The Era of Clausen and Martensen."
[4] Jens Schørring, "H.L. Martensen" in *Teologi og Filosofi. Nogle Analyser og Dokumenter vedrørende Hegelianismen i Dansk Teologi*, op. cit., and his "Martensen," in *Kierkegaard's Teachers*, ed. by Niels Thulstrup and Marie Mikulová Thulstrup, Copenhagen: C.A. Reitzel 1982 (*Bibliotheca Kierkegaardiana*, vol. 10), pp. 177-207.

Hermann Brandt continued the history of this tradition with his book on Martensen's speculative theology.[1] He gave a long "Bibliographical Sketch" (pp. 17-62), which is the first real effort among Martensen scholars to set the sociological context for Martensen's writings, although it is based largely on Martensen's memoirs. His thesis is rather unique in that he argued that Martensen, especially in his dogmatics, was finally more dependent on Schelling than Hegel. In addition, Brandt contended that Martensen exhibited how his understanding of and yearning for "the ideal of the speculative knowledge of God left him radically estranged from the world in which he lived and the church for which he had accepted responsibility."[2] In making his case for Martensen's increasing estrangement from world and church, he picked up on Arildsen's professor/bishop distinction and carried it to the extreme. In fact, he concluded that Martensen's theological work merely gives the appearance of being a speculative theology of mediation because of its ambivalent brilliance and debility, an ambivalence residing finally, he claimed, within Martensen's personality itself. Furthermore, on the basis of a few of Martensen's personal letters written to L. Gude, he argued that Martensen detested his position as bishop because the duties of the office kept him from his contemplation and studies; the office was in this sense Martensen's *purgatorium.*

The first dissertation on Martensen in English was by Robert Leslie Horn.[3] This creative work has recently been published by the Søren Kiekegaard Research Centre in conjunction with C.A. Reitzel's Publishers close to four decades after its original appearance as a Th.D. dissertation in 1969. This is emblematic of the surge of interest in the Martensen-Kierkegaard connection over the past few years. Horn's purpose was "to discuss in detail the development of Martensen's theological position, concentrating upon his theory of religious knowledge and his view of the relation between the historical or positive elements in the Christian faith and his use of the immanent dialectic of the philosophy of Hegel."[4]

---

[1] Hermann Brandt, *Gotteserkenntnis und Weltentfremdung*, op. cit.
[2] Ibid., p. 250.
[3] Horn, *Positivity and Dialectic: A Study of the Theological Method of Hans Lassen Martensen*, op. cit.
[4] Ibid., p. 3.

Horn devoted nearly as much of his dissertation to the thought of J.L. Heiberg as to that of Martensen and admitted that his presentation focused "upon Martensen only insofar as the study of Martensen's thought can be an aid to the understanding of Kierkegaard."[1]

This means that Horn did not deal with any of Martensen's works written after 1850. A second book in English that advanced the history of this tradition was Bruce H. Kirmmse's valuable work on "Golden Age" Denmark.[2] This work, dealing respectively with "Kierkegaard's Denmark" and "Denmark's Kierkegaard," hard-hittingly situated Martensen at the heart of "Golden Age" culture, depicting him, with undoubtedly a good measure of accuracy, as having to walk a fine line: "On the one hand, Martensen could not alienate his early protector and lifelong friend, Heiberg, who was his principal avenue of access to high and refined literary culture. On the other hand, Martensen's solicitude for Heiberg had to be kept from interfering with his relationship to the clerical establishment generally and, specifically, to Bishop Mynster, his second protector."[3] Kirmmse's discussion of Martensen underscores the often forgotten-about need to remember the bourgeois character of Martensen's thought and person, as he, enmeshed in Golden Age culture, is influenced by a social imaginary that is indeed in the service of the status quo. At the same time, the scholar doing the interpretation also needs to remember that both moments of interpretation are needed in giving an account of a figure such as Martensen, both the contestatory discourse and the emancipatory, both the combative and the sympathetic. Only such a balanced hermeneutical approach will yield fruitful results. So the interpreter must be careful not to allow the necessary hermeneutics of suspicion to rule out in advance any possible shred of integrity, nobility, and value in the subject being interpreted that might be recovered in the equally desirable hermeneutics of retrieval.

Within this line of tradition Roger Poole's work on Kierkegaard's indirect communication should also be mentioned.[4] He helped extend

---

[1] Ibid.
[2] Bruce H. Kirmmse, *Kierkegaard in Golden Age Denmark*, Bloomington and Indianapolis: Indiana University Press 1990, especially chapter 12 on "H.L. Martensen," pp. 169-197.
[3] Ibid., p. 183.
[4] Roger Poole, *Kierkegaard: The Indirect Communication*, op. cit.

the focus from Kierkegaard and Hegel to Kierkegaard and Hegel and the Danish Hegelians. For instance he proposes that the interesting question concerning the rhetorical strategies Kierkegaard employs in *The Concept of Irony* is not so much "to what extent was the young Kierkegaard, while writing the dissertation on irony, under the influence of Hegel," but rather "to what extent was the young Kierkegaard, while writing the dissertation on irony, struggling to get free of the influence of Martensen and Heiberg on Hegel?"[1] Poole thinks "the various layers of intention in the dissertation" are "better understood as the efforts to win free of two disliked father figures in the Danish academic establishment rather than to win free of the German philosopher himself."[2] Poole sees the need to take seriously the Danish Hegelians in interpreting Kierkegaard, and this represents an important shift toward recognizing the complexity involved in sorting out Kierkegaard's relations with Hegel and Hegelians. Some of my own work can also be included in this recounting of the history of the Martensenian research tradition as attempting to broaden the focus in Kierkegaard scholarship to include the likes of Martensen.[3]

Two other recent writings by Danish scholars make contributions to Martensen scholarship. The first is Joakim Garff's biography of Kierkegaard, published in Denmark in 2000.[4] Garff weaves into his interesting narrative of Kierkegaard's unfolding life's story a number of discussions of Kierkegaard's relation to Martensen. He has been extremely resourceful in garnering all the loose, extant information about Kierkegaard's life, some of it fairly trivial and tangential, but magically synthesizing it all into a captivating tale that captures the depth and richness of Kierkegaard's personality. The second work is Carl

---

[1] Ibid., p. 39.
[2] Ibid.
[3] See my "H.L. Martensen's Theological Anthropology," *Faith, Knowledge and Action*, ed. by G.L. Stengren, Copenhagen: C.A. Reitzel 1984, pp. 199-216, and reprinted in slightly modified form in *Kierkegaard and His Contemporaries*, op. cit., 164-180; "The Logic of Theonomy: Hans Lassen Martensen's Theological Method," Chicago: Ph.D. dissertation, The University of Chicago 1985; the "Introduction" to *BHK*, op. cit., pp. 1-71; and "From Presupposing Pantheism's Power to Potentiating Panentheism's Personality: Seeking Parallels Between Kierkegaard's and Martensen's Theological Anthropology," op. cit.
[4] Garff, *Søren Kierkegaard*, op. cit.

Henrik Koch's book on Danish idealism from 1800 to 1880, which is volume four in a five-volume work on the history of Danish philosophy during the eight-hundred year period from the mid-twelfth to the mid-twentieth century.[1] Koch devotes a chapter to Hans L. Martensen's thought.[2] He analyzes the 1837 dissertation on the autonomy of human self-consciousness and the 1840 system of moral philosophy as Martensen's two most important philosophical writings, but he also notes as decisive for Martensen's further development his 1834 meeting in Munich with the Catholic theologian Franz von Baader. Martensen was drawn to Baader's willingness to criticize the philosophical tradition of consciousness extending back to Descartes, to Baader's underscoring of the fact that self-consciousness involves and is conditioned by consciousness of the human's divine creator, and to Baader's view that the human in and with the conscience is related to the divine, which renders superfluous every proof for God's existence.[3] Besides making the case for Baader's influence on Martensen, Koch also delves into such issues as Martensen's view of baptism, examining some of the polemical writings of "a persistent critic" of Martensen, namely, Magnús Eiríksson, the Icelandic theological candidate at the University of Copenhagen.

The writings of Jon Stewart at this point need to be lifted up. The second of the two real highlights of Martensen scholarship appeared with Jon Stewart's 2003 book reconsidering Kierkegaard's relations to Hegel.[4] *Kierkegaard's Relations to Hegel Reconsidered* changed radically the landscape of Kierkegaard scholarship by establishing through meticulous argument the complexity of his relations to Hegel and his followers. In establishing this case, which alters the presuppositions out of which Kierkegaard scholars operate, that the Danish Hegelians are often the target of Kierkegaard's criticisms rather than Hegel himself, the important place that Martensen, among others, should assume in these deliberations has also been established. In reading Stewart's encyclopedic book one learns much about Kierkegaard and Hegel as

---

[1] Carl Henrik Koch, *Den danske idealisme 1800-1880*, Copenhagen: Gyldendal 2004.
[2] Ibid., pp. 271-298.
[3] Ibid., p. 278.
[4] Stewart, *Kierkegaard's Relations to Hegel Reconsidered*, op. cit.

well as about nineteenth-century European thought and life in general. We can be grateful that a scholar among us has had the *élan* and passion to plum to the depths within such a broad array of texts and ideas. Kierkegaardians in general and the few in the restricted circle of those interested in seeing scholarship concerning the Kierkegaard-Martensen relation advanced—owe much to Stewart.

Stewart identifies the standard view of the Kierkegaard-Hegel relation as the position articulated most forcefully and one-sidedly by Niels Thulstrup, namely, that Kierkegaard waged a campaign against Hegel's philosophy and Hegel himself, that there was essentially no positive relation between these two since they held absolutely nothing in common. This understanding of Kierkegaard's relation to Hegel, lacking subtlety and nuance, has generally informed mainstream Kierkegaard research up until the appearance of Stewart's book. He contends "that there are many more points of comparison and similarity between the two thinkers than are generally recognized"[1] and "that there are a number of heretofore neglected points of positive influence of Hegel on Kierkegaard."[2] Calling his readers to go beyond this standard view of interpreting Kierkegaard as an utterly anti-Hegelian figure, Stewart endorses instead a view of the relation that accords a much larger place to the Danish Hegelians, and especially H.L. Martensen. Just as there were right- and left-wing Hegelians in Germany, so too were there Danish Hegelians of various persuasions and types in Denmark. In turning to Kierkegaard's texts themselves and to the task of uncovering the ways Danish Hegelians such as J.L. Heiberg, Martensen, and A.P. Adler and critics of Hegel such as F.C. Sibbern, P.M. Møller, and J.P. Mynster are involved in them, it is Martensen who receives the bulk of Stewart's attention. His careful discussion brings more nuance to the Kierkegaard-Martensen relation than has previously been achieved. Stewart is careful not to place Martensen into the same inappropriate orthodox Hegelian box as other Kierkegaard scholars have placed Hegel. Stewart chooses to concentrate on Kierkegaard's published writings that prove valuable in investigating his relation to Hegel and Hegelians, engaging Kierkegaard's

---

[1] Ibid., p. 32.
[2] Ibid., p. 44.

journals, notebooks, and papers only for elucidating or supplementing discussions in the published works. In his analysis Stewart also pays more attention to what he calls anonyms than to Kierkegaard's pseudonyms, giving reasons for why he pays little attention to differentiating positions with respect to Kierkegaard's various pseudonyms.[1] He maintains that Kierkegaard frequently uses anonyms through which by "a kind of code" he makes "hidden references to his contemporaries."[2] By means of these anonyms his contemporary readers were able to identify the real targets of Kierkegaard's criticism and in the restricted confines of Copenhagen life "his intellectual enemies" were given "at least a semblance of anonymity."[3] The concept of anonym, then, plays an important and effective role in Stewart's interpretation of Kierkegaard's relation to the Danish Hegelians, and especially per our concern, to Martensen.

In Stewart's interpretive model he depicts Kierkegaard and Hegel as being about completely different projects, the one religious and the other philosophical. In fact, at the end of the book he controversially suggests, because of the religious character of Kierkegaard's project, that it is not clear why Kierkegaard should be counted among philosophers in the nineteenth-century sense of that word.[4] His investigation seeks "to locate Kierkegaard in his proper historical-philosophical context so that it is possible to obtain a truer picture of his relation to Hegel than the reigning view has provided,"[5] with the main goal of his project being to understand "Kierkegaard as a part of the development of nineteenth-century European thought."[6] Through his labors we have been given a truer picture of the Hegel relation, and to that extent the tradition of Martensen research has at the same time been significantly advanced.

Stewart has continued to advance the Martensenian research program with the publication of additional books. Three books of translations of the philosophical writings of Johan Ludvig Heiberg have at the same time been an indirect notable contribution to Martensen scholarship. These

---

[1] Ibid., pp. 40-42.
[2] Ibid., pp. 42-43.
[3] Ibid., p. 43.
[4] Ibid., p. 640.
[5] Ibid., p. 44.
[6] Ibid., p. 36.

books, which are the first three volumes in the *Texts from Golden Age Denmark* series, include in 2005 *Heiberg's On the Significance of Philosophy for the Present Age and Other Texts*,[1] in 2006 *Heiberg's Speculative Logic and Other Texts*,[2] and in 2007 *Heiberg's Introductory Lecture to the Logic Course and Other Texts*.[3] Stewart is also engaged in writing a three-volume work on *A History of Hegelianism in Golden Age Denmark*. The work's first tome on *The Heiberg Period: 1824-1836* has been published, the second tome concentrating on the years 1837 to 1842 and focusing on Martensen's appropriation of Hegel's thought has just appeared,[4] and the third tome dealing with the years after 1842 and covering many different intellectuals while centering especially on the left Hegelians in Denmark and on the writings of Kierkegaard is forthcoming. Besides all these initiatives, Stewart is the driving force behind numerous series of volumes of scholarly essays on Danish Golden Age figures, and these books too press forward the tradition of Martensen interpretation. One of these volumes that merits inclusion in this account of the research program on Martensen is K. Brian Soderquist's *The Isolated Self*, which includes a deliberation of Martensen's aesthetic views of irony and humor in relation to Kierkegaard's developing views.[5]

## II. Contributing to the Thought-World of Kierkegaard's Reflections

Two comments from long ago can provoke thoughts on Kierkegaard's relation to Martensen. One of these is by C.I. Scharling and the other is by Skat Arildsen. Scharling's early work on Martensen, in addressing the topic of "Martensen and Our Time," compares Martensen and Karl Barth, whom he recognizes as being in so many ways Martensen's "polar

---

[1] *Heiberg's On the Significance of Philosophy for the Present Age and Other Texts*, ed. and trans. by Jon Stewart, op. cit.
[2] *Heiberg's Speculative Logic and other Texts*, ed. and trans. by Jon Stewart, op. cit.
[3] *Heiberg's Introductory Lecture to the Logic Course and Other Texts*, ed. and trans. by Jon Stewart, op. cit.
[4] Stewart, *A History of Hegelianism in Golden Age Denmark, Tome I: The Heiberg Period: 1824-1836*, op. cit. and *A History of Hegelianism in Golden Age Denmark*, Tome II: *The Martensen Period: 1837-1842*, Copenhagen: C.A. Reitzel 2007.
[5] K. Brian Soderquist, *The Isolated Self: Truth and Untruth in Søren Kierkegaard's On the Concept of Irony*, op. cit., especially pp. 181-200.

opposite": "He wants to separate, where Martensen wants to join; he wants to dig a ravine, where Martensen wants to build a bridge."[1] "And yet," he continues, "in the highest questions, in that which so to speak gets them off the ground and becomes the starting point for their entire point of view over against life, there is a deep unity."[2]

> That which Barth has said, so that it has been heard across the land, is the word about the *living* God, the *sovereign* God, the God of *the Bible*, over against whom the human is and remains *the creature*, whose entire glorious culture, whose entire spiritual life of its own making is one great rebellion against God, when it wants to occupy any other place than that of the creature, which in itself is dust and ashes, over against the almighty Creator. Away with every depraved human thought, shouts Barth, which wants to find God in the depths of the human spirit or in the heavenward flight of human thought or altogether any other place than *in God's own revelation*![3]

Then Scharling asks:

> But was it not completely the same ordeal through which Martensen struggled? When in Germany he had his time of spiritual crisis, it was the question of theism or pantheism that was pending for him, and that is to say: the living, personal god, the God of the Bible, that God who has revealed Godself—or the God of the philosophers, the God one senses and feels one's way forward toward, the God the human finds through his or her own, autonomous thought. And the choice, he made, was foundational not merely for his personal relation of faith, but for all his thinking concerning life. If Barth turns in scornful indignation against those who want to allow revelation to fade away, Martensen turns against those who want to think away their creatureliness and allow their human thought to penetrate into God's mysteries outside of the ground of faith and revelation. And if Barth judges the human's entire glorious cultural possession as sin and rebellion

---

[1] Scharling, *H.L. Martensen*, op. cit., p. 149.
[2] Ibid.
[3] Ibid.

against God, so does Martensen judge the human spirit, which like Faust and Prometheus wants to establish itself a kingdom without regarding this kingdom as an entitled estate from God.[1]

Nonetheless there is a difference between Martensen and Barth. "While Barth remains in dualism, in the dialectic of the razor's edge, Martensen seeks—on the ground of faith—to go beyond dualism into synthesis and harmony. The thought of the Creator, which in Barth essentially works negatively, toward maintaining that the human is dust and ashes, is employed in Martensen according to its positive content."[2] For Martensen the God-relation is not just a limit but an empowering presence: "Precisely as God's creature the human stands in an intimate connection with the entire created world, as a microcosmos amidst a macrocosmos; precisely as created in God's image can the human on the ground of faith know God."[3] Faith potentiates the self in such a way that genuine knowledge is grasped in the God-relation, but the theological thematization of this is never going to be exhaustively carried out no matter how longingly the human desires a knowledge that is comprehensive and absolute. Martensen had this desire "for a comprehensive knowledge of existence, a harmonic view of the whole, where *everything* that has worth in human life, indeed in the universe, receives its place."[4] Of course, the desire was not fulfilled: "It can be said that Martensen did not attain the completing of such a view of the whole, that it in many ways remained a glimpse; but his intention is definitely clear enough."[5]

The comparison between these two significant theological figures, Martensen from the nineteenth century and Barth from the twentieth, is an interesting one. And if the comparison works with the early Barth, which is the Barth being described here in 1928, then it surely works with the later Barth of the *Church Dogmatics*. However, the intention here is not simply to lift up the Martensen-Barth relation as intrinsically

---

[1] Ibid., pp. 149-150.
[2] Ibid., p. 150.
[3] Ibid.
[4] Ibid., pp. 150-151.
[4] Ibid., p. 151.

interesting in-and-of-itself, but rather to use it as an illustration of what we can learn about the Kierkegaard-Martensen relation. Martensen and Barth are very different theologically, and yet many points of connection and commonality can be evidenced between them. The typical depiction of the relation between Kierkegaard and Martensen is that of volatility, hostility, conflict, bitterness, and strife. Our long discussion above in the first two chapters of this monograph certifies that such turbulence characterized the relation. But standing convinced that their relationship is finally to be understood as one of diastasis rather than synthesis does not preclude identifying ways in which these two creative thinkers shared common ground. In fact, their discord could not have developed to the level it did, had they not been in mutual agreement on many of the ways in which they perceived and understood their world. On the other hand, as with Barth and Martensen, the emphases of Kierkegaard and Martensen flowing from their affirmation of the Creator/creature distinction differ. Kierkegaard stresses how the infinite qualitative difference between God and the human points to the absolute differentiation between these two. Martensen also affirms the infinite qualitative difference between God and the human but he stresses as well the natural relatedness of God to the human and the possibility for nurturing this natural connection by means of the symbols and myths of religion into a religious relationship, with the religion of Christianity possessing the greatest potency for such nourishing. Kierkegaard, like Barth, continually employs dialectic, using its razor's edge negatively to combat the ever-present human propensity toward selfishness, which sickness is finally labeled and understood religiously as sin, that is, as before or over against God. Martensen again likewise makes use of dialectic, and while sometimes he employs a negative dialectic, he also sees the dialectic functioning in a mediating way, in a way that, as grounded in faith, is able to reconcile opposites and issue in a positive result.

In light of this attempt to acknowledge commonalities and differences between Kierkegaard and Martensen, I want to make a rather mild claim, but one that is not without significance, one that sums up what this monograph has been showing throughout more so than trumpeting what will now be demonstrated in its remainder. The claim is that Kierkegaard was turned to Martensen as surely *a* and possibly *the* thinker among his Danish contemporaries who most determined the thought-world or discourse in terms of which concerns should be considered and who most determined also the issues themselves to be dealt with. Other Danish contemporaries such as J.L. Heiberg, J.P. Mynster, F.C. Sibbern, and P.M. Møller did much as well to shape Kierkegaard's world of thought and his sense for which issues were truly important. Heiberg and Sibbern were philosophers, and while the latter especially demonstrated concern for religious sensibilities, he was not quite on the cutting edge of theological thinking during Kierkegaard's most productive literary years. Mynster was the godfather-figure of Danish Christianity and since Kierkegaard's youth had been a close acquaintance with Kierkegaard's family, so he was to be respected, to be sure, so much so that the "Attack on Christianity" was held off until after Mynster's death. However, Kierkegaard would have sensed that to a real extent time had passed Mynster by, and his anti-rationalist supernaturalism, while maybe preferable to a theologically mediating position such as that of Martensen's speculative theology, and the general theological position undergirding Mynster's daily ecclesial decisions, were no longer in tune with the thinking of the day. It was Martensen of these most significant figures who most set the agenda for Kierkegaard's deliberations. Of course, Kierkegaard would have never agreed with this judgment about how he proceeded in his deliberations of the late 1830s, '40s, and early '50s. As we have seen, Kierkegaard detested Martensen and all the talk of a new age that had been heralded with his speculative theology grounded on the principle of mediation. And yet, at the end of the day in evaluating Kierkegaard's writings, it is the thoughts of Martensen which time and again most come to mind as establishing the discourse, *not* to be sure the particular points of view and nuances of thought and expression, but the discourse in which the thinking is carried out. Kierkegaard followed the chosen one

The second thought from long ago that can provoke further reflection on the Kierkegaard-Martensen relation is from Skat Arildsen. Arildsen raised a question concerning Martensen over seventy years ago when he viewed Martensen's return to idealism in a negative fashion because of how it put Martensen out of touch with modernity:

> If one holds the point of view that the modern theological development takes its beginning in 1835 with Strauss' writing mentioned above [*Leben*

*Jesu*], which both begins an epoch and a crisis, the dissolution of idealism's reconciliation of faith and knowledge and the heralding of a series of meaningful modern problems for the church and Christianity, then it must be said that Martensen considered in relation to the background belongs to the period before 1835. That of course does not annul the contribution he came to make in Denmark, where he proclaimed thoughts partially new in philosophy and completely new in theology; but that does not set aside the fact that the thoughts, ways of presenting problems and points of view which Martensen championed quite certainly had in many places stood on the agenda abroad, but all the same were growing older day by day as the modern theological development took place, more or less imperceptible for those from before 1835, but more clearly for the generation after 1835.[1]

What is Martensen's relation to modernity? Was he as outdated as Arildsen suggests? If with some, we see modernity as having its roots in the Enlightenment, which in some ways reached its culmination point in the idealist tradition, then in continuing to embrace idealism, Martensen was actually also embracing modernity as expressed in one of its finer moments. The same can be said of Kierkegaard, who criticized Enlightenment ways of thinking and being and yet also was thoroughly immersed within those ways. Protestantism's principle of subjectivity, which Hegel sees as the primary feature of the rise of modernity, was fully embraced by Kierkegaard, and by Martensen too. Others see the reaction against the Enlightenment that emerged, in part from idealism, in the form of romanticism, which reaction then continued to develop into other forms of rebellion against the sameness of the Enlightenment, as leading eventually to what is later dubbed postmodernity. Martensen was as much a romantic as he was an idealist; however, he stood in a critical relation to both of these movements. The same can be said for Kierkegaard. Both are committed to fighting for an expansive view of the human personality or freedom, which some cultural forces are at work to delimit and therefore need to be combated.[2]

---

[1] Arildsen, *H.L. Martensen*, op. cit., p. 112.
[2] See the excellent essay by Jørgen Pedersen, "Conception of Freedom. Principal Perspectives," *Some of Kierkegaard's Main Categories*, ed. by Niels Thulstrup and Marie Mikulová Thulstrup, Copenhagen: C.A. Reitzel 1988 (*Bibliotheca Kierkegaardiana*,

Santiago Zabala, in conjunction with Richard Rorty and Gianni Vattimo, differentiates between the pre-Enlightenment world as an "Age of Faith" with duties to God and the Enlightenment world as an "Age of Reason" with duties to reason; but he contends that today we seem to be in an "Age of Interpretation" with less clarity on what our duties are.[1] Both Martensen and Kierkegaard resided in the Age of Interpretation. For Martensen, "speculation" or "mediation" was a method by which perspectives on Christian faith were relativized and which expected that out of the creative mix of plural perspectives a new perspective would emerge, with the full richness of truth residing always in the original experience of the relationship with God, which was the perennial source for regenerated reason's novel theological perspectives. For Kierkegaard, "the paradox" was the watchword for the primacy of absoluteness residing with the incarnate one, in whom, utterly contradictory of reason, eternity has entered into time and calls to the individual in personal fashion to follow him in a life of faith active in love. Both affirm faith as reflected upon by reason and reason as informed by faith, and both recognize that they are in the Age of Interpretation where meaning needs to be created within human experience, even if there is a revelatory given informing freedom's creative meaning-making. Martensen and Kierkegaard alike are consciously engaged in the hermeneutical enterprise.

Nihilism presents itself in this context as another point of commonality. Brian Soderquist has argued effectively that Martensen was fully aware that the ironic consciousness of romanticism "is characterized by a subjective freedom" that "recognizes its own superiority over the 'illusory world' of everydayness" and "leads to an 'inverted world' in which the ironic subject takes his or her own subjective nihilism to be the absolute truth of the world."[2] Martensen recognized the value of this

---

vol. 16), pp. 26-62. This essay does not point out many lines of connection to Martensen, the one exception being his claim that Augustine was important for both thinkers, but it beautifully summarizes Kierkegaard's understanding of freedom so that one who knows Martensen's view of freedom can readily draw those lines of connection.

[1] Richard Rorty and Gianni Vattimo, *The Future of Religion*, ed. by Santiago Zabala, New York: Columbia University Press 2005, pp. 3-4, 71-72.
[2] Soderquist, "Irony and Humor in Kierkegaard's Early Journals," op. cit., p. 151. See Martensen's review of *Fata Morgana*, op. cit.

nihilist vision, but he also saw the need for it to be transcended. Nihilism can serve religion, and when it does it could be called an empowering nihilism. Religious nihilism destroys the pretensions of the human self and can prepare the soil for a more profound relation to the world such as becomes possible in humor. In this sense, as one who affirms religious nihilism, Martensen can be regarded as acknowledging the benefits that can come from a "postmodern" consciousness such as romantic irony. But he always insists on the need to critique such a consciousness and in that sense he would be labeled by some, including likely Arildsen, as maybe "pre-modern," or more appropriately as "late modern."

Kierkegaard learned from Martensen, among others, the discourse that most helpfully penetrates into comedy and its sub-forms of irony and humor. We must remember that there are "subtle differences in tone and emphasis" in Kierkegaard's discourse; "unlike Martensen's happy reconciliation in Christian humor, Kierkegaard's humor contains 'a thorough-going negativity in relation to the world.'"[1] And yet there are parallels in how these two Danes understand the human's relation to life's *nihil* or nothing. Similarities can be seen in their common affirmation of empowering nihilism and in their recognition of the incredible significance of nothing's possibilities as the primary means by which God is at work in the world.

### III. Empowering Nihilism and the Possibilities of a Dipolar God

In the first volume of his three-volume *Christian Ethics*, published in 1871, about two-and-a-half decades after Kierkegaard's death, Martensen points out that the category of "the individual" is common to all those who "want to maintain *the principle of personality*, to maintain the personality of God and of the human in opposition to pantheism."[2] Martensen agrees that Kierkegaard was perfectly justified

---

[1] See ibid., p. 159, and George Pattison, *Kierkegaard, Religion, and the Nineteenth-Century Crisis in Culture*, op. cit., p. 113.
[2] H. Martensen, *Den christelige Ethik*, vols. 1-3, Gyldendalske Boghandels Forlag 1871-1878, vol. 1., p. 279. English translation as *Christian Ethics*, vol. 1, trans. from the Danish by C. Spense, vol. 2, trans. from the German by William Affleck, and vol. 3, trans. from the German by Sophia Taylor, Edinburgh: T. & T. Clark 1873-1882, vol. 1, pp. 220-221.

in making the claim "that with the category 'the individual' the cause of Christianity stands and falls; that without this category pantheism has won unconditionally."[1] He thinks "that S. Kierkegaard should have made common cause with the philosophical and theological movements which precisely wanted to advance the principle of personality against pantheism."[2] We can draw from these comments that Martensen clearly believed that he and Kierkegaard were on "the same side" insofar as both affirmed the principle of personality as central to their causes. To identify the theme of personality as the heart of one's thought is to be endorsing freedom as front and center in one's thinking. Both Martensen and Kierkegaard would assert that human freedom creates itself in relation to other centers of freedom or personalities, and that this self-creation reaches its highest fulfillment only in relation to the divine personality.

From this point on this monograph is largely about nothing. In what follows the discussion will focus on two topics, both of which have to do with nothing or life's *nihil*. The first topic or theme is nihilism. Both Martensen and Kierkegaard recognize that nihilism plays a role in the development of the self. Without nihilism or a nihilistic moment, the self lacks the appropriate consciousness of its shortcomings and is not likely to move beyond its prideful self-absorption. But nihilism can become disabling and enervating if it is not transcended. Both Martensen and Kierkegaard endorse an empowering sort of nihilism. The second theme treats the possibilities which God draws on in creating *ex nihilo* or out of nothing, namely, the possibilities from God's own eternal being. These possibilities are nothing or non-being in that they do not yet exist. As not-yet being, possibilities are nothing, and yet they are the means by which the di-polar God works in the world to further it toward fulfillment. In treating these two topics or themes our discussion will proceed in a somewhat less fettered fashion.

The first theme is empowering nihilism. Both Martensen and Kierkegaard focus on the Idea as the ideal realm of nothing as *meontic* non-being or possibility that stands in relation to the world and becomes ingredient within it. Hegel had understood that process as taking place

---
[1] Ibid., vol. 1, p. 281; ibid., vol. 1, pp. 221-222.
[2] Ibid; ibid., vol. 1, p. 222.

through the dialectical movement of *geist* that negates every particular content in progressing to the next synthesis. Martensen recognized the value of Hegel's vision, but at the same time he did not see this as denying, as Kierkegaard did, according an important place in the shaping of the human personality to existential decisions that overcome life's contradictions. Kierkegaard's analysis of human existence grants significant place to this nothing as non-being or possibilities and to the imagination that is the organ for presenting possibilities to the human or accessing possibilities by the human. This non-being or these possibilities are the breath of fresh air that keeps life vital. At the same time, these possibilities are not-yet being. They possess some actuality, but they are deficient in actuality in that they have not yet been actualized. They are, then, not-yet. To the extent that they are not-yet, they are nothing. Without non-being life shrivels up and dies. With too much of it, life becomes trivialized, unfocused, decentered.

In the *Concluding Unscientific Postscript* Kierkegaard's Johannes Climacus conceptualized the stages on life's way and in this theological anthropology envisioned the human's relation to the Idea as the realm of possibilities through which the divine mystery relates to humans and humans relate to the divine mystery.[1] Irony as the boundary line between the aesthetic and ethical stages can be understood as a higher awareness owing to an accessing of the Idea and bringing it into relation with actual existence. The immediate is therefore recontextualized in light of a larger vision, a vision which sees the immediate particular now from a broader perspective, relativizing the part and disclosing it for the partial reality that it is. Irony, in other words, views the aesthetic from the viewpoint of the ethical, without adopting the ethical through an existential act of will. The ethical standpoint relativizes the aesthetic viewpoint. It does this by revealing the *nihil* quality of the aesthetic. Similarly, the humorous as the boundary line between the ethical and religious stages can be understood as a higher awareness owing to an accessing of the Idea and bringing it into relation again with actual existence. The universal human characterizing the ethical is then recontextualized in light of a

---

[1] See for example the discussion in *SKS* 7, 455-465; *CUP1* 501-513.

yet-larger vision, a vision which sees the ethical now from a broader point of view, relativizing the ethical and making clear how inadequate that mode of existing is in relation to the higher religious viewpoint. The religious perspective relativizes that of ethics, making one see the humor in the serious rigor of the ethical mode. This is done, then, by once again indicating the nothingness of the ethical enterprise. In both irony and humor, therefore, nihilism plays a role. It need not necessarily lead to an existential adoption of the higher level of existence or stage of life, be it relating oneself with dutiful sincerity to the ethical ideal of the universal human or relating oneself with heartfelt fervor to the ultimate religious reality. One can live one's life in the posture of ironist or humorist. But often the one who becomes capable of the ironic will decide to become ethical; and sometimes the one who becomes capable of the humorous will decide to become religious. When this happens, the nihilistic experience involved in relativizing the former stage of life has played its part in the existential advance. In either case, empowering nihilism, as was present in Martensen's thought, would have been a factor.

    We saw that possibilities played a very important function in Martensen's theological understanding. We see the same in Kierkegaard. The full realm of possibilities or *meontic* non-being can serve a very positive function as it is brought into relation to that which has been actualized. It can disrobe the pretention of haughty self-congratulation for achievements in actualization. Comparing actuality to possibility, in other words, keeps us humble. Accessing *meontic* non-being or staying in touch with the not-yet places our actuality, our lived world, within a more expansive context, the context of all that is yet to come, the new heaven and the new earth. From the perspective of the enlarged viewpoint, our endeavors are recontextualized; within that larger framework we can see the humor of the situation. Consideration of the *nihil* allows us to laugh at ourselves. We remember that the divine mystery always has more in store for us. Keeping an eye on the Idea reminds us that we have not yet arrived, no matter what the endeavor. This, it seems, is a nihilistic function: to call to mind the nothingness of our so-called accomplishments. We can speak of "empowering nihilism" because the nothingness of the not-yet points up the need for more work while at the same time putting us in touch with the possible through which the divine mystery is able to lure us ahead into the transforming work that can move the world closer to the Idea or the divine mystery's purpose. Empowering nihilism does not end in cynicism but in meliorism.

Faith, for Kierkegaard as for Martensen, entails what he calls a lowering or humbling of the human. This lowering of the human theme in Kierkegaard points to an endorsement of nihilism as an important part of his understanding of the God-human relation. Loving the divine mystery, on Kierkegaard's view, is "absolute blessedness, is the absolutely unlimited depth of happiness,"[1] and yet "it is also something terrible," for before the divine mystery one becomes nothing; that is why in every person "there is no doubt a prudent fear of really having anything to do with God, because in becoming involved with God he [one] becomes nothing."[2] For the same reason people wisely flee from spiritual trials, never allowing themselves to appear naked before the divine mystery, for as Kierkegaard notes, with a wink, "in the relation to God you must always make sure of having something to hold on to so that he [God] does not absolutely reduce you to nothing."[3] Of course, if one takes the God-relationship seriously, being reduced to nothing is necessarily going to be what happens, because the closer one becomes to God, the more rigorous God becomes.[4] The absolute is the highest ideality, or in religious language this demand of ideality is referred to as divine authority.[5] Kierkegaard's nihilism, to be sure, is not an enervating or disempowering nihilism but an empowering nihilism. It is a form of nihilism that ends not in nothing but in something. It is the case that "every step forward toward the ideal is a backward step, for the progress consists precisely in my discovering increasingly the perfection of the ideal—and consequently my greater distance from it"[6]; and yet in the process one has come closer to God, one relates to God, one is negated, but in and through the negation or reduction to nothing one arrives at a

---

[1] *SKS* 20, 95-96, NB:138; *JP* 2, 1350.
[2] *Pap.* VIII-1 A 63; *JP* 2, 1353.
[3] *Pap.* VIII-1 A 77; *JP* 2, 1354.
[4] *Pap.* X-4 A 132; *JP* 2, 1422.
[5] *Pap.* X-3 A 268; *JP* 2, 1785.
[6] *Pap.* X-3 A 509; *JP* 1, 789.

more profound relating.[1] It is because of this positive dialectical process, this determinate negation, that Kierkegaard proclaims, "Becoming nothing in this world is the condition for being able to become something in the other world."[2]

William James would have rightly included the Danish Socrates in his "Sick Soul" category just as he would have rightly included Martensen within his "Religion of Healthy-Mindedness" category. But here too on the nihilism theme we find tension rather than one-sided negativity. Kierkegaard's commitment to empowering nihilism nudges him to counsel that the whole religious tendency toward stressing nothingness and self-deprecation can be fraudulent if it undermines responsibility.[3] There is finally a transnihilistic character to faith. When religious folk elevate the infinitely sublime divine mystery to such an extent that the divine mystery becomes a triviality and so transcendent that religious relationship is undercut, then religious orthodoxy—"with its doctrine that it is God who works everything in us and that we accomplish nothing at all"—has become a self-deception and the contention of incommensurability an indulgence.[4] If religious nihilism is to serve relating to the divine mystery, then it cannot allow its talk about God's majesty and sublimity to carry the divine mystery away so that "there remains no actual Christian life to speak of."[5] The divine mystery wants to annihilate humans, to be sure, but it is so that humans can become full, free individuals, and so that the divine mystery can use humans, because the divine mystery has need of them.[6] Thus, the world ought not be despised. "Since God himself has *created* and *sustains* this world," Kierkegaard announces, "one ought to guard himself against the ascetic fanaticism which as a matter of course hates it and annihilates it. You are to believe that God is fatherly enough to rejoice in a childlike way with you whenever you according to your human conception are happy."[7]

---

[1] *Pap.* X-4 A 253; *JP* 1, 425.
[2] *Pap.* XI-2 A 123; *JP* 4, 4814.
[3] *Pap.* X-1 A 59; *JP* 2, 1383.
[4] *Pap.* X-1 A 60; *JP* 2, 1384.
[5] *Pap.* X-1 A 64; *JP* 2, 1385.
[6] Ibid.
[7] *Pap.* X-2 A 241; *JP* 2, 1399.

And he even suggests, when wanting to enjoy yourself, "to *pray* God to cooperate with" you and grant that you might really enjoy yourself.[1]

Both Martensen and Kierkegaard would affirm the distinction between an implicit, unintended nihilism of idolatrous commitment that leads to unconscious despair and an explicit, intended nihilism of humorous recontextualizing that leads to hopeful transformation.[2] Here empowering nihilism can be regarded as a moment in the tragicomic sense of life that gives hope. Disempowering or disabling or enervating nihilism, on the one hand, suffers from the fallacy of misplaced absolute affirmation. It leads to unconscious despair because the endpoint of its commitment is unworthy of ultimate allegiance. Significant cultural forms of this type of nihilism are consumerism, moralism, and ecclesiasticism. In each case these cultural forms lead to lives that are empty because they have settled on realities that are not worthy of the ultimate commitment they have been given. Empowering nihilism, on the other hand, enjoys the benefits of recognizing that total presence in the form of an absolute experience of beauty, truth, justice, or love lies beyond the possibility of finite humans. Drawing on the fullness of the Idea and its possibilities for life, one becomes aware of the limitations "non-being" places on "being." In so doing, the one who tends to life's *nihil* acknowledges with a sense of humor the incongruities, ambiguities, and contradictions of existence and is motivated to make incremental changes for the better and to rest content with these finite contributions to the world.

Religious nihilism in the Martensenian and Kierkegaardian form does not have to assume the dualistic shape that it does in Nietzsche's thought. One can place a positive theological spin on nihilism in relation to the divine mystery. Empowering nihilism can be viewed as the divine mystery's "Yes" or positive work being carried out in and through the experiencing of life's grand "No." In his book on medieval mysticism, Martensen included these words of Meister Eckhart: "I tell you on

---

[1] *Pap.* X-2 A 241; *JP* 2, 1399.
[2] See John Marmysz's excellent study of nihilism, *Laughing at Nothing: Humor as a Response to Nihilism*, Albany: State University of New York Press 2003.

account of the eternal and everlasting truth that in every person who has annihilated himself or herself before God, God must pour out Godself so richly, so completely and thoroughly, that in God's life and essence, in God's nature and divinity, nothing is kept back. God must with great fecundity pour out everything."[1] To acknowledge the mysterious divine ground, grace, and goal of life need not, as Nietzsche suggests, pull one away from and out of life; in fact, passionately relating to the divine mystery can direct one with passion into life to join in the important work that is to be done. Committed to the power of life's nothing or non-being or possibilities, or to the *copula* of life as Martensen once put it, to the power of creative transformation that is the locus of spiritual renewal within the cosmos, one appreciates with continual wonder the gloriousness of the concrete, actual, finite reality that one is tasting and feeling and savoring in life. This posture finally opens rather than closes us to life's fullness. Again Martensen's old mystic Eckhart expresses it well: "My outward person tastes all creatures as creatures, wine as wine, bread as bread. My inward person tastes all as God's gifts. But in all God's gifts God gives only Godself."[2] Martensen and Kierkegaard would agree that tending to life's *nihil* or possibilities leads to a religious nihilism that bestows the gift of humor on the one who then lives out her existence, not in world-negating melancholy and fear, but rather in world-affirming joy and hope.

The second theme concerns life's possibilities that are utilized by the divine to further life. Kierkegaard was no less intoxicated by God than were his mentors Martensen and Hegel. However, unlike Hegel and his Danish follower, Kierkegaard emphasizes passionate *relating to God* and gives less explicit attention to a precise *conceiving of God*. Yet, functioning implicitly behind his language of faith and inwardness and subjectivity is a concept of God. One can draw on journal and notebook entries to sketch out the view of God with which Kierkegaard is operating in relating passionately to God and in writing about such religious relating.

---

[1] Cited in *Mester Eckart*, op. cit., p. 26; *Meister Eckhart, BHK*, p. 168.
[2] Cited in ibid., p. 25; ibid., p. 167.

In reconstructing this God it becomes apparent that Kierkegaard, like Martensen, affirms a dipolar God.[1]

We saw above that in his *Dogmatics*, in affirming divine self-limitation, Martensen stated: "that power is the true power, which creates freedom, and which nevertheless is able to make itself all in all."[2] This was in 1849, but this affirmation appears in earlier writings as well.[3] In a fascinating entry to his notebooks Kierkegaard makes a similar claim that the art of power is the ability to make free.[4] In that passage he defines divine power while reflecting on divine omnipotence, seen in God's creation of the free human being. He is in awe of God's incredible power, which is supposed to make dependent but manages to do precisely the opposite. In divine

---

[1] I use the term "dipolar" rather than "bipolar" primarily because of its use by Whitehead and process philosophy and theology. Whitehead writes in *Process and Reality: An Essay in Cosmology*, Corrected Edition by David Ray Griffin and Donald W. Sherburne, New York: The Free Press 1978 [1929], p. 345: "Thus, analogously to all actual entities, the nature of God is dipolar. He has a primordial nature and a consequent nature." Furthermore, Schelling's conception of God is often characterized as being dipolar. Compare, for instance, Philip Clayton's discussion of Schelling's dipolar God in *The Problem of God in Modern Thought*, Grand Rapids, MI: Eerdmans Publishing 2000, pp. 467-505, where he depicts, p. 495, Schelling's God in terms of the framework of "ground and consequent" that facilitates an understanding of "divinity both as the infinite ground of being and as personal being." In choosing to use "dipolar" rather than "bipolar," one also removes the possibility of an easy criticism of the "bipolar disorder" of this notion of God.

[2] Martensen, *Den christelige Dogmatik*, op. cit., p. 81.

[3] For instance, on the notion of divine Providence and how one should believe and act in relation to this, Martensen writes in his 1841 *Outline to a System of Moral Philosophy*, that "this belief and action are moments in Providence itself; only in these does Providence step forward as Providence. What many humans call faith in Providence is only an unconscious fatalism. They do not bear in mind that the will of Providence is only realized through human striving, and they will only have God's support as a Fate, not as a grace. For grace and blessing include the activity of human freedom. Fate excludes this." H. Martensen, *Grundrids til Moralphilosophiens System*, op cit, pp. 22-23; *Outline to a System of Moral Philosophy*, *BHK*, pp. 265-266. This understanding of Providence presupposes an affirmation of genuine divine self-limitation.

[4] *SKS* 20, 57-58, NB:69; *JP* 2, 1251. For a further development of this theme, see my essay, "Interpreting God's Translucent World: Imagination, Possibility, Eternity," *Translucence: Religion, the Arts, and Imagination*, eds. Carol Gilbertson and Gregg Muillenburg, Minneapolis: Fortress Press 2004, pp. 3-37.

omnipotence Kierkegaard sees "the determination to be able to take oneself back again in the expression of omnipotence in such a way that precisely therefore that which has come into existence by omnipotence can be independent."[1] God bestows freedom but in the bestowing is able to take Godself away: the creature does not sense a trace of being dependent upon God. Kierkegaard argues that "[o]nly omnipotence can take itself back while it gives away, and this relation is indeed precisely the independence of the recipient."[2] In a later journal entry Kierkegaard also speaks the language of divine self-limitation. In relation to divine providence he writes that "he does not wish to intervene with power, but he omnipotently constrains his own omnipotence, for it pleases him to see what can come of the whole of existence."[3]

---

[1] Ibid. See also Kierkegaard's development of the independence theme in relation to duty in *Works of Love*, ed. and trans. by Howard V. Hong and Edna H. Hong, Princeton: Princeton University Press 1995, p. 37: "*Only when it is a duty to love, only then is love eternally made free in blessed independence.*" In *Works of Love* Kierkegaard comes back to the theme of freedom in considering the conscience, another category very important to Martensen. Kierkegaard exclaims, p. 147, that the pure heart finds "total freedom in giving itself away." The pure heart must be bound to God without limit: "Therefore, first the infinite unboundedness, and then the talk about freedom can begin" (pp. 148-149). Yet another treatment of the independence theme in *Works of Love* comes in the second series in deliberating on the claim, p. 274: "*Love does not seek its own; it rather gives in such a way that the gift looks as if it were the recipient's property.*" In that deliberation Kierkegaard contends, ibid., that "the one who loves also knows how to make himself unnoticed so that the person helped does not become dependent upon him—by owing to him the greatest beneficence." Standing in the background of *Works of Love* might also be remarks about love Martensen makes in his *Outline to a System of Moral Philosophy*, BHK, p. 281, where he writes two particularly relevant sentences: Love "is the moment of necessity in the freedom of enthusiasm and love." And "love is in and-for-itself so far from excluding the law that it much more is *the fulfilling of the law*, and contains the finest, most conscientious consciousness of duty."

[2] Ibid. Compare also Schelling's comment on power, F.W.J. Schelling, *The Ages of the World*, trans. by Jason M. Wirth, Albany: State University of New York Press 2000, p. 14: "Actual power lies more in delimitation than expansion and that to withdraw oneself has more to do with might than to give oneself."

[3] *Pap.* XI-2 A 170. The translation of this entry is in *The Last Years: Journals 1853-1855*, ed. and trans. by Ronald Gregor Smith, London: The Fontana Library 1968 [1965], pp.273-274.

Furthermore, in his reflections upon God, our nineteenth-century Danish religious thinker insists, as does Martensen, that God is love: "God is eternal love,"[1] love is the one substantive quality of God,[2] love is God's essence,[3] and "God has only one passion: to love and to be loved."[4] God as eternal love is unchangeable, and this theme of the unchangeableness of God is affirmed in the journals as early as 1834.[5] At the end of his life, as the impulse to give expression to the corrective to the established order that levels lives of passion and subjective intensity, Kierkegaard writes more and more frequently of God as love. God is "eternal, unchanged, educating love"; everything moves God, but nothing changes God, that is, God is dipolar, for in being moved by everything God is perfectly relative or in relation to the world, and in being changed by nothing God is perfectly absolute in God's faithfulness to love the world in changeless, eternal fashion.[6]

But Kierkegaard is also fully aware that love does not take place apart from decision or resolution. As he states it: "That by which a beginning is made is a resolution."[7] In God's case, the resolve is eternal, and this eternal divine resolve becomes the model in Kierkegaard's view for human beings as well, as captured in his comment, "A beginning is always a resolution, but a resolution is really eternal."[8] For God, love is grounded in freedom. The God of eternal love is at the same time the God of eternal freedom.[9] However, precisely because this absolute God of freedom is love, this God is not merely absolute, but relative or in relation. Charles Hartshorne reminds us of the link between relationship and relativity, noting: "A personal God is one who has social relations,

---

[1] *SKS* 21, 103-104, NB7:58, 58a; *JP* 2, 1377.
[2] *SKS* 18, 27, EE:62; *JP* 2, 1319.
[3] *Pap.* XI-2 A 99; *JP* 2, 1446.
[4] *Pap.* XI-2 A 98; *JP* 2, 1445.
[5] *Pap.* I A 29; *JP* 2, 1304.
[6] *Pap.* X-4 A 305; *JP* 4, 4891.
[7] *SKS* 18, 288, JJ:442, 442.1, 442.a; *JP* 2, 2292.
[8] *SKS* 18, 224, JJ:264; *JP* 1, 912.
[9] Compare as well Schelling's comment, *The Ages of the World*, op. cit., pp. 82-83: "The eternal only exists through its will. Only through a free resolution does the eternal make itself into that which of Being has being….Hence, just as this decision is a work of the highest freedom, it is also a work of the highest Love."

really has them, and thus is constituted by relationships and hence is relative."[1]

Kierkegaard's God is absolute, but absolute love, and the divine love passionately moves God into relationship. As Kierkegaard so elegantly puts it in an 1850 entry: God "has only one joy: to communicate," i.e., to relate.[2] The almighty lover, desiring to communicate, to relate, creates the world. The absolute God of eternity is creator of the world and the source of its possibilities. As eternal freedom, pure subjectivity, God is absolute; as eternal love, pure communicativity, God is relative. God is dipolar. Kierkegaard embraces a dipolar God as did Martensen.

It seems that for Kierkegaard God is eternal freedom, a burning fire of passionate life characterized by decisiveness, a centered free reality who resolves to love. God, then, is fullness of actuality, being-itself. God is pure actuality. God's self-actualization is perfect, infinite, unconditioned, absolute. God's eternal subjectivity is perfectly intense. Everything is possible for the God of pure subjectivity; in this sense God is absolute.

And yet it must be granted that in relation to the world God is relative. In creating the world and in relating to it, God's actuality becomes the world's ideality: the world relates to God via possibilities. Kierkegaard puts this simply and beautifully: "God is the actuality of the possible."[3] As creator God is the bestower of possibilities.[4] The ideal lures life towards

---

[1] Charles Hartshorne, *The Divine Relativity: A Social Conception of God*, New Haven: Yale University Press 1948, p. x.
[2] *Pap.* X-3 A 585; *JP* 2, 1414.
[3] *SKS* 17, 41, AA:22; *JP* 2, 1190.
[4] Martensen offers an interesting comment on possibilities in his *Den christelige Ethik*, op. cit., vol. 1., pp. 279-280: "While Hegel posits the universal as the in truth existing [*Værende*] and allows this to give itself its determinations, move itself toward its concretions, the later Schelling posits, in this concurring with Aristotle, the individual as the in truth existing. Not as though he denied worth to the ideas, the universal concepts. But the idea only arrives at participating in the actual existent, in existence by becoming an attribute of the individual; and God is to him the absolutely individual being, who enshrouds Godself with the universal. While Hegel says that it is the universal which individualizes itself, Schelling says that, to the contrary, it is the individual which universalizes itself. He inquires from where the universal should receive the power to individualize itself and posit itself in existence, which can also be expressed in this way, that not thought as the universal and ideal, but *the will* as the existential [*Existentielle*] is the prime reality, which

itself. If within God's life God is the actualizer of possibilities, in relation to creation the divine actualizer becomes the possibilizer.[1] God bestows possibilities marked by God's valuation, for such valuing happens in the eternal resolve that constitutes God's eternal reality. In creation these valued possibilities are presented to the creation as candidates for actualization. God's creation project can only be accomplished over time. Therefore, the goodness and love in which God desires the world to share cannot transpire apart from the participation of the cosmos in the divine creativity. This goodness and love must therefore be created conjointly with the created world and can only come about in unfolding fashion. In relation to humans, God as eternal freedom begets freedom: "with the help of the eternal…Christianity at every moment creates fresh air" by giving the possible, the future, and hopeful expectation of the good which is stronger than anything else in the world.[2]

The relativity of God is very apparent when Kierkegaard discusses the human's relation to God, for he claims that in a real sense God is no more than what the human allows God to be. An 1846 entry states that God is present only for the existing person—in faith. It reads:

> Immanently (in the imaginative medium of abstraction) God does not exist or is not *present* [*er ikke "til"*]; God *is* [*er*]—only for the existing person [*Existerende*] is God present, i.e., God can be *present* [*være "til"*] in faith…. Faith, therefore, is the anticipation of the eternal which holds the elements together, the discontinuities of existence [*Existentsens*]. If an existing person

---

has the power to determine itself and the other. Reason is to him only the sum, the totality of the divine *possibilities*, the circles of the *predicates*, through which the absolute individual being makes itself intelligible. Reason, the mere realm of ideas, *is*, but cannot arrive at *existence* except by a will." This quotation cannot be applied directly to our discussion of Kierkegaard's use of Martensen, since it is from a later quotation that bears the imprint of Martensen's intense study of Schelling that began in 1860, as we learn in a letter of Martensen's to his friend Otto Laub. See *Biskop Otto Laubs Levnet. En Livsskildring i Breve*, vols. 1-3, eds. F.L. Mynster and G. Schepelern, Copenhagen: Karl Schønberg 1885-1887, *Andet Tidsrum 1855-1882, Første Afdeling: O. Laubs Brevvexling med H.L. Martensen*, vol. 2, p. 19, where in a letter dated April 6, 1860 Martensen says that Schelling has consumed much of his free time.

[1] On this notion of God as possibilizer see Richard Kearney, *The God Who May Be: A Hermeneutics of Religion*, Bloomington: Indiana University Press 2001.

does not have faith, then [for that person] God neither *is* nor *is* God *present*, although understood eternally God nevertheless eternally is.[1]

Here the ontological status of the eternal God is affirmed in the last phrase, but the point is that the existential payoff of God is contingent upon the openness of faith, which receives the gift of a world that is created by the brackets eternity provides for its disparate perceptions. The person in the God-relation lives in the realm of actuality, but "God is not an actual something in the external sense and does not walk about."[2] And Kierkegaard states, "God is not an external palpable power who bangs the table in front of me when I want to alter his will and says: No, stop! No, in this sense it is almost as if God did not exist. It is left up to me."[3] In Kierkegaard's eyes, divine greatness increases in proportion to human concern.[4] Faith is an existential relation and cannot be reduced to a cognitive assertion. "To believe," clarifies Søren, "is not an *indifferent relation to something* which is true, but an *infinitely decisive relation to something*. The accent falls upon the relation."[5] The very self of God is *how* one involves oneself with God, as Kierkegaard indicates: "In respect to God, the *how* is *what*....In relationship to God one can not involve oneself to a certain degree, for God is precisely the contradiction to all that which is to a certain degree."[6] Here we are close to the alluring understanding of God expressed by Tillich in his notion of faith as religious or ultimate concern. In strongly emphasizing the theme of subjectivity, one needs to be careful not to allow the dialogue with God to become a monologue. Maybe that concern is what prompted Kierkegaard to state that a mediator is needed so one knows it is God and not oneself with whom one is talking.[7]

Eternity was the first attribute of God for Martensen. The absolute aspect of God's being is expressed very clearly by Kierkegaard in the

---

[1] *Pap.* VII-1 A 139; *JP* 2, 1347.
[2] *SKS* 21, 208, NB9:20; *JP* 2, 1382.
[3] *Pap.* X-5 A 13; *JP* 2, 1273.
[4] *SKS* 20, 416, NB5:112; *JP* 2, 1371.
[5] *Pap.* VI B 19:1-10; *JP* 4, 4537.
[6] *Pap.* X-2 A 644; *JP* 2, 1405.
[7] *Pap.* X-4 A 252; *JP* 2, 1424.

notion of eternity. Kierkegaard understands eternity "as a continuous state of fulfillment."[1] "Eternity...does not need men. It is men who need eternity. Eternity does not change."[2] "In eternity a person is not in the succession of time," he notes, "and being *eterno modo* is the most intensive punctuality."[3] Eternity touches temporality in the moment; "the moment is really time's atom, but not until eternity is posited."[4] "A person is out upon the deep only when the eternal is his [or her] sole support."[5] The New Testament criterion for being human, as Kierkegaard identifies it, is: "the eternal," which he takes in this setting finally to mean "to be a single individual."[6] In relation to humans, the eternal means inwardness, subjectivity, ideality, rigor, becoming a full, free individual. Eternal freedom, in relating to humans, desires to beget true freedom. Kierkegaard acknowledges that eternity, as the highest, is always very near to a person, for eternity accompanies a human being through the various ages of life; but he also sees more clearly than most that eternity's ubiquitous presence does not mean that the person's eyes are necessarily open to the eternal.[7] As Kierkegaard warns, God is indeed personal, but it does not follow that God is thereby personal *for you*.[8]

Martensen knew well the tension existing between the absolute and relative aspects of the divine. The tension present in Kierkegaard's dipolar divinity becomes manifest in his concern to maintain both the majesty and sublimity of God and the compassion and love of God. Much is disclosed about Kierkegaard's understanding of this struggle in an entry on the God-relationship, in which Father, Son, and Spirit are discussed.[9] Provided here is a step-by-step account of how God draws one to Godself. This process involves relating to successive prototypes, each of which is required because the previous has become too exalted, and each of which brings God lower and closer to the human—from

---

[1] *SKS* 18, 185, EE:185; *JP* 1 834.
[2] *Pap.* XI-3 B 124; *JP* 1, 846.
[3] *SKS* 21, 228-229, NB9:48; *JP* 1, 842.
[4] *Pap.* V B 55:6; *JP* 3, 2740.
[5] *SKS* 20, 112, NB:184, 184a; *JP* 1, 838.
[6] *Pap.* XI-1 A 130; *JP* 2, 1802.
[7] *SKS* 20, 106, NB:167; *JP* 1, 837.
[8] *Pap.* XI-2 A 175; *JP* 2, 1452. My emphasis.
[9] *Pap.* X-5 A 23; *JP* 2, 1432.

God as Father to God as the Son, and then to God as the Atoner, and finally to God as Spirit. This passage explains how the process begins with the relationship to God as Father, then as one matures and relating to God as Father has become infinitely exalted, God directs one to the Son, the Mediator, and this one is also the prototype. But after a time there is the realization that the Son as prototype is infinitely exalted and far beyond the person's striving, and then the prototype comes to be seen as the Atoner, and this becomes the prototypical exemplar that one strives to be like. Upon further maturing and realizing the momentous nature of the task, the faithful one is led by God to the Spirit and is empowered to live the life of freedom which gives itself in love. Kierkegaard concludes: "Thus it is not the spirit who leads to the Son and the Son who leads to the Father; no, it is the Father who directs to the Son, the Son who directs to the Spirit, and not until then is it the Spirit who leads to the Son, and the son who leads to the Father."

In this process God's majesty, it might be thought, would be compromised as God lowers Godself in relation to the human. But exactly the opposite takes place, according to what Kierkegaard designates as "the law of inversion—that to come closer is to get farther away: infinite majesty!" Despite the relativizing of God, God's absoluteness is protected. At each stage in the process of lowering, there is an elevating of God as the full divine majesty comes to be appreciated ever more profoundly and with the higher conception of God comes a matching humbling or lowering of the human. But, as we have seen, the lowering is really an elevating, the annihilating really a potentiating.

Martensen gave great emphasis to possibilities as the means by which God acts in the world. In Kierkegaard's understanding of the divine, the relative aspect of God finds God making use of possibilities to carry out providential activity. In creatively laboring within the world God works through possibilities. "A possibility is a beckoning by God," writes this religious thinker who could rightly be called a theologian of possibility.[1] Kierkegaard is joyous even amidst his suffering because he remembers

---

[1] *SKS* 21, 126, NB7:93; *JP* 1, 337.

"the millions of possibilities God has at every moment."[1] "God who holds everything in his hand at every moment has possibilities to burn."[2] The modern world has brought about a shrinking of the realm of the possible. Kierkegaard believes that God is the dipolar reality who makes the impossible possible. He explains in NB13:43:

> My imagination almost swoons to think of the millions of possibilities that God has at every moment. I do something wrong. I am aware of it at once. What is to be done now? My gloomy imagination instantly perceives the possibility that this little mistake can ruin everything. But then, the very same moment, I say to God: *Bitte, bitte*. I made a mistake; but even if I am a pest, an impudent pest, O God, make something good out of this very mistake. And then (God who has millions of possibilities at every moment), then the circumstances are combined somewhat differently and, so it is. This very mistake proves to be the right thing. That is how I pray to God. And that is how I get more out of this mistake than out of the most proper thing I ever did.[3]

Kierkegaard's lesson here is that humans dare not compare their reason and imagination with God. Just because the human imagination does not stretch far enough to think of possibilities, does not mean that God does not have possibilities. We should not make a cutoff on possibilities just because we can no longer see any possibility. My blindness in not seeing possibilities, my lack of imagination, does not necessarily mean there are no possibilities.[4]

Jacob Böhme understood God as eternal freedom, Schelling also used that language in speaking of God, Martensen too can be situated within that tradition, and we can attribute this understanding to Kierkegaard as well, for he surely views God as that eternal freedom who lovingly nurtures humans to grow into freedom. Apart from freedom or voluntariness there are no stages on life's way. Kierkegaard maintains

---

[1] *SKS* 22, 379, NB13:43; *JP* 6, 6514.
[2] *SKS* 21, 208-220, NB9:20; *JP* 2, 1382.
[3] *SKS* 22, 379, NB13:43; *JP* 6, 6514.
[4] *SKS* 21, 160, NB8:37; *JP* 3, 3344.

that freedom or "voluntariness is the precise form for qualitatively being spirit": "Voluntariness is the highest form of religiousness and is therefore to be recognized by the fact that here God is most rigorous. Religiousness is classified according to ascending rigor."[1] And it is rather ironic that Kierkegaard, the reputed father of existentialism with its embrace of freedom, would agree with Luther against Erasmus that the human will is bound rather than free in relation to God. There are two levels of freedom: freedom of choice and true freedom, and the latter is attained in giving up the former by choosing, which choice Kierkegaard would say is empowered by grace. He writes in NB12:172: "Freedom really is freedom only when in the same moment, the same second, it is (freedom of choice), it rushes with infinite speed to bind itself unconditionally by the choice of attachment, the choice whose truth is that there can be no question of any choice."[2] He continues: "By staring fixedly at 'freedom of choice' instead of choosing, he [one] loses both freedom and freedom of choice."[3] Kierkegaard is saying that "the most tremendous thing conceded to" the human "is—choice, freedom. If you want to rescue and keep freedom, there is only one way—in the very same second unconditionally in full attachment give it back to God and yourself along with it. If the sight of what is conceded to you tempts you, if you surrender to the temptation and look with selfish craving at freedom of choice, then you lose your freedom."[4] Here Kierkegaard agrees with what Augustine says in distinguishing true freedom from freedom of choice—"namely that a person has the most lively sense of freedom when with completely decisive determination one impresses upon one's action the inner necessity which excludes the thought of another possibility."[5] True freedom, therefore, is embodied in action marked by singularity of possibility and purpose or purity of heart. True freedom also includes what Luther, Nietzsche, and Tillich have called a transmoral conscience. Truly free persons are those who subjectively consult only with God and

---

[1] *SKS* 22, 337-338, NB12:189; *JP* 2, 1258.
[2] *SKS* 22, 325, NB12:172; *JP* 2, 1261.
[3] *SKS* 22, 325, NB12:172; *JP* 2, 1261.
[4] *SKS* 22, 325, NB12:172; *JP* 2, 1261.
[5] *Pap.* X-4 A 177; *JP* 2, 1269.

their conscience; such persons, as Kierkegaard expresses it, do "not give the time of day as to whether there are laws or regulations against" the free act they know is required of them, "for such things are nothing but flimsy thread" to them.[1] Such true freedom is given, then, in the context of faith in which one lives one's existence in the possibilities-bestowing relationship with the loving God.

---

[1] *Pap.* X-3 A 618; *JP* 2, 1264.

# Postlude

Kierkegaard once wrote in his notebooks that in Denmark " 'The System' and the pseudonyms belong essentially together."[1] We might say that both Kierkegaard and Hegel are needed. But if one has entered into the writings of Martensen and has an interest in theological construction, one might think it better to say that both Kierkegaard and Martensen are needed. We can learn from the Danish romantic idealist who would not let go of the distinctiveness of Christian faith as a source of transformative experience. Martensen was a theologian who strove to honor both the scientific-philosophical concerns of Hegel and German idealism and the existential-personal concerns of the religious individual. As a responsible thinker, one needs to take a stand on the nature of reality, looking to the past and making judgments about objective reality, as Hegel does, but one must also recognize the importance of being a person who is open to the future, thinking about subjective realities, and living out of a sense of expectation, as Kierkegaard does. Kierkegaard and Hegel are best understood when they are brought together into dialogue and integrated. But again the same can be said for Kierkegaard and Martensen, who has more to say on specifics of Christian faith and life and therefore brings more nuances to a dialogue with Kierkegaard. As Kierkegaard and Hegel are continually brought into relation to one another, new illuminations will be forthcoming. A similar claim can be made about Kierkegaard and Martensen: bringing them together sheds light on the matter being considered in interesting ways. When Hegel and Kierkegaard are read together and allowed to complement one another, the resultant perspective is appropriately comprehensive in its cosmic grasp and meaningful in its personal passion. When Martensen

---

[1] *Pap.* X-6 B 137.

and Kierkegaard are read together, the complementing is not quite as wide-ranging, but often it is more intense and therefore fructifying.

In 1928 C.I. Scharling wondered whether Martensen's star still dwelt under the horizon because his time had not yet come, but whether it would not soon rise up into the heavens because an entirely new time is coming, a time when there will be use precisely for "Martensen's thoughts—these thoughts which in clear and noble form lie concealed in his long series of writings, all the way from the treatise of his youth about Faust to the *Ethics* and his '*Levnet*.'"[1] Nearly four score years after Scharling, we can ask the same. Kierkegaard followed Martensen even though he identified him as "the cultured public's chosen one." We are able to discern shortcomings in Martensen no less than could Kierkegaard. Nevertheless, I hope it has been established that there are reasons for us also to follow him. Martensen mattered to Kierkegaard. Kierkegaard learned much from Martensen, and so can we.

---

[1] Scharling, *H.L. Martensen*, op. cit., pp. 9-10.

# Bibliography

Bibliographical Note: Entries in the bibliography are divided into three categories: (1) Works by Martensen; (2) Works on Martensen; and (3) Other Works. Works in the first category are listed chronologically. Works in the second and third categories appear alphabetically.

## Works by Martensen

"Priisopgave," unpublished manuscript from the year 1833, in the Martensen Archives at the Royal Library, Copenhagen.

Two sermons on Matthew 4:1-11 and Matthew 13:31-32, unpublished manuscripts in the Martensen Archives at the Royal Library, Copenhagen, May 12, 1833 and January 12, 1834.

"E. G. Kolthoff: *Apocalypsis Joanni Apostolo vindicata*," *Maanedsskrift for Litteratur*, vol. 12, 1834, pp. 1-31.

*Ueber Lenau's Faust*, Stuttgart: Cotta 1936.

"J.L. Heiberg: *Indledningsforedrag til det i November 1834 begyndte logiske Cursus paa den kongelige militaire Høiskole*," *Maanedsskrift for Litteratur*, vol. 16, 1836, pp. 515-528. (English translation: "Review of the *Introductory Lecture to the Logic Course at the Royal Military College that Began in November 1834*" in *Heiberg's Introductory Lecture to the Logic Course and Other Texts*, ed. and trans. by Jon Stewart, Copenhagen: C.A. Reitzel 2007 (*Texts from Golden Age Denmark*, vol. 3), pp. 75-86.

"Betragtninger over Ideen af Faust. Med Hensyn paa Lenaus *Faust*," *Perseus, Journal for den speculative Idee*, no. 1, 1837, pp. 91-164.

*De autonomia conscientiae sui humanae, in theologiam dogmaticam nostri temporis introducta*, Hauniae: J.D. Quist 1837.

"Forelæsninger over Indledning til speculative Dogmatik." Winter Semester lectures from 1837-1838 at the University of Copenhagen, printed in *Pap.* II C 12-24.

"*Fata Morgana: Eventry-Comedie* af J.L. Heiberg," *Maanedsskrift for Litteratur*, vol. 19, 1838, pp. 361-397.

"Forelæsninger over den nyere Philosophies Historie fra Kant til Hegel." Winter Semester lectures from 1838-1839 at the University of Copenhagen, *Pap.* II C 25, in *Pap.* XII, pp. 280-331.

"Forelæsninger over "Speculativ Dogmatik," undated lectures from 1838-1839 at the University of Copenhagen, *Pap.* II C 26-28, in *Pap.* XIII, pp. 3-116.

"Rationalisme, Supranaturalisme og *principium exclusi medii*," *Tidsskrift for Litteratur og Kritik*, vol. 1, 1839, pp. 456-473.

"Philosophiske Beskedenhed i *Kjøbenhavnsposten*," *Fædrelandet*, vol. 1, no. 50, January 29, 1840, columns 259-261.

"Erklæring," *Fædrelandet*, vol. 1, no. 56, February 4, 1840, column 315.

*Mester Eckart. Et Bidrag til at oplyse Middelalderens Mystik*, Copenhagen: C.A. Reitzel 1840. (English translation: *Meister Eckhart: A Study in Speculative Theology*, in *Between Hegel and Kierkegaard: Hans L. Martensen's Philosophy of Religion*, trans. by Curtis L. Thompson and David J. Kangas, Atlanta: Scholars Press 1997, pp. 149-243.)

*Den menneskelige Selvbevidstheds Autonomie i vor Tids dogmatiske Theologie*, trans. by L.V. Petersen, Copenhagen: C.A. Reitzel 1841. (English translation: *The Autonomy of Human Self-Consciousness in Modern Dogmatic Theology*, in *Between Hegel and Kierkegaard: Hans L. Martensen's Philosophy of Religion*, trans. by Curtis L. Thompson and David J. Kangas, Atlanta: Scholars Press 1997, pp. 73-147.)

"*Nye Digte* af J.L. Heiberg," *Fædrelandet*, vol. 2, no. 398, January 10, 1841, columns 3205-3212; no. 399, January 11, 1841, columns 3213-3220; no. 400, January 12, 1841, columns 3221-3224.

*Grundrids til Moralphilosophiens System*, Copenhagen: C.A. Reitzel 1841. (English translation: *Outline to a System of Moral Philosophy* in *Between Hegel and Kierkegaard: Hans L. Martensen's Philosophy of Religion*, trans. by Curtis L. Thompson and David J. Kangas, Atlanta: Scholars Press 1997, pp. 245-315.)

"Nutidens Religiøse Crisis," *Intelligensblade*, vol. 1, 1842, pp. 53-73.

*Den christelige Daab betragtet med Hensyn paa det baptistiske Spørgsmaal*, Copenhagen: C.A. Reitzel 1843.

# Bibliography 187

"Kirke-Aaret," *Urania: Aarbog for 1844*, ed. by J.L. Heiberg, Copenhagen: H.I. Bing 1848, pp. 161-188.
"Litterait Uvæsen," *Berlingske Tidende*, no. 115, April 29, 1844.
*Prædikener*, Copenhagen: C.A. Reitzel 1847.
*Den christelige Dogmatik*, Copenhagen: C.A. Reitzel 1849.
*Prædikener*, Copenhagen: C.A. Reitzel 1849.
*Den christelige Dogmatik*, 2nd ed., Copenhagen: C.A. Reitzel 1850.
*Die christeliche Dogmatik* (translator unnamed), Kiel: Carl Schrøder 1850.
"Sendschreiben an den Herrn Oberconsistorialrath Nielsen in Schleswig," Copenhagen: [n.n.] 1850.
*Dogmatiske Oplysninger. Et Leilighedskrift*, Copenhagen: C.A. Reitzel 1850.
*Mester Eckart*. Ny Udgave, Copenhagen: C.A. Reitzel 1851.
*Den danske Folkekirkes Forfatningsspørgsmaal*, Copenhagen: [n.n.] 1851.
*Prædikener. Tredie Samling*, Copenhagen: C.A. Reitzel 1852.
"Om Gudstjenstens Indretning i den lutherske Kirke," Copenhagen: [n.n.] 1853.
"Prædiken, holdt i Christiansborg Slotskirke paa 5te Søndag efter Hellig-Tre Konger, Søndagen før Biskop Dr. Mynsters Jordefærd," Copenhagen: [n.n.] 1854.
"Til Geistligheden i Sjællands Stift," Copenhagen: [n.n.] 1854.
*Prædikernen. Fjerde Samling*, Copenhagen: C.A. Reitzel 1854.
"I Anledning af Dr. S. Kierkegaards Artikel i *Fædrelandet* Nr. 295," *Berlingske Tidende*, no. 302, December 28, 1854.
*Til Erindring om J.P. Mynster*, Copenhagen: Gyldendal 1955.
"I Anledning af Pastor Grundtvigs Oplysninger om 'Alterbogs-Daaben,'" Copenhagen: Gyldendal 1856.
*Die christliche Dogmatik. Vom Verfasser selbst veranstaltete deutsche Ausgabe*, Leipzig: J.C. Hinrich'sche Buchhandlung 1856.
*Christian Dogmatics*, trans. by W. Urwick [from the 1856 German edition], Edinburgh: T & T Clark 1890.
*Et Gjensvar i Striden om "Alterbogsdaaben*," Copenhagen: Gyldendal 1857.
*Prædikener, holdte i Aarene 1854 til 1858*, Copenhagen: Gyldendal 1859.

*Taler ved Præstevielse*, Copenhagen: Gyldendal 1860.
*Prædikener, holdt i Aarene 1859-1863*, Copenhagen: Gyldendal 1859.
*Til Forsvar mod den saakaldte Grundtvigianisme*, Copenhagen: Gyldendal 1863.
*Om Tro og Viden. Et Leilighedsskrift*, Copenhagen: C.A. Reitzel 1867.
*Den danske Folkekirkes Forfatnings-Spørgsmaal paany betragtet*, Copenhagen: Gyldendal 1867.
*Taler ved Præstevielse, holdte i Aarene 1860 til 1868*, Copenhagen: Gyldendal 1868.
*Prædikener, holdte i Aarene 1864 til 1869*, Copenhagen: Gyldendal 1869.
*Den christelige Ethik. Den almindelige Deel*, Copenhagen: Gyldendal 1871.
*Christi Lidelseshistorie. Tolv Prædikener*, Copenhagen: Gyldendal 1872.
"Til Ministeriet for Kirke- og Underviisningsvæsenet. Svarskrivelse den 12te November i Anledning af Klage fra en Rigsdagsmand over den af Pastor Fibiger holdte Prædiken for Rigsdagen," *Fædrelandet*, no. 282, December 3, 1872.
*Katholicisme og Protestantisme. Et Leilighedskrift*, Copenhagen: Gyldendal 1874.
*Socialisme og Christendom. Et Brudstykke af den specielle Ethik*, Copenhagen: Gyldendal 1874.
*Prædikener paa alle Søn- og Helligdage i Aaret*, Copenhagen: Gyldendal 1875.
*Den christelige Ethik. Den specielle Deel.* Første Afdeling: *Den individuelle Ethik*; Anden Afdeling: *Den sociale Ethik*, Copenhagen: Gyldendalske Boghandels Forlag 1878.
*Prædikener, holdte i Aarene 1875 til 1880*, Copenhagen: Gyldendal 1880.
*Jacob Böhme. Theosophiske Studier*, Copenhagen: Gyldendal 1881.
*Taler ved Præstevielse, holdte i Aarene 1869 til 1882*, Copenhagen: Gyldendal 1882.
*Af mit Levnet*, vols. 1-3, Copenhagen: Gyldendal 1882-1883.
*Leilighedstaler*, Copenhagen: Gyldendal 1884.
*Mindre Skrifter og Taler af Biskop Martensen: Udgivne med en Oversigt over hans Forfattervirksomhed af Julius Martensen*, Copenhagen: Gyldendal 1885.

*Biskop Otto Laubs Levnet: En Livsskildring i Breve*, vols. 1-3, ed. by Frederik Ludvig Mynster, Copenhagen: Karl Schønberg 1885-1887, vol. 1 (*O. Laubs Brevvexling med H. L. Martensen*), p. 299; vol. 2 (*O. Laubs Brevvexling med forskjellige*), p. 407.

*Briefwechsel zwischen Martensen und Dorner*, vols. 1-2, Berlin: H. Reuter's Verlag 1888.

*Biskop H.L. Martensens Breve. Breve til L. Gude 1848-1867*, vols. 1-3, ed. by B. Kornerup, Copenhagen: G.E.C. Gad 1955-1957.

## Works on Martensen

Andersen, J. Oskar, "Biskop H.L. Martensens Ungdom," *Kirkehistoriske Samlinger*, series 6, vol. 1, 1933, pp. 130-237.

———, *Survey of the History of the Church in Denmark*, Copenhagen: O. Lohse 1930.

Andersen, Vilhelm, *Nogle Betragtninger og Studier over og i Sammenhæng med Martensens "Den Christelige Ethik,"* Copenhagen: C.A. Reitzel 1879.

———, *Tider og Typer af dansk Aands Historie*, Første Række: Humanisme. Anden Del: Goethe, vols. 1-2, Copenhagen, Kristiania: Gyldendal, Nordisk Forlag 1915-16, vol. 2, pp. 11-19.

Anonymous, "Biskop Martensen," *London Quarterly Review*, vol. 67, 1884, pp. 74-91.

Anonymous, "Biskop Martensen," *Methodist Review*, vol. 68, 1886, pp. 701-717.

Arildsen, Skat, *H.L. Martensen. Hans Liv, Udvikling og Arbejde. Studier i det 19. Aarhundredes Danske Aandsliv*, Copenhagen: G.E.C. Gad 1932.

Birch, J.H.S., *Denmark in History*, London: John Murray 1938.

Birchedahl, Vilhelm, *Kirkeaaret, et Billede paa den christelige Livsudvikling*, Copenhagen: C.A. Reitzel 1843.

Birkedal, Vilhelm, "Hans Lassen Martensen," in his *Personlige Oplevelser i et langt Liv*, vols. 1-3, Copenhagen: Karl Schønbergs Forlag 1890-91, vol. 1, pp. 187-214.

Bornemann, Johan Alfred, "Af Martensen: *de autonomia conscientiae. Sui humanae*," *Tidsskrif for Literatur og Kritik*, no. 1, 1839, pp. 1-40.

Brandt, Hermann, *Gotteserkenntnis und Weltentfremdung: Der Weg der spekulativen Theologie Hans Lassen Martensens*, Göttingen: Vandenhoeck & Ruprecht 1971.

Brøchner, Hans, "Erindringer om Søren Kierkegaard," in *Det Nittende Aarhundrede, Maanedsskrift for Literatur og Kritik*, vol. 5, March 1877, pp. 337-374. (English translation: "Hans Brøchner's Recollections of Kierkegaard," in *Encounters with Kierkegaard: A Life as Seen by His Contemporaries*, trans. and ed. by Bruce H. Kirmmse, Princeton: Princeton University Press 1996, pp. 225-252.)

———, *Nogle Bemærkninger om Daaben, foranledigede ved Professor Martensens Skrift: "Den christelige Daab,"* Copenhagen: P.G. Philipsen 1843.

Bukdahl, Jørgen K., "Martensen og hans Samtid," *Dansk Udsyn*, no. 1, 1957, pp. 1-6.

Busck, G., *Om Biskop Martensens Grundtvigianisme*, Copenhagen: Karl Schønbergs Forlag 1863.

Buske, Thomas, "Kirche und Gesellschaft. Überlegungen zur "Ethik" von Hans Lassen Martensen," *Neue Zeitschrift für Systematische Theologie und Religionsphilosophie*, vol. 7, 1965, pp. 62-70.

Caron, Jacques, "H.L. Martensen," in his *Angoisse et Communication chez S. Kierkegaard*, Odense: Odense University Press 1992, pp. 46-56.

Christensen, Arild, "Efterskriftens Opgør med Martensen," *Kierkegaardiana*, 4, 1962, pp. 45-62.

Czakó, István, "Das Unbekannte. Die Aufhebung der klassischen *theologia naturalis* in der negativen Theologie des Johannes Climacus," *Kierkegaard Studies. Yearbook*, 2004, pp. 235-249.

Eiríksson, Magnús, *Dr. Martensens trykte moralske Paragrapher, eller det saakaldte "Grundrids til Moralphilosophiens System af Dr. Hans Martensen," i dets forvirrede, idealistisk-metaphysiske og phantastiskspeculative, Religion og Christendom undergravende, fatalistiske, pantheistiske og selv-forguderske Væsen*, belyst og bedømt af Magnús Eiríksson, Cand. Theol, Copenhagen: Klein 1846.

———, *Om Baptister og Barnedaab, samt flere Momenter af Den kirkelige og speculative Christendom*, Copenhagen: P.G. Philipsen 1844.

Fenger, Henning, *Kierkegaard, the Myths and Their Origins: Studies in the Kierkegaardian Papers and Letters*, trans. by George C. School-field, New Haven and London: Yale University Press 1980, pp. 136-142 and passim.

Fick, A.G., "Martensen, Kierkegaard og Grundtvig," *Theologisk Tidsskrift*, 1880, pp. 385-416.

Fuglsang, Damgaard, H., "Martensens Teologi," *Teologisk Tidsskrift*, series 4, vol. 10, 1929, pp. 273-289.

Gosse, Edmund, "Bishop Martensen," *The Expositor*, series 3, no. 1, 1885, pp. 59-68.

Grane, Leif, "Det Teologiske Fakultet 1830-1925," in *Københavns Universitet 1479-1979*, vol. 5, *Det Teologiske Fakultet*, ed. by Leif Grane, Copenhagen: G.E.C. Gad 1980, pp. 325-500.

Green, Allan, "H.L. Martensen," in his *Kierkegaard bland samtida. Personhistoriska skisser*, Eslöv: Förlags AB Gondolin 1995, pp. 77-86.

Hagen, Johan Frederik, "*Mester Eckart, et Bidrag til at oplyse Middelalderens Mystik*, by Dr. H. Martensen, Copenhagen: C.A. Reitzel 1840, 153 Pag. 8°," *Fædrelandet*, vol. 1, no. 279, September 13, 1840, columns 2237-2242.

Himmelstrup, Jens, *Sibbern, en Monografi*, Copenhagen: J.H. Schultz 1934.

Holm, Søren, "H.L. Martensen," in his *Filosofien i Norden før 1900*, Copenhagen: Munksgaard 1967, pp. 86-89.

⸻, *Religionsfilosofiske Essays*, Copenhagen: Gyldendal, Nordisk Forlag 1943, pp. 99-109.

Horn, Robert Leslie, *Positivity and Dialectic: A Study of the Theological Method of Hans Lassen Martensen*, Copenhagen: C.A. Reitzel 2007 (*Danish Golden Age Studies*, vol. 2).

Høffding, Harald, "Heiberg og Martensen," *Danske Filosofer*, Copenhagen: Gyldendal 1909, pp. 129-137.

Kirmmse, Bruce H. (ed.), *Encounters with Kierkegaard: A Life as Seen by His Contemporaries*, trans. by Bruce H. Kirmmse and Virginia R. Laursen, Princeton: Princeton University Press 1996, pp. 196-205, 323-324.

———, "H.L. Martensen," in his *Kierkegaard in Golden Age Denmark*, Bloomington and Indianapolis: Indiana University Press 1990, pp. 169-197.

Kleinert, Markus, "Martensens Rezension von Heibergs Einführungsvortrag," *Kierkegaard Studies. Yearbook*, 2003, pp. 506-522.

Koch, Carl Henrik, "Hans L. Martensen," in his *Den danske idealisme 1800-1880*, Copenhagen: Gyldendal, pp. 271-298, see also pp. 363-378 and pp. 443-447.

Koch, Hal (ed.), *Den Danske Kirkes Historie*, vols. 1-8, Copenhagen: Gyldendal, Nordisk Forlag 1950-66, vol. 6, pp. 318-323.

Kornerup, Bjørn (ed.), *Biskop H. Martensens Breve*, Copenhagen: G.E.C. Gads Forlag 1955.

Krogh, W., *Biskop Martensen og Kong Frederik den Syvende*, Copenhagen: A. Giese 1883.

Lein, Bente Nilsen, "Biskop Martensen og den etisk-kristelige sosialisme: H.L. Martensens tanker om den 'ethiske Socialisme' som kristelig alternative til økonomisk liberalisme og revolusjonær socialisme," *Norsk Teologisk Tidsskrift*, vol. 81, 1980, pp. 233-247.

Lübcke, Poul, "Guds og verdens visdom. Troen og forargelsen hos Kierkegaard, Mynster og Martensen," *Filosofiske Studier*, vol. 14, 1994, pp. 131-195.

———, "Indirect Communication and Kierkegaard's Transcendental Existential Perspectivism," *Søren Kierkegaard and the Word(s): Essays on Hermeneutics and Communication*, ed. by Poul Houe and Gordon D. Marino, Copenhagen: C.A. Reitzel 2004, pp. 28-37.

Lunddahl, Andr. P., "Fra Martensens første Docenttid," *Teologisk Tidsskrift*, vol. 5, 1888, pp. 321-331.

Madsen, P., "Biskop Martensen som Theolog. Et Foredrag i Kjøbenhavns Præsteconvent," *Teologisk Tidsskrift*, vol. 50, 1884, pp. 398-409.

Martensen, Josepha, *H.L. Martensen i sit Hjem og blandt sine Venner*, Copenhagen: J. Frimodts 1918.

Martensen, Julius (ed.), *Mindre Skrifter og Taler af Biskop Martensen, Udgivne med en Oversigt over hans Forfattervirksomhed*, Copenhagen: Gyldendalske Boghandel 1885.

Martensen-Larsen, H., *Paludan-Müller og Martensen*, Copenhagen: J. Frimodts Forlag 1923.

Mynster, Jakob Peter, "Rationalisme, Suprarationalisme," *Tidsskrift for Litteratur og Kritik*, vol. 1, 1839, pp. 249-268.

Nannestad, V., *H. L. Martensen. Nyt Bidrag til en Charakteristik af Dansk Prædiken i det nittende Aarhundredes sidste Halvdel*, Copenhagen: Karl Schønberg 1897.

Neiiendam, Michael, "Martensen, Mynster og Kierkegaard," in *H.L. Martensen. Hans Tanker og Livssyn*, ed. by C.I. Scharling, Copenhagen: P. Haase & Søns Forlag 1928, pp. 94-127.

Nielsen, Rasmus, *Mag. S. Kierkegaards "Johannes Climacus" og Dr. H. Martensens "christelige Dogmatik". En undersøgende Anmeldelse*, Copenhagen: C.A. Reitzel 1849.

Paludan-Müller, J. *Om Dr. Martensens christelige Dogmatik*, Copenhagen: C.A. Reitzel 1850.

Pattison, George, *Kierkegaard, Religion and the Nineteenth-Century Crisis of Culture*, Cambridge: Cambridge University Press 2002, pp. 96-115.

————, *Kierkegaard: The Aesthetic and the Religious*, New York: St. Martin's 1992, pp. 18-21 and passim.

Pedersen, Jørgen, "Conception of Freedom. Principal Perspectives," *Some of Kierkegaard's Main Categories*, ed. by Niels Thulstrup and Marie Mikulová Thulstrup, Copenhagen: C.A. Reitzel 1988 (*Bibliotheca Kierkegaardiana*, vol. 16), pp. 26-62.

————, "Et møde med perspektiver eller perspektiver i et møde. Martensen hos Baader i München 1835," *Kirkehistoriske samlinger 1976*, Copenhagen 1976, pp. 150-181.

Plekon, Michael, "Kierkegaard, the Church and Theology of Golden Age Denmark," *Journal of Ecclesiastical History*, vol. 34, no. 2, 1983, pp. 245-266.

Poole, Roger, *Kierkegaard: The Indirect Communication*, Charlottesville and London: University Press of Virginia 1993, pp. 37-41, pp. 144-148, pp. 262-269 and passim.

Scharling, C.I., J. Fog-Petersen, and M. Neiiendam, *H. L. Martensen. hans Tanker og Livssyn*, Copenhagen: P. Haase & Sons 1928.

Schjørring, Jens, *Teologi og Filosofi. Nogle Analyser og Dokumenter vedrørende Hegelianismen i Dansk Teologi*, Copenhagen: G.E.C. Gad 1974, pp. 27-35.

———, "Martensen," *Kierkegaard's Teachers*, ed. by Niels Thurlstrup and Marie Mikulová Thulstrup, Copenhagen: C.A. Reitzel 1982 (*Bibliotheca Kierkegaardiana*, vol. 10), pp. 177-207.

Soderquist, K. Brian, "Irony and Humor in Kierkegaard's Early Journals: Two Responses to an Emptied World," *Kierkegaard Studies. Yearbook*, 2003, pp. 143-167.

———, "Kierkegaard's Contribution to the Danish Discussion of 'Irony,'" *Kierkegaard and His Contemporaries: The Culture of Golden Age Denmark*, ed. by Jon Stewart, Berlin and New York: Walter de Gruyter 2003 (*Kierkegaard Studies. Monograph Series*, vol. 10), pp. 78-105.

———, *The Isolated Self: Truth and Untruth in Søren Kierkegaard's On the Concept of Irony*, Copenhagen: C.A. Reitzel 2007 (*Danish Golden Age Studies*, vol. 1).

Sponheim, Paul, *Kierkegaard on Christ and Christian Coherence*, Masters of Modern Theology Series, ed. by Jaroslav Pelikan, New York: Harper & Row 1968, pp. 58-66.

Stewart, Jon, *Heiberg's Introductory Lecture to the Logic Course and Other Texts*, ed. and trans. by Jon Stewart, Copenhagen: C.A. Reitzel 2007 (*Texts from Golden Age Denmark*, vol. 3).

———, *Heiberg's On the Significance of Philosophy for the Present Age and Other Texts*, ed. and trans. by Jon Stewart, Copenhagen: C.A. Reitzel 2005 (*Texts from Golden Age Denmark*, vol. 1).

———, *Heiberg's Speculative Logic and Other Texts*, ed. and trans. by Jon Stewart, Copenhagen: C.A. Reitzel 2006 (*Texts from Golden Age Denmark*, vol. 2).

———, *A History of Hegelianism in Golden Age Denmark,* Tome I: *The Heiberg Period: 1824-1836*, Copenhagen: C.A. Reitzel 2007 (*Danish Golden Age Studies*, vol. 3).

———, *A History of Hegelianism in Golden Age Denmark,* Tome II: *The Martensen Period: 1837-1842*, Copenhagen: C.A. Reitzel 2007 (*Danish Golden Age Studies*, vol. 3).

———, "Kierkegaard and Hegelianism in Golden Age Denmark," *Kierkegaard and His Contemporaries: The Culture of Golden Age Denmark*, ed. by Jon Stewart. Berlin and New York: Walter de Gruyter 2003 (*Kierkegaard Studies. Monograph Series,* vol. 10), pp. 106-145.

_____, "Kierkegaard's Criticism of Martensen in the *Concluding Unscientific Postscript*," *Revue Roumaine de Philosophie*, tome 45, nos. 1-2, 2001, pp. 133-148.

_____, *Kierkegaard's Relations to Hegel Reconsidered*, Cambridge and New York: Cambridge University Press 2003.

_____, "Martensen's 'Rationalism, Supernaturalism and the *principium exclusi medii*,' " trans. and introduced by Jon Stewart, *Kierkegaard Studies. Yearbook*, 2004, 583-598.

_____, "Mynster's 'Rationalism, Supernaturalism,' " trans. and introduced by Jon Stewart, *Kierkegaard Studies. Yearbook*, 2004, 565-582.

_____, "Schleiermacher's Visit to Copenhagen in 1833," *Journal for the History of Modern Philosophy*, vol. 11, issue 2, 2004, pp. 279-302.

_____, "The Paradox and the Criticism of Hegelian Mediation in *Philosophical Fragments*," *Kierkegaard Studies. Yearbook*, 2004, pp. 186-209.

Teisen, N., *Kort Indlæg i Sagen mellem S. Kierkegaard og H.L. Martensen. Et Lejlighedsskrift*, Copenhagen: Karl Schønbergs Forlag 1884.

Thompson, Curtis L. and David J. Kangas (eds.), *Between Hegel and Kierkegaard: Hans L. Martensen's Philosophy of Religion*, trans. by Curtis L. Thompson and David J. Kangas, Atlanta: Scholars Press 1997.

Thompson, Curtis L., "From Presupposing Pantheism's Power to Poten-tiating Panentheism's Personality: Seeking Parallels between Kierkegaard's and Martensen's Theological Anthropology," *The Journal of Religion*, vol. 82, 2002, pp. 225-251.

_____, "H.L. Martensen's Theological Anthropology," in *Faith, Knowledge and Action*, ed. by G.L. Stengren, Copenhagen: C.A. Reitzel 1984, pp. 199-216, and reprinted in slightly modified form in *Kierkegaard and His Contemporaries: The Culture of Golden Age Denmark*, ed. by Jon Stewart, Berlin and New York: Walter de Gruyter 2003 (*Kierkegaard Studies. Monograph Series*, vol. 10), pp. 164-180.

_____, *The Logic of Theonomy: Hans Lassen Martensen's Theological Method*, Chicago: Ph.D. dissertation, Chicago: The University of Chicago 1985.

Thulstrup, Marie Mikulová, "Plato's Vision and its Interpretation," *Kierkegaard's Classical Inspiration*, ed. by Niels Thulstrup and Marie Mikulová Thulstrup, Copenhagen: C.A. Reitzel 1982 (*Bibliotheca Kierkegaardiana*, vol. 14), pp. 63-103.

Thulstrup, Niels, *Kierkegaard's Relation to Hegel*, trans. by George L. Stengren, Princeton: Princeton University Press 1980.

———, "Martensen's *Dogmatics* and its Reception," *Kierkegaard and the Church in Denmark*, Copenhagen: C.A. Reitzel 1984 (*Bibliotheca Kierkegaardiana*, vol. 13), pp. 169-197, and reprinted in slightly modified form in *Kierkegaard and His Contemporaries: The Culture of Golden Age Denmark*, ed. by Jon Stewart, Berlin and New York: Walter de Gruyter 2003 (*Kierkegaard Studies. Monograph Series*, vol. 10), pp. 181-202.

Waaler, Arild, and Christian Fink Tolstrup, "*Philosophical Fragments*—in Response to the Debate between Mynster and Martensen," *Kierkegaard Studies. Yearbook*, 2004, pp. 208-234.

Wolff, A.A., *Talmudfjender. Et Gemæle mod de seneste Angreb paa Jøderne og Jødedommen*, Copenhagen: C.A. Reitzel 1878.

*Other Works*

Adorno, Theodor W., *Kierkegaard: Construction of the Aesthetic*, trans., ed., and with a foreword by Robert Hullot-Kentor, Minneapolis: University of Minnesota 1989.

Arbaugh, George E. and George B. Arbaugh, *Kierkegaard's Authorship: A Guide to the Writings of Kierkegaard*, Rock Island, IL: Augustana College Library 1967.

Baader, Franz, *Sämmtliche Werke*, vols. 1-16, ed. by F. Hoffmann, Leipzig: Hermann Bethmann Verlag 1851.

Bowen, Ralph H., *German Theories of the Corporate State: With Special Reference to the Period 1870-1919*, New York: Russell & Russell 1947.

Clausen, Henrik Nicolai, *Optegnelser om mit Levneds og min Tids Historie*, Copenhagen: G.E.C. Gad 1877.

Clayton, Philip, *The Problem of God in Modern Thought*, Grand Rapids, MI: Eerdmans 2000.

Cole, J. Preston, *The Problematic Self in Kierkegaard and Freud*, New Haven and London: Yale University Press 1971.

Collins, James, *The Mind of Kierkegaard*, Chicago: Henry Regnery 1953.

Connell, George B. and C. Stephen Evans (eds.), *Foundations of Kierkegaard's Vision of Community: Religion, Ethics, and Politics in Kierkegaard*, Atlantic Highlands, N.J. and London: Humanities 1992.

Croxall, T.H., *Kierkegaard Studies*, London and Redhill: Lutterworth 1948.

Daise, Benjamin, *Kierkegaard's Socratic Art*, Macon, GA: Mercer University Press 1999.

Dibner, Bern, *Oersted and the Discovery of Electromagnetism*, New York: Blaisdell 1962.

Dorner, I.A., *Entwicklungsgeschichte der Lehre von der person Christ*, vols. 1-4, Stuttgart: [n.n.] 1839. (English translation: *History of the Development of the Doctrine of the Person of Christ*, vols. 1-5. Edinburgh: [n.n.] 1861-1863.)

Dupré, Louis, *Kierkegaard as Theologian*, London and New York: Sheed & Ward 1963.

Elrod, John W., *Being and Existence in Kierkegaard's Pseudonymous Works*, Princeton: Princeton University Press 1975.

———, *Kierkegaard and Christendom*, Princeton: Princeton University Press 1981.

Evans, C. Stephen, *Kierkegaard's Ethic of Love: Divine Commands and Moral Obligations*, Oxford: Oxford University Press 2004.

———, *Kierkegaard on Faith and the Self: Collected Essays*, Waco, TX: Baylor University Press 2006.

———, *Kierkegaard's Fragments and Postscript: The Religious Philosophy of Johannes Climacus*, Atlantic Highlands, N.J.: Humanities Press International 1983.

———, *Søren Kierkegaard's Christian Psychology: Insight for Counseling & Pastoral Care*, Grand Rapids, MI: Zondervan 1980.

Fenger, Henning, *The Heibergs*, trans. by Frederick J. Marker, New York: Twayne 1971.

Fenves, Peter, *"Chatter": Language and History in Kierkegaard*, Stanford: Stanford University Press 1993.

Ferguson, Harvie, *Melanchology and the Critique of Modernity: Søren Kierkegaard's Religious Psychology*, London and New York: Routledge 1995.

Feuerbach, Ludwig, *The Essence of Christianity*, trans. by George Eliot, with an introductory essay by Karl Barth and a Foreword by H. Richard Niebuhr, New York: Harper & Row 1957.

Fichte, Johann Gottlieb, *Science of Knowledge (Wissenschaftslehre): With the First and Second Introductions*, ed. and trans. by Peter Heath and John Lachs, New York: Meredith Corporation 1970; reissued edition, Cambridge: Cambridge University Press 1982.

Gadamer, Hans-Georg, *Truth and Method*, trans. by Garrett Barden and John Cumming, New York: Seabury 1975.

Gardiner, Patrick, *Kierkegaard*, Oxford: Oxford University Press 1988.

Gouwens, David J., *Kierkegaard as Religious Thinker*, Cambridge: Cambridge University Press 1996.

Green, Garrett, *Imagining God: Theology and the Religious Imagination*, New York: Harper & Row, San Francisco 1989.

Green, Ronald M., *Kierkegaard and Kant: The Hidden Debt*, Albany: State University of New York 1992.

Grundtvig, N.F.S., *Udvalgte Skrifter*, vols. 1-10, ed. by H. Begtrup, Copenhagen: Gyldendal 1904.

Hall, Amy Laura, *Kierkegaard and the Treachery of Love*, Cambridge: Cambridge University Press 2002.

Hall, Ronald L., *Word and Spirit: A Kierkegaardian Critique of the Modern Age*, Bloomington and Indianapolis: Indiana University Press 1993.

Hannay, Alastair, *Kierkegaard: A Biography*, Cambridge: Cambridge University Press 2001.

———, *Papers and Journals: A Selection*, trans. with introductions and notes by Alastair Hannay, London: Penguin Books 1996.

Hartshorne, Charles, *The Divine Relativity: A Social Conception of God*, New Haven: Yale University Press 1948.

Hegel, G.W.F., *The Encyclopaedia Logic. Part One of the Encyclopaedia of the Philosophical Sciences*, trans. by T.F. Gerats, W.A. Suchting, and H.S. Harris, Indianapolis: Hackett 1991.

———, *Hegel's Aesthetics. Lectures on Fine Art*, vols. 1-2, trans. by T.M. Knox, Oxford: Clarendon Press 1975.

_____, *Hegel's Phenomenology of Spirit*, trans. by A.V. Miller, Oxford: Clarendon Press 1977.

_____, *Hegel's Philosophy of Mind. Part Three of the Encyclopaedia of the Philosophical Sciences*, trans. by William Wallace and A.V. Miller, Oxford: Clarendon Press 1971.

_____, *Hegel's Philosophy of Nature. Part Two of the Encyclopaedia of the Philosophical Sciences*, trans. by A.V. Miller, Oxford: Clarendon Press 1970.

_____, *Hegel's Science of Logic*, trans. by A.V. Miller, London: George Allen and Unwin 1989.

_____, *Lectures on the History of Philosophy*, vols. 1-3., trans. by E.S. Haldane, London: K. Paul, Trench, Trübner 1892-1896; Lincoln and London: University of Nebraska Press 1955.

_____, *The Philosophy of History*, trans. by J. Sibree, New York: Willey 1944.

_____, *Sämtliche Werke. Jubiläumsausgabe in 20 Bänden*, ed. by Hermann Glockner, Stuttgart: Friedrich Frommann 1928-1941.

Heiberg, Johanne Luise, *Et liv genoplevet i erindringen*, vols 1-4, Copenhagen: Gyldendal 1973.

Herbert, R.T., *Paradox and Identity in Theology*, Ithaca and London: Cornell University Press 1979.

Houe, Poul and Marino, Gordon D. (eds.), *Søren Kierkegaard and the Word(s): Essays on Hermeneutics and Communication*, Copenhagen: C.A. Reitzel 2003.

Houe, Poul, Gordon D. Marino, and Sven Hakon Rossel (eds.), *Anthropology and Authority: Essays on Søren Kierkegaard*, Amsterdam and Atlanta, GA: Rodopi 2000.

Hovde, B.J., *The Scandinavian Countries, 1720-1865: The Rise of the Middle Classes*, vols.1-2, Ithaca: Cornell University Press 1948.

Johnson, Howard A. and Niels Thulstrup (eds.), *A Kierkegaard Critique*, Chicago: Henry Regnery Company 1962.

Kangas, David J., *Kierkegaard's Instant: On Beginnings*. Bloomington and Indianapolis: Indiana University Press 2007.

Kant, Immanuel, *Religion Within the Limits of Reason Alone*, trans. with an introduction and notes by Theodore M. Greene and Hoyt H. Hudson with a new essay The Ethical Significance of Kant's Religion by John R. Silber, New York: Harper & Row, Harper Torchbooks 1960.

Kelly, George Armstrong, *Idealism, Politics and History: Sources of Hegelian Thought*, Cambridge: Cambridge University Press 1969.

Kierkegaard, Søren Aabye, *The Book on Adler*, trans. by Howard V. Hong and Edna H. Hong, Princeton: Princeton University Press 1998.

_____, *Breve og Aktstykker vedrørende Søren Kierkegaard*, vols. 1-2, ed. by Niels Thulstrup, Copenhagen: Munksgaard 1953-1954.

_____, *Christian Discourses. The Crisis and a Crisis in the Life of an Actress*, trans. by Howard V. Hong and Edna H. Hong, Princeton: Princeton University Press 1997.

_____, *The Concept of Anxiety*, trans. by Reidar Thomte in collaboration with Albert B. Anderson, Princeton: Princeton University Press 1980.

_____, *The Concept of Irony; Schelling Lecture Notes*, trans. by Howard V. Hong and Edna H. Hong, Princeton: Princeton University Press 1989.

_____, *Concluding Unscientific Postscript*, vols. 1-2, trans. by Howard V. Hong and Edna H. Hong, Princeton: Princeton University Press 1992.

_____, *The Corsair Affair; Articles Related to the Writings*, trans. by Howard V. Hong and Edna H. Hong, Princeton: Princeton University Press 1982.

_____, *Early Polemical Writings: From the Papers of One Still Living; Articles from Student Days; The Battle between the Old and the New Soap-Cellars*, trans. by Julia Watkin, Princeton: Princeton University Press 1990.

_____, *Eighteen Upbuilding Discourses*, trans. by Howard V. Hong and Edna H. Hong, Princeton: Princeton University Press 1990.

_____, *Either / Or*, vols. 1-2, trans. by Howard V. Hong and Edna H. Hong, Princeton: Princeton University Press 1987.

_____, *Fear and Trembling; Repetition*, trans. by Howard V. Hong and Edna H. Hong, Princeton: Princeton University Press 1983.

_____, *Johannes Climacus, or De omnibus dubitandum est*, trans. by Howard V. Hong and Edna H. Hong, Princeton: Princeton University Press 1986.

_____, *Kierkegaard: Letters and Documents*, trans. by Henrik Rosenmeier, Princeton: Princeton University Press 1978.

———, *Kierkegaard's Writings*, vols. 1-26, trans. by Howard V. Hong and Edna H. Hong, Princeton: Princeton University Press 1978-2000.

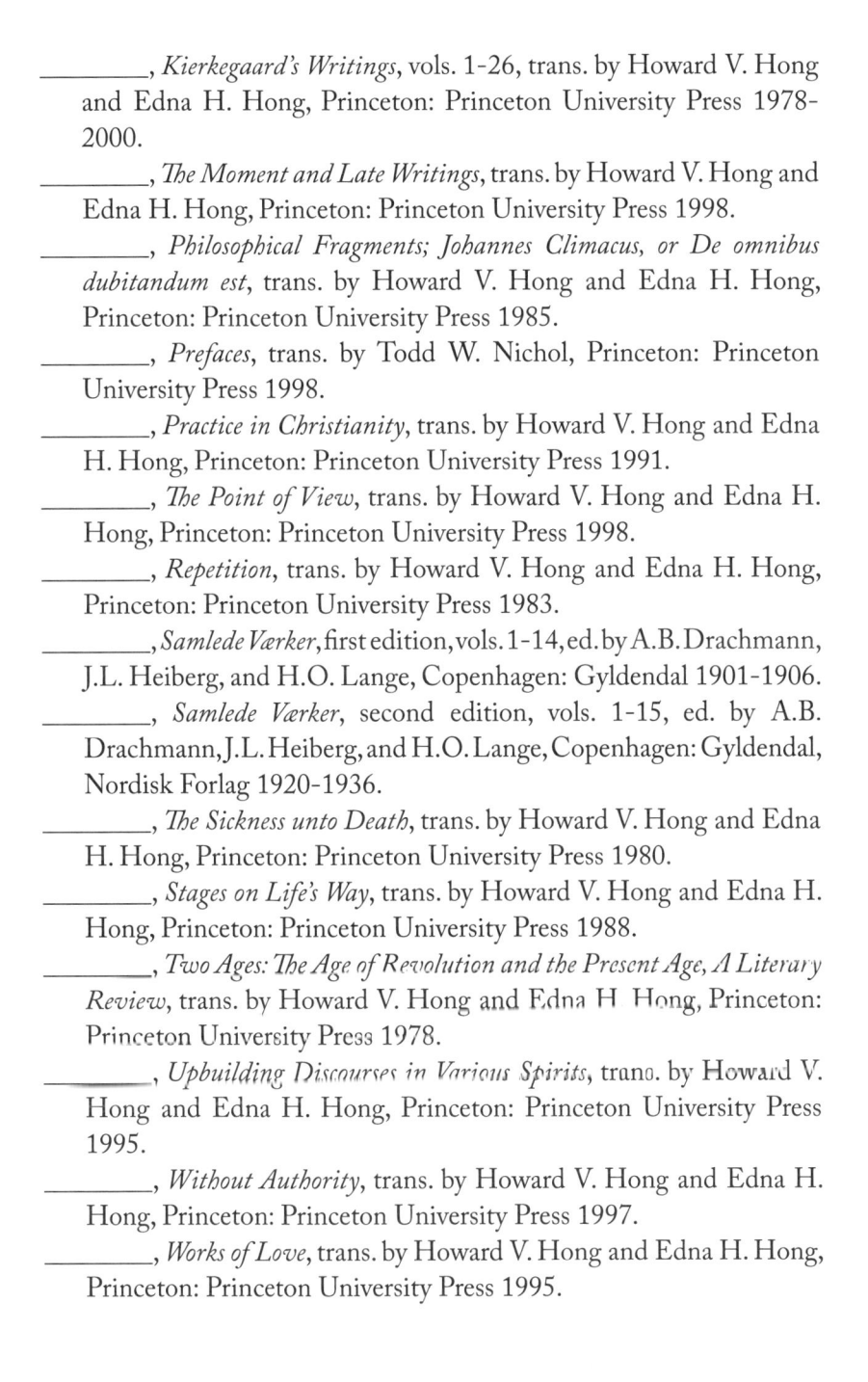

———, *The Moment and Late Writings*, trans. by Howard V. Hong and Edna H. Hong, Princeton: Princeton University Press 1998.

———, *Philosophical Fragments; Johannes Climacus, or De omnibus dubitandum est*, trans. by Howard V. Hong and Edna H. Hong, Princeton: Princeton University Press 1985.

———, *Prefaces*, trans. by Todd W. Nichol, Princeton: Princeton University Press 1998.

———, *Practice in Christianity*, trans. by Howard V. Hong and Edna H. Hong, Princeton: Princeton University Press 1991.

———, *The Point of View*, trans. by Howard V. Hong and Edna H. Hong, Princeton: Princeton University Press 1998.

———, *Repetition*, trans. by Howard V. Hong and Edna H. Hong, Princeton: Princeton University Press 1983.

———, *Samlede Værker*, first edition, vols. 1-14, ed. by A.B. Drachmann, J.L. Heiberg, and H.O. Lange, Copenhagen: Gyldendal 1901-1906.

———, *Samlede Værker*, second edition, vols. 1-15, ed. by A.B. Drachmann, J.L. Heiberg, and H.O. Lange, Copenhagen: Gyldendal, Nordisk Forlag 1920-1936.

———, *The Sickness unto Death*, trans. by Howard V. Hong and Edna H. Hong, Princeton: Princeton University Press 1980.

———, *Stages on Life's Way*, trans. by Howard V. Hong and Edna H. Hong, Princeton: Princeton University Press 1988.

———, *Two Ages: The Age of Revolution and the Present Age, A Literary Review*, trans. by Howard V. Hong and Edna H. Hong, Princeton: Princeton University Press 1978.

———, *Upbuilding Discourses in Various Spirits*, trans. by Howard V. Hong and Edna H. Hong, Princeton: Princeton University Press 1995.

———, *Without Authority*, trans. by Howard V. Hong and Edna H. Hong, Princeton: Princeton University Press 1997.

———, *Works of Love*, trans. by Howard V. Hong and Edna H. Hong, Princeton: Princeton University Press 1995.

*Søren Kierkegaard's Journals and Papers*, vols. 1-7, ed. and trans. by Howard V. Hong and Edna H. Hong, Princeton: Princeton University Press 1967-1978.

*Søren Kierkegaards Papirer*, vols. 1-16, ed. by P.A. Heiberg, V. Kuhr, and E. Torstin, Copenhagen: Gyldendal 1908-1948; supplemented by Niels Thulstrup, Copenhagen: Gyldendal 1968-1978.

*Søren Kierkegaards Skrifter*, vols. 1-28, K1-28, ed. by Niels Jørgen Cappelørn, et al., Copenhagen: Gad 1997-.

Lichtenberger, F., *History of German Theology in the Nineteenth Century*, trans. and ed. by W. Hastie. Edinburgh: T & T Clark 1889.

Lippitt, John, *Kierkegaard and* Fear and Trembling, London and New York: Routledge 2003.

Lowrie, Walter. *Kierkegaard*, vols. 1-2. New York: Oxford University 1938; reprint edition, New York: Harper & Brothers, Harper Torchbooks 1962.

Malantschuk, Gregor, *Kierkegaard's Concept of Existence*, ed. and trans. by Howard V. Hong and Edna H. Hong, Milwaukee: Marquette University 2003.

―――――, *Kierkegaard's Thought*, ed. and trans. by Howard V. Hong and Edna H. Hong, Princeton: Princeton University Press 1971.

Marino, Gordon, *Kierkegaard in the Present Age*, Milwaukee: Marquette University 2001.

Marmysz, John, *Laughing at Nothing: Humor as a Response to Nihilism*, Albany: State University of New York 2003.

Matuštík, Martin J. and Westphal, Merold (eds.), *Kierkegaard in Post/Modernity*, Bloomington and Indianapolis: Indiana University 1995.

Mooney, Edward F., *Knights of Faith and Resignation: Reading Kierkegaard's* Fear and Trembling, Albany: State University of New York 1991.

―――――, *Selves in Discord and Resolve: Kierkegaard's Moral-Religious Psychology from* Either/Or *to* Sickness Unto Death, New York and London: Routledge 1996.

Mynster, C.L.N. (ed.), *Breve til og fra F.C. Sibbern*, vols. 1-2, Copenhagen: Gyldendal 1866.

Mynster, Jakob Peter, *Om Begrebet af den christelige Dogmatik*, Copenhagen: Gyldendal 1831.

_____, *Betragtninger over de christelige Troeslærdomme*, 3rd ed., vols. 1-2, Copenhagen: Deichmann 1846.

_____, *Blandede Skrifter*, vols. 1-6, Copenhagen: Gyldendal 1856.

_____, *Meddelelser om mit Levnet*, Copenhagen: Gyldendal 1854.

Ørsted, Hans Christian, *Aanden i Naturen*, Copenhagen: A.F. Høst 1850. (English translation: *The Soul of Nature, with Supplementary Contributions*, trans. from the German by Leonora and Joanna B. Horner, London: Henry G. Bohn 1852.)

Pattison, George, *Kierkegaard's Upbuilding Discourses: Philosophy, Theology, Literature*, London and New York: Routledge 2002.

Rée, Jonathan and Chamberlain, Jane (eds.), *Kierkegaard: A Critical Reader*, Oxford and Malden, MA: Blackwell 1998.

Ricoeur, Paul, *Time and Narrative*, vols. 1-3, Chicago: University of Chicago 1984-1988.

Roberts, David E., *Existentialism and Religious Belief*, New York: Oxford University Press 1959.

Rorty, Richard, *Contingency, Irony and Solidarity*, Cambridge and New York: Cambridge University Press 1989.

Rorty, Richard and Vattimo, Gianni, *The Future of Religion*, ed. by Santiago Zabala, New York: Columbia University Press 2005.

Schelling, F.W.J., *The Ages of the World: (Fragments) from the Handwritten Remains, Third Version (c. 1815)*, trans. by Jason M. Wirth, Albany: State University of New York 2000.

_____, *Sämmtliche Werke*, vols. 1-14, ed. by K.F.A. Schelling, Stuttgart: J.G. Cotta 1856ff.

_____, *Of Human Freedom*, trans. with a critical Introduction and Notes by James Gutman, Chicago: Open Court 1936.

Schiller, Friedrich, *An Anthology for Our Time*, in new English translations and the original German, with an account of his life and work by Frederick Ungar, New York: Frederick Ungar 1959.

Schleiermacher, Friedrich, *The Christian Faith*, English translation of the second German edition, ed. by H.R. Mackintosh and J.S. Stewart, Edinburgh: T.&T. Clark 1928.

Smith, Ronald Gregor, *Journals 1853-55*, London: Collins 1965.

Sontag, Frederick, *A Kierkegaard Handbook*, Atlanta: John Knox 1979.
Sponheim, Paul R., *Faith and the Other: A Relational Theology*, Minneapolis: Fortress 1993.
―――――, *God—The Question and the Quest: Toward a Conversation Concerning Christian Faith*, Philadelphia: Fortress 1985.
―――――, *The Pulse of Creation: God and the Transformation of the World*, Minneapolis: Fortress 1999.
―――――, *Speaking of God: A Relational View*, St. Louis: Chalice 2006.
Stack, George J., *Kierkegaard's Existential Ethics*, University, AL: University of Alabama 1977.
Steffens, Henrich, *Indledning til philosophiske Forelæsninger*, Copenhagen: Gyldendal 1803.
Stendahl, Brita K., *Søren Kierkegaard*, Boston: G.K. Hall & Co. 1976.
Strauss, David, *Life of Jesus*, vols. 1-2, trans. by George Eliot, London: [n.n.] 1843.
Strawser, Michael, *Both/And: Reading Kierkegaard from Irony to Edification*, New York: Fordham University 1997.
Taylor, Mark C., *Journeys to Selfhood: Hegel & Kierkegaard*, Berkeley: University of California 1980.
―――――, *Kierkegaard's Pseudonymous Authorship: A Study of Time and the Self*, Princeton: Princeton University Press 1975.
―――――, *The Moment of Complexity: Emerging Network Culture*, Chicago: University of Chicago 2003.
Theunissen, Michael, *Kierkegaard's Concept of Despair*, trans. by Barbara Harshav and Helmut Illbruck, Princeton: Princeton University 2005.
Thompson, Curtis L., "Interpreting God's Translucent World: Imagination, Possibility, Eternity," *Translucence: Religion, the Arts, and Imagination*, ed. by Carol Gilbertson and Gregg Muillenburg, Minneapolis: Fortress 2004, pp. 3-37.
Toews, John Edward, *Hegelianism: The Path toward Dialectical Humanism, 1805-1841*, Cambridge: Cambridge University 1980.
Walker, Jeremy, *To Will One Thing: Reflections on Kierkegaard's Purity of Heart*, Montreal and London: McGill—Queen's University Press 1972.

Walsh, Sylvia, *Living Poetically: Kierkegaard's Essential Writings*, University Park, PA: The Pennsylvania State University 1994.

Westphal, Merold, *Becoming a Self: A Reading of Kierkegaard's* Concluding Unscientific Postscript, West Lafayette, IN: Purdue University 1996.

―――――, *Kierkegaard's Critique of Reason and Society*, Macon, GA: Mercer University Press 1987.

Weston, Michael, *Kierkegaard and Modern Continental Philosophy: An Introduction*, London and New York: Routledge 1994.

Whitehead, Alfred, *Process and Reality: An Essay in Cosmology*, Correted Edition by David Ray Griffin and Donald W. Sherburne, New York: The Free Press 1978 [1929].

# Index

**absolute Spirit**, Hegel's view of discussed in *Autonomy* 13, in *Faust*, idea of as freedom 17, as God, who views people metaphysically as well as ethically 21.
**absolute truth**, ironic subject's subjective nihilism as 161.
**actuality**, in relation to God's possibilities 117, possibilities or non-being possess some 164, comparing to possibility, 165, God as pure actuality 173, God as not an actual something 175.
**Adler, Peter**, 108, 153.
**aesthetics**, 18, Hegel's *Aesthetics* 27.
**Andersen, J. Oskar**, 147.
**Anselm of Canterbury**, 67.
**apocalyptic poetry**, 6–9, 11, 17, 20, 102–103, 109, 114–115.
**appropriation**, 8–9, 36, Kierkegaard's, of Martensen xvii, Martensen's, of Hegel's thought 135.
**Aquinas, Thomas**, 67.
**Arildsen, Skat**, 147–149, 155, 159, 160–161.
**Aristotle**, 22.
**Art**, Faust-poem artistically expresses a theological vision 17, new form, speculative poetry, as transformative 19, artistic means of bringing emancipation 20, artistic aims of the state 31, as religious surrogate 31, power of 170.
**Athanasius of Alexandria**, 67.
**Augustine of Hippo**, 67, 11, 179
**authority**, 7, 42, 71, 79, 97, 100–101, 123, 35, 166.
**autonomy**, of natural theology as speculative theology 4, dissertation on 12–13, 68, 94, 109, 132, sectarian Anabaptists insist on relinquishing of 32.

**Baader, Franz von**, 9, 76, 152.
**Baggesen, Jens**, 113.
**baptism**, 36–37, 40–41, 43–44, 46–47, 100–101, 107–108, 115–119, 122–123, 152.
**Barth, Karl**, 155–158.
**belief**, existential crisis of 11, spiritless 71, against unbelief 72, 82, in theology as praxis-oriented 80, how skeptical doubt casts light on 195, attending baptism 109, and action as moments of Providence 170. *See also* faith.

Bidoulac, Virginie Henriette Constance, 47.
Birchedahl, Vilhelm, 44–45.
Böhme, Jacob, 178.
Bornemann, Frederik Christian, 2, 3, 9, 22.
Bornemann, John Alfred, 22.
Brandes, Georg, 17.
Brandt, Hermann, 10, 148.
Bremer, Fredrika, 48–49.
Brøchner, Hans, 30.

Catholicism, 28, 44, 72, 152.
Christ, as alpha and omega 69, and baptism 117, being united with God in 26, 39, biblical 43, 108, come to Jesus, or believe in him 38, and culture 36, equipping and endowing the baptized 40, as the eternal founder of the cultus 42, faith bound to 119, as the founder of faith 39, grasped by 36, has constituted the church 39, eternal, metaphysical relation of, to the human race 69, the imitation of 26, 88, the incarnate 24, includes the entire fullness of churchly life 40, kingly office of 43, new creation and redemption of human nature by 46, as an omnipresent idea 43, an organ, instrument, or organism of 39, personality of 12, 41, the preacher has been appropriated by 100, preachers come in the name of 39, relating to believers 41, the revelation of 24, 37, 45, royal will of 116, sacramentally reproduces his historical presence 43, as the Son of Man 87, and the Spirit 118, true human ideal found in 88, view of Jesus as the 108, who lives in the church's thought, faith, and devotion 43, would still have come, if no sin 69.
Christian, doctrine 44, humor 22, 162, tradition 7, paradox 128.
Christian the Eighth, King, 75.
Clausen, Henrik Nicolai, 17, 136.
comedy, 19–21, 93, 99, 114, 130, 162
comic, comical, 20–21, 11, 114-115, 122, tragicomic 168.
conscience, 7, 10, 64, 70, 72, 152, 171, 180, as witness of the Spirit 7, transmoral 179.
consciousness, absolute power in 15, believing or reborn 37, cultural 72, divine enlivening human 24, 35, duty- 11, 171, eternal 107, ethical 19, humoristic 20–21, identical with revelation 25, of the infinite 20, ironic 20–21, mystical 25–26, 95, nihilistic 19, philosophical tradition of 152, political 74, 76, postmodern 162, of reconciliation and revelation 63, 71–72, relations of, attractive and repulsive 62, religious 4, 31, 70, 75, self- 12, 25–26, 28, 35, 68, 152, of sin 70, 107, singular 20, 25, speculative 19, urge toward God's kingdom in 70, world 31.
Creator, divine creating, 10, 24, 52, 69, 87, 152, 156–157, 167, 170, 173–175.
creature, creaturely, 13, 53, 116, 156–158, 169, 171, 173–174.

## Index

Dante Alighieri, 109.
Daub, Karl, 64.
*De omnibus dubitandum est*, 93–94, 99, 101, 106, 112. *See also* doubt.
Descartes, René, 102–103, 112, 152.
dialectic, dialectical, 3, 9, 21, 50–51, 57, 98, 105, 116, 126, 130, 157–159, 164, between comedy and tragedy 21, dialectician 127, immanent, of Hegel 149, living 24, as mediating 159, method 25, 87, negative 121, 158, positive 167, thinking 25, 87, validity of 117, *See also* logic.
dogma, dogmatic, 29-74 passim, Anabaptist view of 103, Christian 45, 48, 79, 144, 147, 179, concept 50, and ethics 143, infant baptism, justified 36–37, modern 71, publics of dogmatic theology 1, 44, 74, Schleiermacher's 3, 6, speculative 16, 46, 50, 67, 94, 110, 127, theology 4, 5, 30, 46, 48, 50, 67–68, 71, 74, thinker 116, Straussian 34, of the Trinity, 72–73.
Dorner, Isaak August, 30, 90.
doubt, 32, 103, self-doubts 79, doubting everything 99, 101–103, 105–106, 112. *See also de omnibus dubitandum est.*

Eckhart, Meister, 26, 168–169.
Eiríksson, Magnús, 46, 152.
Either/Or, 23. *See also* mediation.
Engelstoft, Christian Thorning, 95–96.
Erasmus, Desiderius, 179.

ethical, the, 19, 21, 26–28, 109, 121, 123, 141, 164 –165.
evil, 21, 32, 102, 110, 132.

faith, 5, 7, 15, 20, 29, 31, 34, 37–44, 48–49, 51, 56–57, 59–60, 62–67, 71–72, 74, 89, 102–104, 108–109, 119, 121, 130–131, 135, 149, 151, 156–158, 160–161, 166–167, 169–170, 174 –175, 177, 180– 181. *See also* belief.
Fall, the, fallen, 21, 74, 110.
Faust, 182.
Fenger, Henning, 99.
Feuerbach, Ludwig, 31.
Fichte, Johann Gottlieb, 3, 30.
Frederick VII, King, 99.
freedom, 3, 7–8, 12, 15, 17, 19-20, 26–29, 35–36, 38, 44, 46, 52–53, 72, 78, 80, 87, 104, 111, 121, 131–132, 145, 160–161, 163, 170–174, 176–180.

Gadamer, Hans-Georg, 145.
Garff, Joakim, 93, 98–99, 151.
Girard, René, 129.
God, as the actuality of the possible 173–174, of the Anabaptists 32, autonomy of 13, becoming human 24, 69 71, 96, bestower of freedom 172–173, can change everything into a sacrament 117, and Christ, too little of in church 34, Christ's individuality includes the entire fullness of 44, Christian concept of 51–54, Christian worship of 80, commitment of, to the church 39, comprehensibility of 65,

**God** (cont.)
of conventional religion 25, cultus and 42, dipolar 162–163, 170, 172–173, 175, disclosing Godhead is revelation 25, in *divina comedia*, as absolute spirit 21, doctrine of 64, duties to, as opposed to duties to reason 161, essence of and kingdom of 12–13, essence of reflected in the word of reconciliation 73, as eternal freedom 174, 178, eternal resolve of 174, as Father, Son, and Spirit 176–177, has chosen the lonely xv, 123, human being united with 26, humans created in the image of 87, human's separation from and unity with 4, as infinite personality in Christian religion 4, 11, 176, infinite qualitative difference between human and 158, Karl Barth's view of 156, Kierkegaard's attack attracted deniers of 84, Kierkegaard emphasizes more relating to than conceiving of 169, knowledge of, conditioned by faith 63, 65, light of 72, as love or loving 172–173, 180, mystery of the kingdom of 146, as most rigorous in relation to voluntariness 179, nihilism as part of the human's relation with 166–167, 169, parallel views of Kierkegaard and Martensen on human's relation to 131, as possibilizer 174, practical and contemplative relations to 63, as present 175, proclaiming word of, to king and queen 45, has possibilities at every moment 178, proof of, rendered superfluous by conscience 152, as pure actuality 173, relation with as empowering presence 157, religious righteousness as before 111, same revelation of, in kingdoms of nature and grace 88, speculative knowledge of 149, urge toward kingdom of 70, when kingdom of, had become just like nature 41, working through possibilities 119, 145.

**Godhead**, 25, 39.
**Goethe, J.W.**, 2, 19, 87.
**Göschel, K.F.**, 9.
**grace**, 21, 37–38, 42, 46–47, 88, 108, 111, 116–119, 170, 179.
**Grane, Leif**, 12, 148.
**Gregory of Nazianzus**, 67.
**Gregory of Nissa**, 67.
**Grundtvig, N.F.S.**, 44, 78.
**Grundtvigian**, 7.
**Gude, Ludvig Jacob Mendel**, 88–89, 149.

**Hartshorne, Charles**, 172.
**Hegel, Georg Wilhelm Friedrich**, 3–4, 9–10, 13, 15, 24–25, 27–28, 35, 48, 66, 92–94, 97–98, 103–105, 109, 111–112, 115, 121–122, 148–149, 151–155, 169, 181.
**Heiberg, Johan Ludvig**, xvi, 3, 13, 18–20, 30, 68, 88–89, 93–94, 96, 98–99, 102–193, 109, 111, 113–115, 121, 123, 150–151, 153–155, 159.
**Herder, J. G.**, 6.

history, 6–8, 12–13, 15–17, 26, 33, 41, 63, 67, 71, 73, 78, 81, 85–86, 94, 102, 108, 112, 117–118, 145–146, 148–152. *See also* positivity and tradition.
Holberg, Ludvig, 112.
holy, the, amidst the sects 39, baptism 41, chain of witnesses to the truth 134, 139, community of, is presupposition for, individual 39, every, consumption can become a Eucharist 117, polemic *ad extra* 33, and the profane 32, relation of the will to God 65, *See also* "Scriptures" and "Spirit."
Horn, Robert Leslie, 4, 149–150.
humor, humoristic, the, 20 –22, 59, 61, 95–96, 115, 123, 155, 162, 164–165, 168–169.

idea, the, 4, 6–7, 12–13, 17, 33 –34, 40, 50, 67–68, 118, 163–166, 168, Christian 7, or the divine mystery's purpose 166, of Faust 68, the fundamental 50, a great coherent 67, infinite possibilities of 118, Kierkegaard's work in the service of 141, of personality 28, practical 28, speculative 17.
illusion, 122, 130.
image, imagery, 25, 43–44, 62, 87, 57.
imagination, 109, 178, as captured by philosophy 102, as organ for presenting possibilities 164.
immediacy, 94, 112, 131.
incarnation, 12, 23–24, 54, 69, becoming human 69-71, 96.
indirect communication, 58–59, 134, 150.

intuition, 5, 50–51, 63, 66–67, 73.
inwardness, 110, 124, 169, 176.
Irenaeus, St., 50, 67.
irony, 19–21, 29, 59, 95, 97–98, 151, 155, 162, 164–165, along with humor, encompassed by irony 20, 62, as the boundary between the aesthetic and the ethical 164, as having less skepticism than humor 95, as a negative form of the comical 21, nihilism plays a role in 165, situated at the heart of romanticism 19, 162.

Jacobi, Friedrich Heinrich, 86.
James, William, 167.
Justice, 72, 81, 168.

Kant, Immanuel, 12, 15, 66, 94.
Kierkegaard, Peter Christian, 101, 126–127.
Kierkegaard, Søren Aabye,
*The Concept of Anxiety*, 100, 108–112.
*The Concept of Irony*, 18, 29, 92, 95, 97–98, 151, 155.
*Concluding Unscientific Postscript*, vols. 1-2, 100, 115, 119–121, 134, 164.
*The Battle between the Old and the New Soap-Cellars*, 98–99.
*Either/Or* 102–103.
*Fear and Trembling*, 100, 103.
*Johannes Climacus, or De omnibus dubitandum est*, 84, 100–101, 103.
*The Moment and Late Writings*, 82, 135–139, 141–145.
*Philosophical Fragments*, 104–108, 115.
*Prefaces*, 100, 111.
*Practice in Christianity*, 133.

**Kierkegaard** (cont.)
*Repetition*, 103–104.
*The Sickness unto Death*, 130–131.
*Stages on Life's Way*, 112-115.
*Two Ages*, 100.
*Upbuilding Discourses in Various Spirits*, 100.
*Works of Love*, 171, 174.
**Kirmmse, Bruce H.**, 150.
**knowledge**, 13, 26–28, 33, 37, 48, 51–52, 56–68, 98, 104, 107, 113, 120, 141, 148–149, 157, 160, comprehensive, of the concept 28, 157, ethical 27, rational 13, speculative 52, 149, theological 65–66.
**Koch, Carl Henrik**, 152.
**Kolthoff, E.G.**, 6.

**Laub, Otto**, 90.
**Lenau, N.F.N.** (von Strehlenau), 10–11, 17, 93, 102.
**Lessing, G.E.**, 87.
**Logic, logical**, 115, 22, 63, Hegel's 13, 93, Heiberg's 26, 155, of theonomy 63, 80, 88, 98. See also dialectic.
**love**, 72, 88, absolute, as relational 173, of the arts 144, creation's longing after the perfect community of, with God 70, divine attributes united in 54, duty to, in which God desires the world to share 174, human freedom empowered to give itself in 177, makes free 171, eternal 52, faith active in 161, faith and 39, freedom's fulfillment in 12, goodness revealed as 54, humor contains the fullness of 21, matrimonial 59, as the one substantive quality of God 172, as part of God's dipolarity 176, total presence of, as beyond humans 168, turning to fanaticism 32, as unchangeable 172, united with God in 26.
**Luther, Martin**, 38, 44, 50, 67, 125, 179.
**Lutheran Church**, 36–37, 71, 78, 80, 100.

**Marheineke, Philipp**, 30.
**Martensen, Anna Marie**, 2.
**Martensen, Hans Anderson**, 2.
**Martensen, Hans Lassen**,
"Priisopgave," 4–6, 51.
"*E.G. Kolthoff: Apocalypsis Joanni Apostolo vindicata*," 6–9, 103.
*Ueber Lenau's Faust* and "Betragtninger over Ideen af Faust. Med Hensyn paa Lenaus Faust," 9–11, 17–18, 68, 93, 102, 113–114, 182.
"Review of the *Introductory Lecture to the Logic Course at the Royal Military College that Began in November 1834*," 13–15, 26.
*The Autonomy of Human Self-Consciousness in Modern Dogmatic Theology*, 12–13, 15, 22, 66, 94, 109, 152.
"Forelæsninger over Indledning til speculative Dogmatik." 16, 94, 102.
"*Fata Morgana: Eventyr-Comedie* af J.L. Heiberg," "Forelæsninger over den nyere Philosophies

# Index

Historie fra Kant til Hegel," 16, 94, 102.
"Forelæsninger over "Speculativ Dogmatik," 16, 46, 50, 94, 102, 110, 131.
"Rationalisme, Supranaturalisme og principium exclusi medii," 22–23, 35, 106.
"Filosofiske Beskedenhed i Københavnsposten" and "Erklæring," 30.
*Meister Eckhart: A Study in Speculative Theology*, 25–26, 168–169.
"*Nye Digte* af J.L. Heiberg," 20, 22, 94, 114–115.
*Outline to a System of Moral Philosophy*, 26–28, 94, 110, 131, 152, 170–171.
"Nutidens Religiøse Crisis," 30–36, *Den christelige Daab betragtet med Hensyn paa det baptistiske Spørgsmaal*, 36–44, 46–47, 100–101, 103, 106–108, 115–119, 122–123, 152.
"Kirke-Aaret," 44-47.
"Litterait Uvæsen," 46.
*Christian Dogmatics*, 45, 48, 51–54, 124, 130.
"Sendschreiben an den Herrn Oberconsistorialrath Nielsen in Schleswig," 79
*Dogmatiske Oplysninger*, 54–74
"Om Gudstjenstens Indretning i den lutherske Kirke," 80.
"Sermon Delivered in Christiansborg Castle Church on the Fifth Sunday after Epiphany, February 5, 1854, the Sunday before Bishop Dr. Mynster's Funeral," 135.

"Til Geistligheden I Sjællands Stift," 82.
"On the Occasion of Dr. S. Kierkegaard's Article in *Fædrelandet* , no. 295," 82.
*Til Erindring om J.P. Mynster*, 85–88.
*Christian Ethics*, 74, 162.
*Af mit Levnet*, 2, 6, 9–11, 13, 29–30, 36, 45, 47, 55–56, 75, 78–79, 81–82, 84, 86.
Martensen, Virginie Henriette Constance Bidoulac, 47.
mediation, 24–25, 50, 68, 105–106, 111, 149, 159, 171.
method, 12, 28, 557, 58, 84, 112, 161, dialectical 97, speculative 51, 66, syllogistic 56, theological 50, 54, 63.
modern philosophy, 15, 17, 67, 94.
Møller, Poul Martin, 17, 153, 159.
moment, 102, 174, 179, of the church's unity 37, contemplative, of faith 43–44, of cultus and culture 31, 34, of individuality and of the race 110, of infinite beginning 40, liberalism destined to become subordinate 77, of passion 64, single understanding as 28, subjective 7, of substantiality 27, three, of mimesis 19, three, of mystical consciousness 25–26, of truth 33.
Monrad, Ditler Gothard, 77–78.
Mynster, Jakob Peter, xvi, 22–23, 30, 35–36, 44–45, 64, 68, 79, 81, 85–88, 91, 101, 123, 133–135, 137–140, 150, 153, 159.
mystery, 24–26, 40, 42, 47, 52, 104, 146, 164–169.

mythology, myths, 7, 33, 134, 158.

Nannestad, V., 146–147.
natural theology, 4.
necessity, Christi's sacramental presence as merely an immediate natural 117, faith as a freedom containing but transcending 121, faith as more than 15, inner, as impressed upon one's action 179, love as the moment of, in freedom 171, of means of grace 117, of not stopping with faith 109, rational, of objectivity 24, of thought 4, unconditional, of emergency baptism 118.
negation, 166–167.
Nielsen, N., 79.
Nielsen, Rasmus, 54–56, 58, 60–62, 64–66, 68, 109, 111, 120, 125–126.
Nietzsche, Friedrich, 26, 168–169, 179.
Novalis (Georg Philipp Friedrich Freiherr von Hardenberg), 2.

Origen Adamantius of Alexandria, 67.

Palludan-Müller, Jens, 69–70.
Pattison, George, 100, 131.
Paradox, 44, 48, 56, 62, 104, 128, 161.
Paulli, Just, 134.
Pelagius, 111.
Perkins, Robert, 139.
personality, 4, 11–12, 25–29, 38, 41–43, 54, 131–132, 145–146, 149, 151, 160, 162–164.
Petersen, Lauritz Vilhelm, 104.

Poole, Roger, 97, 150–151.
positive, 4–6, 21, 63, 86, 87, 92, 118, 149, 157–158, 165, 167–168.
positivity, 14, 33, 63, 111.
presupposition, 25, 28, 37, 39, 56, 67, 73, 80, 117, 121, 148, 152.
Protestantism, 7–9, 31, 37, 43–44, 69, 71–73, 89–90, 113, Protestant principle as principle of subjectivity 7, 44, 160, Protestant Reformation 71–72.
providence, 53–54, 170–171.
public, the, 68–69, 1115, 131–133, 140, of the academy 21, 29, attack 135, of the church 21, 44, 57, 74, good 103, of society 21, 74, 80.

rationalism, 2, 15, 22–23, 35, 68, 82, 106.
reason, 11, 15, 38, 72, Age of 161, as autonomous 52, and faith 88, 102, human's cannot compare with God's 178, immediate certainty of 10, paradox as contradictory of 161, regenerated 72, 161, and revelation 4, in Schelling 174, universals of 3.
reconciliation, 21, 28, 35, 63, 71–73, 110, 160, 162.
Reitzel, Carl Andreas, 128–129.
religion, 3–4, 6, 10, 115, 23–25, 27, 30–32, 34–35, 38, 64, 75, 78, 84, 87, 95, 101, 107, 113, 119, 121, 134, 158, 162, 167.
revelation, 4, 8–9, 12, 17, 24–26, 31, 33, 37, 45, 52–53, 63–64, 67, 71–73, 88, 116–117, 119, 156.
Ricoeur, Paul, 19.

Rorty, Richard, 11, 161.
Scharling, C.I., 147, 155–156, 182.
Schelling, F.W.J., 3, 149, 178.
Schilller, Friedrich, 2.
Schlegel, Friedrich, 29.
Schleiermacher, F., 3, 6, 12, 63, 93.
science, 4, 7, 9, 13–14, 20, 27–28, 31, 34–35, 60, 72, 88.
Schjørring, Jens Holger, 99, 148.
Scriptures, 38, 41–42, 53, 69.
secular, secularize, 31, 40, 78, 127.
self-consciousness, 12, 25, 28, 35, 68, 152.
Shakespeare, 2.
Sibbern, Frederik Christian, 10, 153, 159.
sin, 12, 21, 33, 54, 69–70, 95, 107–108, 110–111, 156, 158.
speculation, 35, 50, 53, 62, 66–68, autonomic 68, Christian 24, 26, dogmatic 67, market 75, or mediation 161, modern, in Germany 73, modernity's 117, philosophical 67, poetic 45, theological 48, tension with faith's intuition 81.
speculative, abstract, standpoint 148, or aesthetic interest 15, form of the comical 21, as dialectical thinking 25, discoveries, ala Niels Klim 113, drama 114-115, the, Idea 17, knowledge 52, 149, method 50–51, 66, 128, modern, direction 104, modernity's 117, mysticism 117, philosophy 114, 121, reflection 64–65, poetry 17, 19, 114, thaumaturgist 114, theology(ian) xvi, 4–5, 16, 24–25, 45–46, 50–51, 67, 102, 105, 119, 127, 131, 149, 159, thinker 11, thoughts on astronomy 45, view on baptism 43, views of Jesus 108, way 62.
Spirit, apostolic 42, 100, of authentic New Testament Christianity 32, brothers and sisters of the Free Spirit 94, Christ has given us the same measure of the 42, the Christ has made himself the principle of the 39, Christ is present in his church as 43, the church year's higher laws of the 45, concept of freedom is one with self-consciousness or 28, conscience as witness of the 7, divine thought as immanent cannot be without 25, emancipated 30, Father, Son, and 176–177, as free, hovers above phenomenal life in artistic comedy 19, God as, in all spirits 53, God is 51, God in the depths of the human 156, great wealth of, in Kierkegaard's writings 85, human reason enlightened by 52, mystic's 25, Jacobi as Mynster's kindred 86, of Martensen 61, 107, the outpouring of 37, of peace 88, of the time xvi, of the world and modern culture 31. *See also* Holy Spirit.
Steffens, Henrich, 9, 17.
Stewart, Jon, 92, 99, 105, 111, 121, 152–154.
Strauss, D.F., 31, 34, 159.
sublate, 21, 24–25, 35, 42, 45, 131.
supernaturalism, 22–25, 35, 46, 68, 106, 159.

**system, systematic**, 48, 50, 57, 60, 66–67, 74, 98, absence of ethics in the 121, antiquated, Copernican 45, cultural, of leveling 133, elements that elude the philosophical 15, of German philosophy 14, churchly 9, Gnostic 72, Hegel's or Hegelian 10, 13, 24, 103–104, Martensen and his 133, Martensen promised the 124, of moral philosophy 26–27, 29, 94, 110, 131, 152, 170, philosophical 68, and the pseudonyms as belonging together 181, of subjectivity 27, as unfinished until culminating in practice 28, waiting for one to bring the 105.

**theonomy**, 63, 88, 151.
**Tieck, Johann Ludwig**, 2, 9.
**Tillich, Paul**, 175, 179.
**tradition**, 5, 7, 14–15, 72–73, 80, 140, 145–146, 148–152, 154–155, 160, 178. *See also* authority, history, and positivity.
**Thulstrup, Marie**, 95, 148.
**Thulstrup, Niels**, 48, 99, 120, 148, 153.
**tragic, tragicomedy**, 21, 161.
**Trinity**, 24, 72–74.

**understanding**, 9, 12–13, 23–24, 28, 30, 35, 39, 44, 49–50, 52, 61, 76, 101, 104–105, 108, 123, 142, 148–150, 153, 161, 165–166, 170, 175, 177–178.
**Vattimo, Gianni**, 161.
**vision**, 17, 20, 53, 95, 101, 162, 164–165.

**Walsh, Sylvia**, 109.
**Watkin, Julia**, 99.
**Werner, Friedrich Ludwig Zacharias**, 2.
**will**, altering God's 175, Christ's royal 116, divine, cannot be bound 116, divine, has freely couched itself in 117, divine, in relation to sacrament 117–118, the eternal exists only through its 172, as the existential 173, existential act of 164. free, as the presupposition of moral philosophy 28, a free revelation of 116, a higher 10, human, as bound 179, of Providence 170, reason cannot arrive at existence except by a 174, relation of, to God 65, self exercises, and rests in the power 131, subjective, as evil by nature 110. *See also* freedom.

**Zabala, Santiago**, 161.
**Zeller, Eduard**, 30.